Bioplanning
A North Temperate Garden

T4

Gratitude to the Unknown Instructors

   What they undertook to do
   They brought to pass;
   All things hang like a drop of dew
   Upon a blade of grass.

         — *William Butler Yeats*

Bioplanning
A North
Temperate
Garden

by
Diana Beresford-Kroeger

Photographs by
Christian H. Kroeger

Foreword by
The Hon.
Miriam Rothschild

QUARRY
PRESS

HERITAGE

The publisher gratefully acknowl-
edges the support of The Canada
Council and Department of Canadian
Heritage for the arts of writing and
publishing in Canada.

ISBN 1-55082-152-0 paperback
ISBN 1-55082-257-8 clothbound

Design by Susan Hannah.

Printed and bound in Canada by
AGMV/Marquis Inc., Quebec

Published by Quarry Press Inc.,
P.O. Box 1061, Kingston, Ontario
K7L 4Y5 Canada
www.quarrypress.com

Cover: *Cheiranthus allionii* 'Orange'
massed in the background, *Gypsophila
repens* 'Alba', *Paeonia lactiflora,* and
Thymus pseudolanuginosus 'Rosea' in
the foreground.

Previous page: *Dianthus chinensis*
'Heddwigii' combined with *Paeonia
lactiflora* 'Sarah Bernhardt' creating a
pink fragrant walk-way.

Following page: Oriental hybrid lilies
viewed through a veil of *Gypsophila
paniculata.*

*For my husband,
   Christian Hinrich Kroeger,
and my daughter,
   Erika, and the children of the world.*

Nomenclature

The Latin name of all plant species as well as the common name, in some cases,
is used in the text. Where specific cultivars are mentioned, the cultivar name
follows the Latin species name. For example, in *Aquilegia vulgaris* 'Flore Pleno',
the double flowering common columbine, *Aquilegia vulgaris*, in italics, denotes
the specie and 'Flore Pleno', in single quotation marks, the cultivar. The genus,
i.e. *Aquilegia*, always appears with the first letter in uppercase and subsequent
specie descriptors appear in lowercase letters.

Generally, *Hortus Third* was used for definitive naming, definition, and
spelling of plant genus and specie names. In many instances, common Latin
synonyms are provided as well as common names. The Latin synonyms were
chosen, often, to assist the European reader in cross-identification.

For each genus monograph, the following convention was used: first
appears the genus name, followed by the common name or names, followed by
the family name, terminating with the climate zones in which the particular
species of the genus chosen for discussion in this text can be expected to grow.
An example follows:

Genus	*Aquilegia*
Common Name	Columbine
Family	*Ranunculaceae*
Climatic Zone	Zones 2–9

Photography

Photographs for this text were taken with a Canon TL-QL 35 mm SLR camera
using the following Canon lenses: FD 70-210 mm zoom F/4, FL 50 mm F/1.8 and
an FD 28 mm F/2. For virtually all the photographs, Kodachrome 64 color
transparency film was used. The photographs were taken in the garden of the
author with the exception the photograph on page 257 taken on a roadside
near Cragside, Northumberland, England.

Contents

Foreword

Time separates a garden from a Nature Reserve, for gardens are ephemeral due to the frequent change of ownership or the whims and fancies of the gardeners themselves. In this book, however, the author, with a felicitous combination of the love of horticultural plants and wild life, seems to have achieved a harmonious and lasting union. Others are bound to follow . . . .

Every gardener and every teacher of biology should buy this volume, and instil each child with the message contained in the garden Bioplan, and utilise the phenomenal accumulation of practical information and research which is both original and crucial. *Bioplanning A North Temperate Garden* provides one answer to 'Silent Spring' as it brings happiness onto the doorstep — we do not have to pack into the car or bus to visit some distant Nature Preserve to experience what E.O. Wilson describes as the sheer biophysical pleasure from propinquity of animals and plants. And cohabitation with the angelic butterfly.

— *Miriam Rothschild*

Introduction
Of Oatmeal, Apricots & Cardinals

As a very young child I was attracted like a magnet to anyone bearing a shovel. If, by chance, the shovel was connected to a garden, any garden, I was around. There was one garden in particular that I used to haunt when I was playing with dolls. The gardener's name was Mr. Teegan and he owned an overgrown rose garden which to me seemed like paradise. I would sit perched up on the stone flag terrace above the garden, dangling my legs and admiring his roses. In the afternoons when I knew he was taking tea and thinly sliced cucumber sandwiches with his aging mother, I would lever my body down off the terrace. I did this gingerly because my legs were so short that I never quite knew where I would land, always hoping to miss the thorns. I remember looking up at the nodding ocean of large pink open roses above my head. Then I would start hopping and jumping at them in some vain attempt to get closer to the source of their wonderful fragrance.

Mr. Teegan must have known full well there were more than robins and insects tramping in his garden, for one day he invited me to help him plant a new Tea Rose. These roses could quite easily have been either the Wild Tea Rose (*Rosa gigantea*) or one of the new hybrids then coming into the Irish market. In any case, I remember huge bull-wood canes with great, thick thorns that were as big as my fingernails. Mr Teegan propped the rose against my small body, and as I hung onto one of the least thorny spots, he dug what seemed to me to be an enormous hole at the time. Then he went indoors and came out with a big bag of Quaker rolled oats. I asked him if he was going to make porridge, something I thoroughly disliked at the time, though I hoped he was going to continue planting the rose bush because by now I was also hanging on to his spade. He had a decided twinkle in his eye as he silently poured the oats into the pit. When we had tramped the soil back around the newly planted rose and had watered it in thoroughly, he informed me of the reason for the oatmeal. "A fine, slow-release fertilizer for my roses," he said. "Keep an eye on this beauty for me and tell me what you think of her next summer. Then ye'll know!"

That was to be my first lesson in organic gardening at the blissful age of four. The rose grew to gigantic proportions. I knew it did because I took great care to watch it every day, rain or shine (mostly rain because it was during an Irish winter), until it bloomed the following spring. Of course, I thought of the porridge feeding it all the time, and I started to eat it myself, although I still cannot profess to eating porridge often now.

Despite Mr. Teegan's tutoring, my first garden was a total unmitigated disaster. I carried the sense of failure over it with me for years afterwards. It was like a kind of deep mourning for something I really could not do. On the surface of it, gardening itself seemed so easy — after all, everybody in my household said so.

I was given a three penny bit for my weekly allowance. The bronze coin had King George on the back and red-blossomed clover on the front. I looked at it and immediately decided to try my first garden with my newly found wealth. Unknown to any members of my household who thought I was happily playing outside, I walked downtown and found the nearest Woolworths store. I knew they carried seeds and other garden plants because I had seen them before — they were next to the toy counter! So my threepence and I were parted. I carried home hidden on my person a package of lettuce seeds. The package itself looked so professional with its lettering and photograph of huge bunches of lettuce on the front. I was sure I would succeed with anything that looked so good.

I went home, carefully, hoping that I would not be spotted crossing the thoroughfares. I went around to the back of the house, which

Previous page: The native *Vitis lambrusca* with its sweetly fragrant flowers, a favorite haunt for small birds and a grand entrance to Carrigliath.

involved climbing a hill and somehow getting over a ten-foot stone wall that had an ample share of glass shards on the top of it. I selected a spot in the garden behind a huge pear tree and in front of a sweet chestnut tree for my first garden. It had to be in the deep shade because I did not want to be spotted from the house and scolded for being in forbidden territory. I used a stick to make a long row and loosened the earth which looked nice and rich and damp. Then I opened my package and sewed the black seeds in a row. I carefully covered them up, again following the instructions written on the back of the package. I waited.

During my wait I decided to build a fort out of old tree limbs and branches to hide my project and shelter me from the rain while I waited for the row of little green seedlings to break through the ground. As I waited patiently, I built a bigger fort which cast even more shade over the area. I sat in deep gloom until the end of the summer, after which the leaves began to fall in October. I climbed the wall for one last look. I saw nothing, absolutely nothing, not even one little tiny black seed. Then I turned and slinked off back to the house with my deep dark black secret and nobody could figure out why I glowered so much at the bowls of green Boston lettuce on the dining room table in front of me.

I have continued to garden avidly, nevertheless. Today, gardening is an all-consuming occupation for me, an extension of my education as a classical botanist and my professional research in medical biochemistry and human physiology at the University of Ottawa School of Medicine. Happily, I can say my gardening skills have improved since I was a child as my knowledge of gardening has increased.

Gardening first in Ireland and now just south of Ottawa near the village of Merrickville, I am well-acquainted with the north temperate climate, both the challenges and the delights such weather offers the avid gardener. The global gardening area is very large for the north temperate garden, encompassing roughly two-thirds of the northern hemisphere, from the Arctic Circle to the Tropic of Cancer. For the gardener, this area is divided into growing zones based on plant hardiness. Unfortunately, a scheme for global zoning has not been devised yet. Most nurserymen in North America use the United States of America Department of Agriculture (U.S.D.A.) map. This map of North America is read in degrees Fahrenheit. In Europe, horticulturalists use the European Garden Flora Zones in degrees centigrade. Since hardiness depends on many other factors apart from temperature, it is in the gardener's best interest to add a little personal observation to a knowledge of zone differences. For instance, a well-drained winter soil will increase plant hardiness as will winter shade and a deep snow cover.

On the North American U.S.D.A. map, the zones are divided from one to ten, zone 1 being the coldest near the Arctic Circle, zone 10 being the southernmost tip of the Florida peninsula (and some areas of arranged micro-climate on the southwestern coast of Canada). On some maps, zones 2–10 are further subdivided into A and B, with A being colder than B.

In general on the U.S.D.A. map, the annual average minimum temperature in degrees Fahrenheit for zone 1 is -50F, though temperatures often go below this average figure, of course. For zone 2, temperatures vary from -50F to -40F, though with a high wind-chill factor average temperatures in any given year can go below these figures. In Canada, zone 2 is a gardening area where such cold is compensated for by a rapid growing season of long days and short nights. Zone 3, the zone in which my garden grows, has temperatures of -40F to -30F. Fortunately, this zone has a high winter snowfall. My friends to the south are in zone 4 with temperatures of -30F to -20F. In zone 5, temperatures of -20F to -10F prevail, which, to my mind, marks the beginning of the warm area of the north temperate region. Zone 6 has temperatures of -10F to 0F. Many southern city gardens in Canada will experience zone 6 conditions because of the surrounding winter heating from buildings acting as a micro-climate. Zone 7 has temperatures of 0F to 10F, and in zone 8 frost and cold are rare with temperatures of 10F to 20F. Zone 9 has temperatures of 20F to 30F, which entices many Canadian and Northern American "snowbirds" to the American South in the winter. In zone 10, temperatures range from 30F to 40F, such that

A delightful mixture of *Gypsophila paniculata* 'Rosensheier' and *Lychnis coronaria* 'Atrosanguinea'.

many north temperate species, bulbs especially, become a challenge to grow due to a lack of winter dormancy.

The European Garden Floral zones can be compared approximately to the U.S.D.A. zones as follows. Zone H1 (European) is similar to zone 3 (American); zone H2 to zone 4; zone H3 to zone 5; zone H4 to zone 6; and zone H5 to zone 7. Zone G1 is equivalent to the combined zones 8 and 9, and zone G2 can be directly compared to zone 10. Incidentally, I gardened in European zone G1 and G2 while growing up in Southern Ireland.

My eastern Canadian garden, Carrigliath, a Gaelic name meaning grey stones, is set against the huge skies of Canada, which are like

North Temperate Climatic Zones

°F	U.S.A.	CANADA	EUROPE	°C
32	Zone 10	Zone 10	Zone G2	0
20	Zone 9	Zone 9	Zone G1	-5
10	Zone 8	Zone 8		-10
			H5	-15
0	Zone 7	Zone 7	H4	-20
-10	Zone 6	Zone 6	H3	-25
-20	Zone 5	Zone 5	H2	-30
-20	Zone 4	Zone 4		
-30	Zone 3	Zone 3	H1	-35
-40	Zone 2	Zone 2		-40
				-45
-50	Zone 1	Zone 1		-50
	USDA	CPH	EGF	°C

USDA — United States Department of Agriculture

CPH — Canadian Plant Hardiness Zones

EGF — European Garden Floral Zones

nowhere else in the world. The patina of the seasons is very different in a Canadian garden. The spring, except for zones 7, 8, and 9, is almost non-existent. The summer, with its high solar exposures, much higher than in Europe, means that the sun-loving plants such as phlox and the shorter day plants such as asters can be grown extremely well. The translation of solar exposures means that European shade plants, indeed most European plants, will take more shade in a north temperate garden. The higher solar exposures with resulting glare means that color design is more difficult, the so-called hot colors are even more dramatic, but the blue range species, which require a softer cloud-reflected light, do not stand out so well as they do in an English garden. The winterscape with its accompanying silence is magnificent in a Canadian garden. The winter garden has three dominant characteristics — silence, non-fragrance, and dormancy. Snow has a very interesting muting effect on the airways, which compartmentalizes the gardening space, shutting the gardening area and changing the vista entirely. The chemicals of fragrance do not act or react in the cold, still air, killing all smell, odor and fragrance, thus magnifying the thrill of spring and early summer, because renewed growth is accompanied by an avalanche of fragrance. The dormancy of winter is wonderful because the garden and gardener can have a true rest.

For these reasons, perhaps, a distinctive style of gardening has developed in Canada which is very different from Irish, English or European gardens. The gardening style is somewhat looser and fits in with the wilderness of the landscape, its many creatures and high insect population. This gardening style has probably subconsciously followed the landscape style of Canada's greatest artists in painting a "reduced" art nouveau wilderness. From the tangled gardens of J.E.H. MacDonald and the muted greenery of A.J. Casson to the huge North American trees on the black canvases of M. A. Fortin, from the biological dissections of Jack Shadbolt to the magic haybales of Jamie Wyeth — all are attuned to a natural world at once wild and tamed. My own garden, Carrigliath, which is featured in the photographs throughout this book, taken by my husband, is one version of this wild-tamed Canadian design. The other garden designs presented in the book — notably the Canine Loggia, the Suburban, and the Mutchmor School plans — have been created to achieve a similar harmony between nature and culture, man and beast, wilderness and civilization.

To describe this harmony I have coined a new word, *bioplan*. Bioplanning involves taking organic gardening one step further and creating the multitude of habitats necessary for beneficial predation. The world as a biosphere has undergone unique changes in the past 50 years. Agricultural technology has removed wildlife habitats by enlarging fields into vast areas of monoculture with an accompanying desertification of species, and suburban sprawl has likewise destroyed these habitats in large areas. Yet the gardener expects the balance of nature to be somehow self-correcting and is surprised when this balance shifts to leave large numbers of otherwise beneficial organisms, such as earwigs, tent caterpillars, cut-worms, fungi, bacteria and viruses, to decimate precious plantings.

To garden successfully in this new environment, another dimension of planning has to be considered. This I call designing for life or *bioplanning.* To bioplan a garden, one must realign the dimensions of the garden to encourage its use as a natural habitat. As soon as nature enters the garden, a much more harmonious system will be in place, which in turn will be healthier and more beneficial for the residents, man included. Bioplanning involves restoring equilibrium among soil, water, fauna, and flora. Success is when the summer tanager, the butterfly, and the toad come to reside again in the garden with man. The balance is restored; the cycle of nature begins again.

Bioplanning a North Temperate Garden has been written in the context of this concept of bioplanning such that the descriptions of species are focussed on the ecological function of the plant. In my descriptions of these north temperate flower species, I am guilty of coining another new word, *ecofunction*, into which fits the chemistry and biochemistry of a plant and how it relates to its environment, man included.

Plants, all plants, are silent organisms. They take the energy of sunlight and trap it into chemical bonds that amass to create a rather extraordinary body of living tissue. All of these structures are made up of carbon, hydrogen, oxygen, sometimes sulphur and nitrogen in different chemical combinations. Knowledge of these chemical structures is the basis of ancient and modern medicine: 50 percent of all medicines used all over the world come from plant origins and are made of one or another combination of these chemicals. These are the chemicals lurking in plants which are so important to our well being and whose importance to the natural world I have called *ecofunction.* As a scientist and as a gardener I have studied the chemistry and ecofunction of the species described in this book, a story previously untold in gardening books.

The plants of a north temperate garden can withstand considerable cold during dormancy, many more degrees of frost than is realized by the gardening community of Europe. Snow acts as an insulating blanket for underground plant material, and well-fed plants can be super-cooled because of a high P/K ratio (phosphate/potassium ratio) and many plant structural modifications found in the physiology of these plants. The north temperate plants discussed in detail in this book will form a hardy backbone for any garden in zones 2–9. The choice is large, being approximately 1200 hardy species. This group of plants is growing rapidly with the development of new hardy cultivars on this continent. With the shifts of climate in Europe, the nurserymen of Europe could well do some investigation of the huge numbers of hardy species which are almost completely unknown there.

One such example is the marvelous Louisiana iris group, as well as the new hybrid American lilies and the Vesper iris. Over the years, I have become very interested in the Iris group of plants and have run hardiness trials on species unknown to this part of the world. At the same time, I have kept a keen, acquisitive eye open for many heritage plants. I have pulled from the brink of extinction the *Peony lactiflora* 'Chocolate Soldier' which came to me from Cambridge in tissue culture form. Because of my scientific background, I knew how to make this plant thrive. Gooseberry species and others have been left to me by will, and some others like my heritage phlox collection have come to me by sheer chance — they were snatched from the path of a bulldozer. I have found new species and I have bred a few experimental mixes in my own garden. Some I am little more than pleased with, while others like the bi-colored perennial pea (as yet not named) thrills me when it breaks into its masses of blooms. But the crowning glory of the garden are the nuts I have waited 17 years to fruit, the resistant shagbark hickories, *Carya ovata*. No! — maybe it is the purple-stemmed *Clematis virginiana* I found one day in an old quarry, or maybe it is the native *Lonicera* species that interest me so much . . .

Detailed growing instructions are given with the perennials, biennials, and bulbs. An emphasis is placed on organic care and protection. The major diseases in some instances are discussed with suggestions how they can be avoided. These really are the parameters of organic gardening, a method of gardening which involves the use of the least toxic methods of insect control and puts an emphasis on the maintenance of health and prevention of disease. If disease does occur, then a serious effort is made to find a cure which is ecologically acceptable. It is my wish that children of all ages can lounge on the lawn and chew on a blade of grass without the fear of poisoning.

Gardening is one of the few occupations that reduces the greenhouse effect for pleasure. The very act of gardening is beneficial and more necessary now than it ever was. If gardening can become biogardening, then our children will have a future. Step by step we can restore our harmony with nature.

Many people do not realize that gardens are built step by step. I find that aspiring gardeners come into my garden and say I would like a border like this or an espalier fruit tree like that or a water-garden, maybe a little smaller, but one just like this one here. Gardening, like anything else in life, requires dedication if one is to succeed. I will not even mention the word *work*. I have completely worn out my first steel shovel and now have a shiny new one, so I suppose you could call me a two-shovel person.

About fifteen years ago when I was barely taking off the edge of my first shovel, I planted two apricots, one a tree, a Harcot, and the other a manchurian shrub apricot, outside of the bedroom windows. Now, the shrub is taller than the tree, which in turn is taller than the house — which begs the question, what is a shrub? They are both espaliered in an informal way and make splendid viewing in the spring when they are covered with pink blossoms at the same time as the thousands of daffodils planted all over the garden are blooming in great yellow hosts.

A few years ago a cardinal decided to make the Harcot apricot his territory and would dart and flash his scarlet way around the spreading limbs. He would also wake me early in the mornings by attacking his mirrored image in the window and squawk at this improper imposter posing as himself.

Early one morning as he woke me with his antics and I comfortably watched his primary color swoon in and out of the tree, I suddenly realized that I had indeed built a garden, for me, for this beautiful bird, and for the world. May all readers of this book do the same.

Bioplanning for the Future

Design

Soil

Water

Airways

Fragrance

Flora

Fauna

Orchestration

The native biennial *Rudbeckia hirta*
or Black-eyed Susan.

Bioplanning for the future

Scientific research is a creative process. As well as intelligence, perseverance and patience, it requires discipline and a lively sense of humor because without that you cannot look back and examine your mistakes evenly with the degree of justice required to put the next foot forward without feeling despair, for all of science is based on the tenuous testing for error.

I have spent a great deal of my life in science. At one time, I worked in heart research, where the protocol was so demanding and lengthy that you came home completely exhausted both physically and mentally. Since it was simply out of the question to have an active social life, I began to garden. As time went by I found that the process of gardening was spiritually refreshing. I tackled the problems I encountered in research with a renewed vigor and insight. So the garden was born.

Then something strange happened in my life. I found that gardening rubbed away the arrogance of science, for you simply cannot sit in the mud for a long time in the spring swatting black flies and mosquitoes and depositing sedimentation on your face without questioning what you are doing, full stop. I began to realize that I was doing something different from other gardeners, horticulturists, and people I had read about in books or magazines. I was putting into action a design in the garden that encircled something very big — a design for life I called the bioplan.

We are poisoning our natural world with the chemicals we created for the battle fields in World War I and II. This is continuing to happen with the widespread use of 'designer' pesticides, insecticides, herbicides, and hormonal compounds. Ironically, the chemical balance of nature is being destroyed by such chemicals introduced in 'unbalanced' amounts. This balance must be restored if our human species is to survive, let alone various plant, insect, and animal species. This must be done because all evidence shows that these man-made chemical compounds developed to 'enhance' nature are killing us slowly, now trapped in the molecules that make up man. We, the community of gardeners all over the biosphere, must lead the way, rethinking what we are doing. We must learn how to bioplan for the sake of all the creatures great and small within our stewardship. If we do this, I believe as a scientist and a gardener, we shall begin to spin a silken thread of change which our children can weave into their lives in the next millennium.

Design

Morning mist over the main perennial border.

The basic bioplan design presented on page 40 of the "Bioplan" chapter can be used on part of an existing garden, or, better still, on all of the garden. It can be scaled down to fit a small garden by reducing the number of plant species, or it can be expanded to increase the number of species, keeping the three-dimensional spacings the same. In gross design terms, this means that one area of the garden should have tall trees with sweeping boughs, one area should have a flat surface with open space overhead, one area should have hedging and perennials of varying heights, one area should have a sheer vertical surface, and one area should have a water surface. From the onset of planning the garden, the gardener must consider the garden to be a biomass. From this, one must mould the dimensions to fit nature, and, of course, accent the housing area. These dimensions are established by a multitude of plant, water, and other surfaces within the garden which fade and change from spring to fall. This living topography is the life source of the biological systems within the garden. These, in turn, depend on a healthy soil with its own micro-system of sustainability. The maintenance of health depends on the gardener's skill — the gardener orchestrates the living topography of the garden to taste.

Soil

The urn fungus, *Urnula craterium*, of North America, one indicator of a healthy soil.

The soil is a complex ecosystem: it is alive and gives life. The soil is being intensely studied by soil chemists, but is not, as yet, fully understood. What is known is that the soil can be killed; that is, the living organisms in the soil can be either so seriously damaged that they do not function properly or can be killed outright. In either case, the soil is said to be sterile and will not support life. Nuclear radiation will cause this, as will spills of toxic chemicals, acid rain, and some of the arsenal of pesticides for domestic and farm use. In the latter case, a lack of understanding of dilution commonly causes havoc in the soil. In any case, this understanding of the soil as a live ecosystem is the first stage of successful bioplanning.

All soil consists of the earth's crust ground up into rock fragments in all sizes mixed with decaying plant and animal matter called humus and living soil organisms, both micro and macro in size. The rock fragments can be considered to be crystalline carriers enabling both humus and micro-organisms to get together to reproduce, dissolve the rock, and make more soil. To make more soil, micro-organisms need nitrogen (NO_3^-, NH_4^+), potassium (K^+), calcium (Ca^{++}), phosphorous (H_2PO_4), magnesium (Mg^{++}), and sulphur (SO_4^{--}) in their diet. As occasional treats, the soil needs iron (Fe^{++}, Fe^{+++}), chlorine (Cl^-), copper (Cu^{++}), manganese (Mn^{++}), zinc (Zn^{++}), molybdenum (MoO_4^{--}), and boron (BO_3^{--}, $B_4O_7^{--}$). Required in minute amounts by soil organisms are cobalt (Co^{++}), sodium (Na^+), aluminum (Al^{+++}), and silicon ($H_2SiO_4^{--}$), which is required also by some specialized land and marine plants. Seaweed concentrates are excellent sources of these elements for supplementing the garden soil micronutrient levels. A fertile garden soil is a soil which has all these elements amongst others in balance.

In addition, growing plants need large amounts of nitrogen, potassium, and phosphorous. Thus the soil needs to be replenished with these three elements regularly. The normal garden practice is to replace them once or twice a year in spring and winter depending on the climate. Additional potassium and phosphorous is needed in a north temperate gardening area to induce increased frost resistance. These three elements are in perfect proportions in all animal manures, which are broken down into more soluble units for plants to use by soil organisms in several processes called the nitrogen cycle, the phosphorous cycle, and possibly the sulphur cycle. The recently discovered sulphur cycle is a complex chemical, marine, and land ecosystem cycle which also benefits plant growth.

Humus from animal and plant sources acts as an air-conditioner in the soil. Humus also considerably modifies the availability of water for plant growth. Humus, air, and water are needed for the aerobic micro-organisms in the soil. The anaerobic micro-organisms do not need air. These micro-organisms are involved in specific stages of decomposition and recycling of carbon, nitrogen, phosphorous, and sulphur.

The soil fungi form a large part of the soil ecosystem and act as caregivers to the higher plants. Since fungi are in the lower order of plants and are still heavily dependent on water in their life cycle, their fragile, cellular constituents are easily damaged by "adverse" chemicals in the environment. The fungi are an enormous group of plants, playing an important role in the soil. Their delicate root-like growth or mycelial hyphae are normally invisible to the gardener. What is occasionally seen are the products of sexual reproduction. These are mushrooms. Mushroom growth is a sign of a living, healthy soil. Fungi have an enormous beneficial role in the soil's ecology as parasites, saprophytes, and general scavenger plants. But when this balance changes from beneficial to pestilent, the result is the cause of great human misery. One such fungus, *Phytophthora infestans*, caused the great potato famine in Ireland in 1845 to 1847, and so was responsible for the death of over three million people. Another such fungus was *Plasmopara viticola*, a mildew fungus which almost destroyed the entire French wine industry. Yet another such ecological disaster, the death of world forests, is on our doorstep. Acid rain is thought to be killing the mycorrhizal growth on tree roots.

The bird's nest fungus, *Scleroderma nidiformis*, looks like a miniature bird's nest complete with eggs. Common in Europe as well as North America, this fungus helps to digest woodchips in a quality garden soil.

Many, if not all, of the soil fungi called mycorrhizae have a symbiosis with the roots of the higher orders of plants such as flowers, shrubs, and trees. Mycorrhizal growth on roots has a felt-like appearance. It seems that the plants supply sugars, amino acids, and many valuable organic chemicals to the fungi, which, in turn, repay with dissolved minerals in a form which the plant can transport all through its vascular system for growth, development, and fruiting. It appears that acid rain is destructive to this mycorrhizal growth, which, subsequently, results in the death and destruction of huge tracts of forest, such as the maple forest regions in Canada and the Black Forest in Germany.

The gardener in his small terrain can broadcast ground dolomitic limestone around his large trees once in every five years to form an increased bicarbonate buffer in the soil to reduce the crippling effect of acid rain. This remedy can be put into action as a makeshift plan for the present time.

It should not be forgotten that some of the soil fungi manufacture some of the most sophisticated, potent compounds known to man. One such fungus is *Claviceps purpurea*, which is a parasite of rye, *Secale cereale*. It caused havoc in the middle ages by felling the inhabitants of entire villages. People got a disease from eating rye bread made from rye flour which was milled from grain infected with the claviceps fungus. The disease was known as St. Anthony's Fire, which we now know as ergotism. *Claviceps purpurea* was also the initial source of D - Lysergic acid diethylamide, commonly known as LSD. The fungus is now extremely important in the manufacture of ergotamine, which is used in the treatment of migraines.

Another important part of the soil ecosystem are the unicellular and multicellular algae. Some of these algae are astonishingly similar to bacteria. One such large group is comprised of the Blue-green algae, which, despite its name, is responsible for the color or bloom of the Red Sea. These algae are extremely important inhabitants of the soil and, from recent research in England and Australia, appear to be strongly connected with the world's nitrogen recycling system in plants.

Apart from the soil bacteria, viruses, slime molds, hosts of fungal spores, zygotes, yeasts, and pathogens of every kind, the soil also teams with life which is more familiar to the gardener — spiders, millipedes, centipedes, beetles, and many kinds of ants, earthworms, slugs, snails, and earwigs. Many of these creatures are predators, all are beneficial, and all work toward a balance to maintain their own integrity as a species.

Water

Water, as an integral part of bioplanning, helps to restore the declining population of frogs and other amphibians. A hardy water lily hybrid, *Nymphaea* 'Pink Sensation', hosts a variety of frog species in late summer.

Water is an integral part of bioplanning. Not only is it essential for plant life, but it is also necessary for the animal kingdom within a garden. Without it, the garden assumes the aspect of a desert for many species. Water can take the form of a series of artistically arranged shallow bowls with pebbles placed as small islands in the bowls, a birdbath, an artificial bog garden, a small water garden, or a running water feature of some kind. The latter is water in its ideal form. The sound of running water, splashing and gurgling with its amplified resonance, has a magical, pleasing, and relaxing quality to the human ear.

Ponds large and small in a north temperate climate add a dimension to gardening that is as filled with pleasure as it is astonishing. The numbers of common skimmers, most usually dragon flies, seen flying over the smallest surface of water is a visual treat taken for granted in North America but noticeably absent in an English garden due to the demise of so many species. Many birds flop down for private bathing, and many garter and various water snakes take an elegant swim. Birds seem to be reassured by the presence of water and will usually nest nearby. In my water garden, fish multiply with astounding genetic diversity and compete with a 26-year-old eastern Ontario painted turtle for protein. Frogs of all kinds are attracted by the call of water.

A few years ago, I saw something swim across the water-garden between the water lilies and water irises, dodging the floating pink flowering candles of water goosefoot. When I crept closer to examine the creature, I saw, to my intense astonishment, that it was a young milk snake (*Lampro peltis triangulum*). It was way out of its natural range. It was the first of many such creatures to find refuge in the garden.

A bird bath, however, is the most common water feature in the garden. It should be placed near shrubbery so that the shy birds have perching ability to enable them to scan the area before they expose themselves to drink or bathe. Birds and insects will queue up for this precious commodity. In times of drought or water restriction, a floater (a small piece of softwood) should be placed in the birdbath. The small insects, honey bees, wasps, butterflies, and many other beneficial insects will use this as a drinking fountain. If honey bees are closely watched drinking, their pumping mechanism can be observed. Bees, while pumping water, are intent on their business and completely ignore human inspection of their work habits. Bird baths should be kept clean and topped up with fresh water as needed.

I have a dog, but he is not your average run of the mill any old dog. He was beaten and very badly abused as a young pup, so he prayed to God to find him a big garden in which to bury his bone. God answered his prayer by pointing his wet nose in my direction. When he came to me he was like a cotton bag with some bones inside. It took me a full month of hand feeding to bring him back to life. When I saw him I knew that he was not at the pinnacle of his canine career, and taking into consideration his murky genetic blending which spills out into pointing not for birds but for squirrels, being an excellent mouser, herding the chickens and counting them if necessary, I decided to call this future companion, Finnegan's Wake. This posh name comes not from my own pomposity because, for although I have read my countryman, James Joyce, I decided to pinch the title of his famous book with a fond wish that I might be able to endow this scrawny animal with a certain nobility where absolutely none exists!

Finnegan also guards the water garden, the frogs, and the fish, probably because my Gaelic call reminds him of his own origin. Another master also guards the water garden, a blue heron. This heron sneaks on to the stone terrace around the water garden with his pipe, a chair, and a comfortable attention to his favorite study, fish anatomy. Now, the fish do not appreciate this kind of dedication because the results are detrimental to their health and neither does the dog who believes he has a god-given appointment to be master of all he surveys.

A vista of colors created by blending the yellow of the antique Rose *Rosa* 'Harisonii' with the *Iris pseudacorus* and the tiny bayonets of the native water plant *Nymphoides peltata*.

The scenario is as follows every morning after mid-July. The heron flaps in. He then stands on the edge of a stone and peers down into the water with deadly seriousness. The fish, who are no fools, being Gaelic bred though not born, dive to the bottom of the water garden and hang on to the Cabomba, the *Nymphoides peltata,* and to the water lilies for dear life. The dog is alerted to this impending disaster by his canine sixth sense borrowed no doubt from one of the cats, probably Piano-Toes, for the occasion. The dog becomes a hunting dog and stalks the heron, crouching on his belly when he comes near the bank of Thyme for his deadly attack. The dog springs. The bird flies. He goes up to an overhanging limb of the American Elm and pretends to be a twig. The bird aligns his body in a sort of miraculous parallax with the branches and the poor dog, whose vision is in inverse proportion to his sense of smell, retreats in a deep funk to the Birds Nest Spruce for another try.

The heron has never caught a fish. The dog has not caught the bird. And I wait for another morning hoping to catch some sleep!

Airways

An eastern Ontario meadow of native species in June.

It is astonishing what little thought is given to airways and airflow within the garden. Airways are essential to the success or failure of an orchard and to the garden bioplan. Birds need unblocked airways just as airplanes do. Birds are necessary in the garden for insect patrol. In eastern North America, house wrens, bluebirds, tree swallows, and martins need appropriate housing in appropriate locations. These air and ground insect-eating birds are marvelously beneficial. In western Canada the house wren, the bluebird, tree swallow, the violet-green swallow, and the northern flicker need housing in gardens. In both eastern and western Canada the house finch is very beneficial when feeding its young as they require a large protein component in their diet which is in a noxious insect in larval form.

Birds are flying machines — they soar, glide, land, and take off again to do their insect patrol. They need to be furnished with adequate landing strips to carry on with their work. The longitudinal section of lawn (A) in the bioplan design is an ideal area for bird flight. The gardener should situate this airstrip to facilitate observation of the birds from the home.

To maintain a stock of birds within a bioplan, birds must have food sources both in summer and winter. Winter feeding should take place in at least three separate locations. Ground feeding of large sunflower seeds should take place on a low 6" (15 cm) table of some kind in the middle of the lawn area to afford protection against marauding felines. Cardinals, grosbeaks, and blue jays are examples of ground feeding birds. Little seed and large seed feeders should be hung or placed near shrubbery well off the ground. Fat strips should also be hung for the fat-loving birds. Winter feeding should begin with the onset of cold weather in October and should continue until spring. Summer feedings of saturated solutions of sugar for the nectar loving hummingbirds should begin with the warm days of spring. A saturated solution is made up by adding sugar to warm water and mixing until no more sugar dissolves; free crystals of sugar are seen to float at the base of the mixing container. Hummingbird feeders should be replenished all summer.

Perching for birds must be provided by hedges, shrubbery, and trees. Birds need to groom. Their grooming is a finely tuned biochemical process whereby the sun's rays change the deoxy form of Vitamin D on the bird's feathers to the oily Vitamin D which the birds preen and thereby ingest for their health and benefit. Wind protection while perching is supplied by evergreens in sections (J) and (F) of the bioplan.

A bat house should be erected in an out-of-the-way place to entice bats into the garden, as these much maligned beneficial creatures may eat many times their own weight in mosquitos and other predacious insects in an evening's hunt.

My friends don't even know this, but I wear the same jacket every day feeding the birds during the cold winter months. I always use the same feeding call. Now the birds follow me around when I cross country ski during the winter or work in the garden during the summer. One day my husband threw on his old jacket and was so impressed that the birds were so friendly around him. I did not say anything. I had been wearing his jacket all these years. Some things are better unsaid.

One day after I had been working in the perennial borders and I went for a walk into the cedar forest behind our house, I was wearing my husband's old jacket. That day I was a bit lonely for Ireland. I get homesick sometimes for the green across the Atlantic. I called the birds. They came down out of the air: there must have been about a hundred birds of every sort and kind. They perched on my shoulders, my arms, and even on my head. I stood stock still trying not to frighten them. Then I got alarmed and wondered if we were going to have an earthquake because I had never seen the birds behave like this before. I ran for the house. It has never happened to me again.

Fragrance

There is probably no other tree or plant that produces the amount of nectar as does the fragrant lime tree, *Tilia americana,* in July.

The Trumpet hybrid lily, *Lilium* 'Pink Perfection ', is exquisitely fragrant in July.

To live in or near a lush garden undoubtedly increases the oxygen (O_2) levels and decreases the carbon dioxide (CO_2) levels in the immediate environment; in fact, it decreases pollution by a factor of about 25 percent. However, warmed spring and summer air also carries another important host of chemicals beneficial to man, fragrance. Fragrance is a non-verbal communication system in the plant and animal world. Every attempt should be made to fill the garden with as much fragrance as possible over the entire gardening season. The combined effects of fragrance on man is little understood, but recent research has indicated that a fragrance such as peppermint increases brain function by as much as 20 percent.

It is quite often forgotten that many evergreens, such as pines and cedars, are fragrant. The indigenous basswood or lime tree, *Tilia americana*, has intensely fragrant flowers in July which stay in bloom for seven to ten days. There is probably no other tree or plant that produces the amount of nectar as does the lime tree. All the nectar seeking beneficial insects can work the tiny open chalice-like flowers of the lime. On the west coast of Canada, a member of the Ericaceae family *Arbutus menziesii* produces plentiful nectar and pollen in the dense clusters of pitcher-shaped fragrant flowers. This beautiful tree is known as the "oriental strawberry tree." Another strawberry tree, *A. unedo*, indigenous to the south of Ireland, is an equally handsome and beneficial feeding tree for insects for milder coastal zones.

Flora

The gardener has to choose the plants carefully to fit the garden's bioplan. The plants should match the soil type within the garden. Extremely acidic or alkaline soils will require planting species matched to their required pH range. Climatic and microclimatic conditions must be known and understood. The gardener should err on the side of increased plant hardiness for an enduring garden. The plants in the bioplan should serve as a continuous and reliable supply of nectar, pollen, and other food for insects, amphibians, and birds. Circumspection must be given to the planting of certain species such as the Rhododendrons, for even though the flowers are attractive to honey bees, the resulting honey is toxic to man.

In consideration of the various plant groupings of the garden bioplan, the flowering hedge (C) can be a mixed hedge of fragrant shrubs. It can also be a hedge of a single species that flowers in early, mid, or late spring. The various cultivars of the Preston lilac in zones 3 to 9, which are in flower approximately two weeks after the common lilac species, may be used. This lilac flowers almost all of June into the beginning of July and is more adaptable to moister soils. The Preston lilac has a fragrance similar to carnations and the flowers are very attractive to hummingbirds and the beautiful, hovering, large sphinx or hawk moths which are quite often mistaken for hummingbirds and the monarch butterfly. Another fragrant shrub is *Viburnum farreri* (*V. fragrans*), zones 4–9, whose intensely fragrant pink flowers open in May. There is a white version, *V.f.* 'Album' and a dwarf form, *V.f.* 'Nanum'. The flowers open before the foliage, which makes this shrub ideal for underplanting with early spring bulbs, daffodils, or tulips in a fine spring display. Colder gardening areas can grow *Ribes odoratum* 'Crandall', zones 2–9, whose fragrance is very similar to the trailing arbutus, *Epigaea repens*, or the native Canadian lily, *Lilium canadense*. This ribes has wonderfully fragrant yellow flowers in May and has an annual bonus of a large crop of black berries which are superior to black currants as a kitchen fruit. If a shorter hedge is required in area (C), any pink, July-flowering cultivars of spirea are ideal, such as *Spiraea japonica* 'Alpina'. The quiet pink and dainty habit will counterbalance the border area (E) across the lawn from it.

Spires of *Digitalis purpurea* in a shaded woodland setting.

The feeding hedge (D) of the bioplan should combine flowering characteristics in spring which supply nectar and pollen for beneficial insects and a good supply of fall berries for the migratory bird population. A honeysuckle called *Lonicera tatarica* 'Claveyi' (syn. *Lonicera x xylosteoides* 'Clavey's Dwarf') fits this criterion for zones 2–9. This Lonicera species forms an informal hedge which grows to about 4' (120 cm) high and just as wide. The hedge itself is a fine vase shape and lends itself to underplanting of spring bulbs, daffodils, early and late tulips. It can also have an attractive foreplanting of mid-summer and fall Hemerocallis species. The fragrant flowers of *L.t.* 'Claveyi' are cream and white and are in flower with the tall bearded iris group. The foliage is blue-green and is very dainty. This species of Lonicera is the nearest shrub to a deciduous evergreen in zones 2–4 because it looses its foliage so late in the season, usually in December. This shrub is remarkably drought tolerant and frost resistant. In spring the flowers are favored by bumblebees, honey bees, hummingbirds, beneficial wasps, Hawk moths, and butterflies of all kinds. In zones 2–5, where the butterfly bush, *Buddleia davidii*, species can only be treated as annual shrubs, *Lonicera tatarica* 'Claveyi' is a generous compromise for attracting many Lepidoptera species and should be included in a butterfly garden.

In warmer zones 7–9, the choices of species which can be used for a feeding hedge (D) in the bioplan becomes greater. Many cultivars of *Enkianthus campanulatus* can be used in the acidic sandy soils of the Western seaboard. Choice cultivars are *E.c.* 'Albiflorus', which has nearly white flowers, or *E.c.* 'Palibinii', which has more intensely red veins in the flowers and is more showy than the other species. The foliage of all species of Enkianthus turns a magnificent fall red color.

Cultivars of *Berberis thunbergii* are also useful species for feeding hedges (D) of the bioplan. Berberis species grow happily in poor, dry soils and are useful both on the Western seaboard and in gardens from zones 3 to 9, depending on the cultivar. *Berberis thunbergii* 'Atropurpurea' cultivars co-host a black stem rust fungus of wheat on its overwintering deciduous leaves. Because of new strains of this fungus now infecting certain cultivars of *B.t.* 'Atropurpurea', the Canadian government has banned all deciduous species of this red-foliaged barberry. It should not be grown near wheat fields. The foliage of Berberis is somewhat barbed and is like a gentle version of holly. It forms an effective barrier shrub. The edible yellow flowers have a plentiful supply of nectar in nectaries at the base of the petals and pollen is ejected on contact. This shrub is a good food supply for winged beneficial insects as are the berries for birds. *B.t.* 'Minor', a fine 3' (.9 m) dwarf with green foliage, which broadens attractively with age, and *B.t.* 'Sparkle', a compact shrub with fine shiny rich green foliage, are both good modern cultivars.

Damp or wet gardening areas in zones 4 to 9 greatly benefit from planting deciduous holly, of which *Ilex verticillata* 'Winter Gold' is a particularly handsome, yellow-fruited cultivar with an abundant fruit crop for hungry fall birds.

The area (E) of the bioplan should consist of a border of flowers. It can be an annual or perennial border or a grouping of perennial plants. These plants should be grouped in various heights. At the back, the tall species should be planted with medium height plants midway and the smaller plants to the foreground. This border of plants should be trimmed back in early spring, as birds such as goldfinches and black capped chickadees will make good use of the standing seed crop for winter feeding.

Color planning is an important part of flower design, but it is also useful as a calling card for the insect world. Bees and butterflies see ultraviolet light. They are geared to see a larger part of the light spectrum than the human eye. The color scheme of the garden should incorporate this. For instance, bees will visit all the flowers they are fond of irrespective of colors. Yellows look like blues to them because of the ultraviolet spectrum, but the food they are after, pollen, has its own ultraviolet coloring in beautiful shades visible only to the bee. Many flowers have their own ultraviolet accentuated visual landscape, which bees use. A fine example of this is the cone

A Callippe Fritillary enjoys a snack on an *Echinacea purpurea* 'Bright Star'. This butterfly is abundant in Carrigliath probably because of the banks of *Viola cornuta* 'Royal Robe' and *V.c.* 'White Czar' which act as host plants for egg laying. *Phlox paniculata* 'Bright Eyes,' also a feeding station, is in the background.

shaped 'guide cells' on the bearded iris. These cells guide the insect towards the source of nectar and pollen on the iris flower. The cells are laden with pigments. In this case these are chemicals, which, when irradiated with ordinary light, will fluoresce both normal and ultraviolet light, thus acting as traffic signals for busy flying insect populations in their search for pollen and nectar.

All the Lepidoptera, butterflies and moths, see ultraviolet light, but this group of insects show a preference for colors in the red and the deep pink color range, as do hummingbirds. Some effort should be made to seek out flowers in this color range. In addition butterflies are attracted to sweet violets, wallflowers of the Cheiranthus species, honesty, Aubrieta species, Alyssum species, all lilacs, the white cultivars of Nicotiana, all species of Buddleias, pinks and carnations, honeysuckle, both shrubs and climbing species, ice plant Mesembryanthemum species, all species of asters both wild and cultivated, and also,

A honey bee, *Apis mellifera*, works the florets of *Echinops ritro* in August.

because of its extraordinary design versatility, *Humulus lupulus* 'Aureus', the golden common hop vine.

The perennial area (E) of the bioplan should have flowers of different morphology to supply the different needs of insects and birds. The greater the diversity of morphology the greater the diversity of beneficial insects will be 'moved' into the garden. Long tubular flowers with nectaries at the base are much loved by hummingbirds and many flying insects. What is not so well known is that the tiny chalice shaped flowers with an open form are necessary for the small beneficial insects. Tiny parasitic wasps, like the Trichogamma wasps, revel in such tiny open flowers, finding it easy to maneuver in such a form. Tiny flowers, such as *Gypsophyla repens*, *Spiraea japonica* species, and members of the *Chenopodiaceae* or goosefoot family, also have good lysine rich pollen and nectar at mid-summer when needed by these wasps. Many of the Encyrtid, Chalcid, and Braconid wasps are also attracted by tiny flowers. Some of these wasps are poly-embryonic; that is, from one small egg up to 1000 young can develop. They make up for their small size in this way. Another ubiquitous parasitic wasp group is the *Ichneumonidae* family. These small fierce looking wasps do not sting but depend on their nasty looking appearance for survival. These parasitic wasps are of great value in controlling noxious insects in the garden. *Trachnid* flies, which look like a hairy version of a bee, and *Syrphid* flies, which are found hovering around dish-shaped flowers, produce larvae which parasitize noxious insects and should be part of the normal balance within a garden. There is another group of beautiful beneficial insects called lacewings which have delicate, beaded, green or brown, attractive, transparent wings. These delicate insects are often found perched on damp green leaves, resting. Both the adults and larvae are predaceous on noxious insects. These graceful insects should be carefully nurtured within a garden. Another gardener's friend is the Antlion, which looks like a damselfly whose larvae dig cone shaped holes in the garden into which ants or other small roaming insects may fall. These succulent insects become the prey of the Antlion.

If the perennial area (E) is mulched with grass clippings or stable manure mixed with wood chips and a little soil in spring before serious growth begins, the worm population in the soil will increase. The mulch will foster increased populations of ground and rove beetles and fire-flies due to a moderated, cool and damp soil surface area. This will in turn attract a greater flying insect, toad, and bird population.

Mulching is important in some areas of the garden as it modifies the microclimate of the soil and reduces weeding. It also supplies nest-ing materials which are sparse in a suburban setting. For this reason, little pieces of groomed dog or cat fleece placed near a composter in spring are invaluable building materials for birds. This composted organic matter also acts as a mineral salt-lick for butterflies.

The area (F) of the bioplan is a protection hedge and a visual back-drop for the flowering border area (E). This hedge should be of local hedging plant species that are proven dependable and maintenance free. For instance, in eastern North America, it can be of Eastern white cedar, *Thuja occidentalis*. By contrast, in the maritime milder areas of Europe, where the growing season is extremely long with very little or no dormancy to check growth, the maintenance of this type of hedge becomes a full time job for the gardener. On the Western seaboard of North America and in milder climates, the slow growing fragrant Langley escallonia, *Escallonia edinensis*, with its pale pink flowers can be grown. The finest cultivar of this escallonia is *E.e.* 'Slieve Donard', which grows to a fine compact 6' (2 m) form ideal for small gardens.

The specimens (J), (K) and (L) of the bioplan should be a mix-ture of evergreen trees and deciduous trees. The specie for (J) should be an evergreen of a weeping or slightly weeping habit to contrast the vertical lines of the house nearby. Such trees as the Eastern hemlock, *Tsuga canadensis*, or the Nootka cypress, *Chamaecyparis nootkatensis* (zones 5–9), are ideal and will add grace to the garden. If the garden-er wishes to plant any species of the Ribes family for kitchen fruit, then (J) should not be a western or eastern white pine, *Pinus monticola* or *P. strobus*, or the whitebark pine *P. albicaulis* or any of the five needled pines, as Ribes co-host the pine blister rust fungus. The pine species *Pinus pence* is said to be resistant. *Ribes nigrum* 'Consort' is the only immune, non-transmitting currant cultivar that can safely be planted with these species. The deciduous trees (K1, 2) can be apple, pear, or cherry trees, hop hornbeam *Ostrya virginiana*, lime trees *Tillia* species, nut trees, or mulberries such as *Morus rubra*. Open trees, such as the apple, will attract many songbirds, including bluebirds. A nesting box for this beautiful bird can be discreetly placed 6' (2 m) high with a southeast facing aspect near the tree. The garden provides an ideal sheltered habitat. The hop hornbeam is a good winter feeding tree for such species as partridge and overwintering birds. Nut trees will attract early hairstreak butterflies as well as being a food source. Mulberries will attract an enormous number of birds into the garden with their sought after dark red to black edible fruit which resembles the blackberry. The deciduous tree (K3) should be a top-grafted weeping tree to add grace to the growing lines of the garden and to act as a visual counterbalance to (J), (K1), (K2), and (L) groupings. The tree (L) should be somewhat smaller in stature than (K1) and (K2) and should be a small shrub or tree. If possible, the shrub should have a low bridging effect between (K1) and (K2) to give variation in the tree line. Suggested plants for this area are the Russian olive, *Elaeagnus angustifolia*, with its handsome silver shimmering foliage and its annual June crop of fragrant yellow flowers. The native billowy shadblow or downey serviceberry, *Amelanchier canadensis,* which shows a soft pink in its early unopened flower racemes and on its streaked trunk, will be the first small tree to show spring growth and flowering in cold gardening areas. Its edible fruit tastes like a blueberry and is very attractive to a host of birds.

The areas (G), (H) and (I) of the garden bioplan are part of a small kitchen garden, the size of which is dependent on the household. The areas called (G) are a series of raised beds; (H) is the composting area; and (I) is a trellis for practical vertical plant growth and design. The kitchen garden beds should have some annuals broadcast on them and subsequently be treated as weeds. The single cultivars of *Papaver sominiferum* entice beneficial insects into the vegetable rows. In addition, some marigolds should be planted in areas designated for radishes and turnip varieties. Marigolds secrete chemicals which act as a nematicide, keeping nematodes out of these kitchen crops. One planting of marigolds will secrete sufficient nematicide for a five-year protection period. The flowers also invite beneficial insects into the vegetable garden both for control and pollination. The trellising area (I) around the kitchen crops will give insect eating birds protection and the opportunity to stalk pestilent insects.

Fauna

Within the bioplan and depending on the gardener's taste, some small natural niches should be arranged for the indigenous fauna. An area of natural stonework, preferably employing drywall building techniques, will considerably increase and aid the snake population. Snakes are very beneficial and should have habitat provided for them. Open stonework in a damp area provides cover for frogs, toads, lizards, and salamanders. In recent years a marked decline in the amphibious species has been observed. A watergarden with open stonework is a superb habitat for the encouragement and preservation of these creatures, provided some shade is also supplied. The increase in U.V. light caused by the ozone (O_3) depletion of the atmosphere is damaging to all amphibians in varying degrees. U.V. light causes DNA damage to amphibians, which is in turn repaired by an enzyme called photolyase. Amphibians seem to vary in their ability to produce this enzyme. Those species who have a lot of it survive, those who do not are becoming endangered. Water and shade in the garden provide a temporary helpful measure for the time being.

An eastern garter snake, *Thamnophis sirtalis sirtalis,* rests in a sour cherry tree.

Occasionally to preserve a garden from the predations of dogs, cats, and squirrels which may become pestilent, Rue, a known deterrent, is planted as an inoffensive yet effective means of keeping other people's pets at bay. For design purposes *Ruta graveolens* 'Variegata' can be used, though the common Rue is a chemically similar plant. Rue contains d-limonene, rutin, and coumarin in the glandular tissue of the leaf. Monarda species, dill (*Anethum graveolens*), and caraway (*Carum carvi*) also contain d-limonene. These chemicals are strongly irritating to dogs, cats, and any other fur bearing mammals. These compounds dissolve into the oils on their fur, which they groom and thus have a lesson in avoidance therapy for that particular garden.

 **Orchestration**

Many years ago I began to realize that I was gardening differently. As the garden evolved over time I realized that the reason why the bird population was so high and the insect population so varied was that I had a masterplan in my head that met all the myriad needs of the creatures and flowers under my care. Now, the garden has matured. It looks as if it has been there forever. Indeed, it must seem so to the flowers also, because they are busily setting seed in a pattern such as I have never seen before. The tiny bulbs of wild-crossed daffodils are coming up everywhere, in the lawn, in the edging area, in the borders and I do so hate to treat them as weeds. I wonder what I will do, there are so many this year!

We kept honeybees for almost 20 years until two black bears decided to go shopping for honey in the garden. One particularly fine spring day I noticed that the bees were making use of the thousands of daffodils planted in the garden. Since the flowers are so large, I became curious. I found that the bees had eaten a small hole at the base of the corona just at the position where the daffodil cup sits in the daffodil saucer. The hole was just large enough for the honey bee to collect nectar secreted at the base of the trilocular ovary. Different creatures shop in different ways!

I make a great use of bulbs in the landscape. One particular bulb that I am very fond of is the Summer Hyacinth, *Galtonia candicans*. Since all the literature on this bulb indicates that it is fragrant, I have invited hundreds of people to smell them when they are in bloom. To date, nobody has discovered the fragrance of those flowers. I think I can safely stop worrying about my olfactory senses.

I always watch for winter aconite on St. Patrick's Day, the 17th of March. The yellow heads rarely fail me. They are the affirmation that spring is beginning and that I will soon hear the honking of the great flocks of Canadian Geese above the house flying so high that only their giant V formation can be seen, an echo of their collective voice, moving in their ancient airways towards their breeding grounds in the waking north.

When bioplanning comes together with soil and water, airways and fragrance, flora and fauna in harmony, something is created that is not quite heard, not quite seen, and not quite felt, but nonetheless very real — something we sense every summer evening in our own garden.

The whip-poor-wills plop about 50 feet away from the front door and sing to their cousins who answer by echo until the whole garden is alive with sound in the diminishing light. The nighthawks clip their sharp jag of catch overhead in their intense joy of the hunt. The little puffs of saw-whet owls chirp over the barn sills, while their larger cousins ho-ho through the tall trees in a laugh for their own regime. The darkening airways are filled with lightning bugs and criss-crossed with the sonar of bats as they break their daily dormancy for the insect delights of the night. The flying squirrels soar overhead from limb to limb in a marvel of upward thrust. Dark bandit forms loom down from trees in a tapered family of grim distrust, while a buck grunts to a doe to be silent as we wander through the garden among the glow beetles giving off a luminescence suggesting that all is not darkness out there in the world.

On the way back to the house, wave upon wave of fragrance hits us, made all the more keen by the looming moth-filled flowers as they burst forth their odors. The breeze winds the smells around us, and we stop to breath these airs into our soul. Is not the intent of nature to tease the mind skyward, for does not nature mimic the very House of God?

Bioplans

The bioplan is the blueprint for all connectivity of life in nature. It is the fragile web which keeps each creature in balance with it's neighbor. It is predation and prey. It is the victor and the victim in a vast cycle of elemental life which is almost beyond our comprehension. It is the quantum mechanic of the green chloroplast without which we would all die. It is the domatal hairs on the underside of deciduous trees harboring the parasites for aphids. It is the U.V. traffic light signalling system in flowers for the insect world. It is the terpine aerosol S.O.S. produced by plants in response to invasive damage. It is the toxin-trick offered by plants for the protection of butterflies. It is the mantle of man, in his life and in his death, a Divine Contract, to all who share this planet.

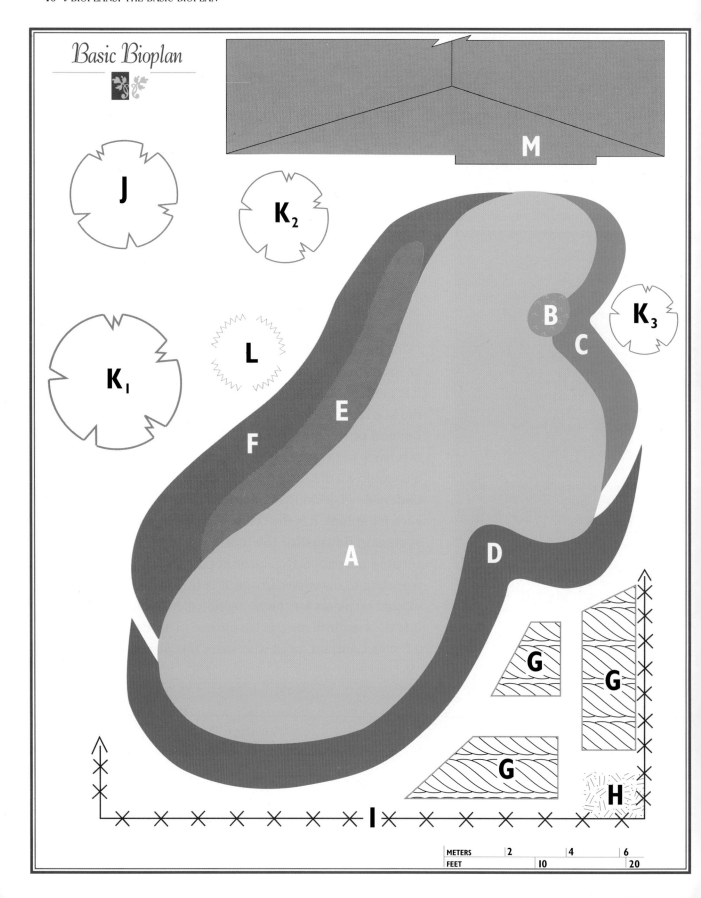

Basic Bioplan

Legend

A. Lawn Area
B. Water Feature
C. Flowering Hedge
D. Feeding Hedge
E. Perennial Border
F. Evergreen Hedge

G. Kitchen Garden Area
H. Composting Area
I. Trellis
J. Evergreen Tree
K. Deciduous Trees
L. Flowering Shrub
M. House

Page 38-39: The single open flower of *Rosa carolina* begins a pink opening to the white border.

Suburban Bioplan

This bioplan is designed to serve a small suburban home situated on a typical subdivision lot of 40 x 80 feet (18 x 36 metres), re-instating the balance of nature upset during the development of the subdivision and the construction of the house. This plan transforms the home into a biosphere sanctuary, with plantings of *Geranium sanguineum* 'Lancastriense', *G.S.* 'Album' and *G. cinerum* 'Subcanlescens' providing avian protection around the water features.

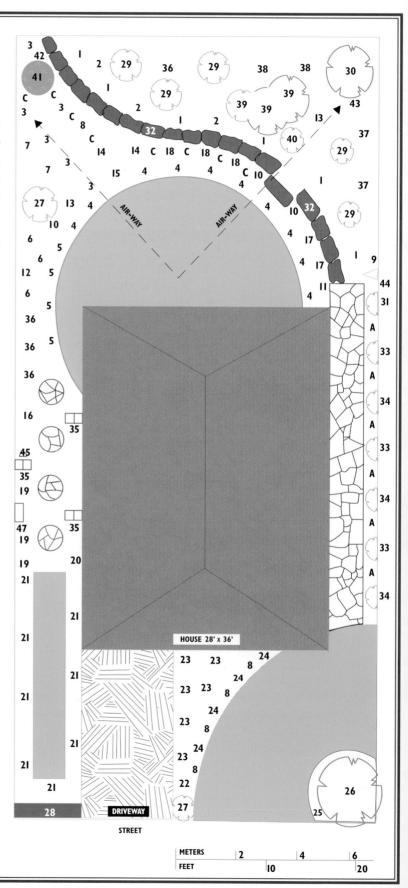

HOUSE 28' x 36'

AIR-WAY

AIR-WAY

DRIVEWAY

STREET

| METERS | 2 | 4 | 6 |
| FEET | 10 | | 20 |

Suburban Bioplan

SPECIE	BIOPLAN CODE
1. *Geranium sanguineum* 'Lancastriense'	Anti-feline, bird protection
2. *Geranium sanguineum* 'Album'	Anti-feline, bird protection
3. *Geranium cinerum* 'Subcaulescens'	Anti-feline, bird protection
4. *Gypsophila repens* 'Rosea'	Beneficial insect
5. *Gypsophila paniculata* 'Rosenscheier'	Beneficial insect
6. *Iris germanica* 'Beverley Sills'	Bees, ambush bugs
7. *Iris siberica* 'Rigugi-sakura'	Humming birds
8. *Iris siberica nana alba*	Beneficial amphibian
9. *Iris dichotoma* 'Alba'	Humming bird
10. *Allium oreophilum* 'Zwanenburg'	Anti-aphid, allelochemical
11. *Lilium regale* 'Album'	Fragrance, tree frogs
12. *Lilium* 'Thunderbolt'	Fragrance, beneficial insect
13. *Lilium* 'Journey's End'	Humming birds, night moths
14. *Aquilegia vulgaris* 'Nora Barlow'	Butterflies
15. *Aster ericoides* 'Ester'	Butterflies, beneficial insects
16. *Aster divaricatus*	Fragrance, lacewings, ground beetles
17. *Campanula carpatica* 'White Chips'	Small beneficial wasps
18. *Aster* 'Royal Amethyst'	Admiral butterfly
19. *Digitalis purpurea* 'Alba'	Honey bees, beneficial humming birds
20. *Arisaema triphyllum*	Amphibians
21. *Erythronium revolutum* 'Jeanette Bickell'	Amphibians
22. *Narcissus* 'Cassata'	Humming birds, beneficial insects
23. *Hemerocallis* 'Evening Gown'	Fragrance
24. *Hemerocallis* 'Pardon Me'	Fragrance
25. *Phlox divaricata* 'Fuller's White'	Fragrance, small beneficials
26. *Sorbus folgneri*	Berries for winter birds
27. *Rosa* 'Nevada'	Small beneficials and wasps
28. *Thuya fastigiata*	Hedge for Winter protection, nesting
29. *Lonicera x xylosteoides* 'Clavey's Dwarf'	Hummingbirds, bee, moths lepidoptera, berries for birds
30. *Picea omorika*	Perching, protection, U.V. resistant
31. Duchess of Oldenberg dwarf apple	Blue bird habitat, kitchen
32. Stone wall	6" (15 cm) rise
33. Meteor sour cherry	Beneficial insects, kitchen
34. North star sour cherry	Beneficial insects, kitchen
35. *Hydrangia anomala* sp. *petiolaris* 6' open trellis as visual baffle	Shade beneficial insects, allelochemicals
36. *Clematis tangutica*	Beneficial insects, seeds for small birds, nesting for hummingbirds
37. *Clematis tibetana* ssp. *vernayi* 'Ludlow and Sherriff'	Beneficial insects, seeds for small birds, nesting for hummingbirds
38. *Clematis virginiana*	Beneficial insects, seeds for small birds, nesting for hummingbirds and fragrance
39. *Daphne cneorum*	Fragrance
40. *Salix pendula* (dwarf)	Honey bees, pollen
41. Water feature	Water for Bioplan amphibians
42. Toad house	Insect patrol
43. Blue bird house 6', S–E	Insect predation
44. Hummingbird feeders	Saturated solution of glucose, hummingbirds
45. Wren house	Morning, evening predation
46. Bat house	Mosquito predation

Underplanting	
A *Trillium grandiflorum*	Allelochemical
B *Chionodoxa luciliae* 'Pink Giant'	Pollen, Nectar
C *Narcissus jonquilla* 'Rip Van winkle'	Fragrance, Ambush Bug predation

Canine Loggia Bioplan

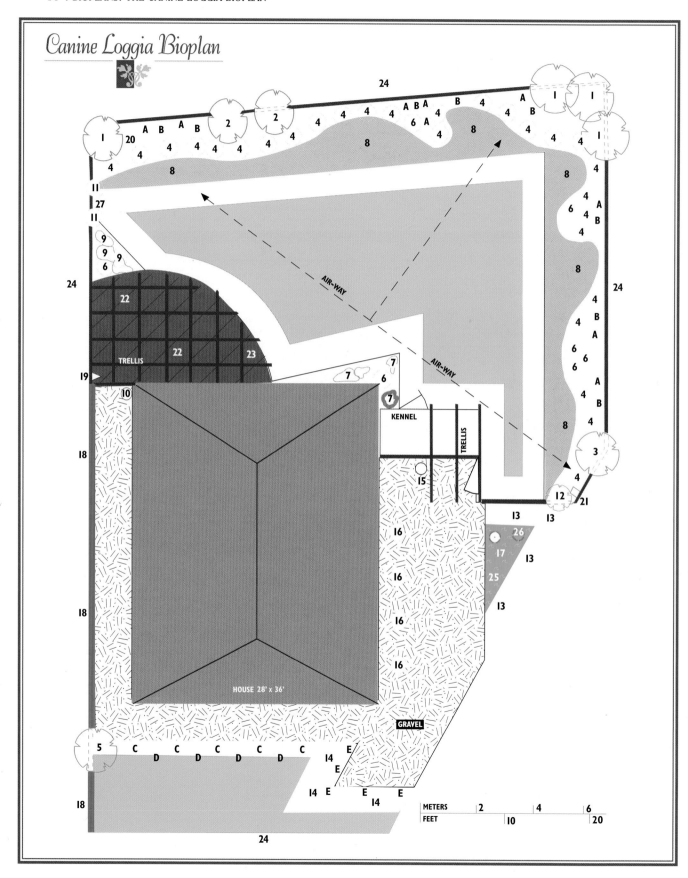

Canine Loggia Bioplan

This bioplan plan was designed for a corner lot of uneven shape which is also the home of the family pet. The predominant design color is shimmering white. The plantings are canine friend-ly, offering U.V. protection for the animal and producing Thymol from *Thymus pseudolanuginosus* in the airways which has a beneficial effect on the dog's well-being because it is antiseptic, anthelmintic (kills intestinal worms), and detoxifies urine. Thymol is also of benefit to flying insects, including honey bees.

SPECIE	BIOPLAN CODE
1. *Cornus alternifolia* 'Argentea'	Beneficial insects, berries for birds and mammals
2. *Sambucus nigra* 'Pulverulenta'	Beneficial small flying insects; berries for birds, mammals and kitchen
3. *Lonicera tatarica* 'Alba'	Beneficial insects, Lepidoptera, moths, hummingbirds, berries for birds
4. *Spirea japonica* 'shirobana'	Beneficial wasps
5. *Corylus avellana* 'Contorta'	Spring pollen source
6. *Yucca gloriosa* 'Variegata'	Water collection for beneficial insects
7. *Ruta graveolens* 'Variegata'	Canine deterrent from digging, bactericide
8. *Thymus pseudolanguinosus*	Trampleproof canine plant, fragrant
9. Large rocks, *Opuntia humifusa*	Sun bathing, vit. D absorption by canine, opuntia fruit for kitchen, medicine
10. *Vitis lambrusca* (Fox Grape)	Fragrant in July, berries for birds, mammals and kitchen, wren habitat
11. *Clematis paniculata* (zone 4 – 9)	Small, beneficial wasps, winter seed feed
12. *Thuya occidentalis* 'Columbia'	Winter bird protection, nesting and perching
13. *Phlox divaricata* 'Fuller'sWhite'	Fragrant, U.V. protection for amphibians
14. *Hemerocallis* 'Kwanso Variegata'	Ambush bugs, water collection for beneficial insects, amphibians
15. *Wisteria venusta* (zones 6 – 9)	Soil conditioner, beneficial insects, foliar feed
Wisteria floribunda (zones 5 – 6)	
Wisteria virginiana (zones 2 – 9)	
16. *Gypsophila repens* 'Alba'	Small flying beneficial wasps
17. *Iris pseudacorus* 'Alba'	Water pumping station, amphibians
18. *Thuya fastigiata* (hedge)	Winter protection, nesting, perching and fragrance
19. Wren box	Pest patrol
20. Blue bird box	Pest patrol
21. Tree swallow box	Mosquito patrol
22. Shade arbour	Ultra-violet irradiation protection for canine and household members
23. Wooden deck 6" (12cm) rise	
24. Ornamental victorian trellis wall	Perching for airways
25. Water-garden 2 ft (60 cm) deep, reflective	Amphibian habitat
26. *Lemna minor* (oxygenator)	Natural oxygenator of water, U.V. protection for amphibians
27. *Trompe de l'oeil*, long, mirror underneath	Space amplification

Underplanting

A. *Allium giganteum*	Soil protector, beneficial flying insects
B. *Narcissus* 'Papillion blanc'	Fresh pollen and nectar source
C. *Pulsatilla occidentalis* 'Alba'	Nectar source
D. *Crocus chrysanthus* 'Snow Bunting'	Fresh pollen source
E. *Fritillaria meleagris* 'Alba'	Fresh pollen, nectar

Mutchmor School Bioplan

| METERS | 2 | 4 | 6 |
| FEET | 10 | | 20 |

TEACHING CODE

1. Flower head, dried bird food, string heads for feeding birds, Oct, Nov
2. Caterpillars, pupate, paper making, edible
3. Edible plant, paper making, pupate
4. Science of flight, biological limits
5. Kindergarten, broadcast seeds, seed capsules, art class, seeds in cookies
6. Observation
7. Edible plant, butterfly plant, very fragrant
8. Butterfly plant, pupation
9. Bird-house from coconut, bathouse
10. Bird house gourd, dry gourds in classroom over winter for birdhouse. Paint, art class
11. Edible plant, pepper taste
12. Edible plant, hot taste
13. Boardwalk, motor skills, route to feeder
14. Edible peas, dry pod, Mendel's law of inheritance, racial discrimination
15. Nitrogen fixation in roots. Bacteria; stain, use of microscope and hand lens
16. Two foot long cucumbers edible, male and female flowers, pollenation
17. Small pumpkins, self-sufficiency. Art class
18. Textures, amphibian and ground beetle watch
19. Child's domain
20. Hummingbirds can be observed inside bean castle
21. Fresh water daily, pine floaters with water. Honey bees and Lepidoptera

Mutchmor School Bioplan

This bioplan was designed for a nearly barren, elementary school yard, not only to restore biological diversity to the yard but also to teach students the basics of bioplanning and good gardening. The bioplan thus serves as an introduction to the science program at the school and can be used as a metaphor for peace among nations as students work to create a harmonious balance among the species in the garden.

SPECIE	BIOPLAN CODE
1. *Helianthus annus* 'Mammoth Russian'	Beneficial insects; pollenators
	Giant Sunflowers
2. *Brassica oleraceae* 'Osaka Pink'	Lepidoptera, cabbage butterflies
	Flowering Cabbage
3. *Brassica oleraceae* 'Nagoya Rose'	Lepidoptera, cabbage butterflies
	Flowering Kale
4. Bean castle of Scarlet Runner Beans	Humming birds; moths
5. *Papaver somniferum* 'Carnation Strain'	Bees, wasps, beneficial insects
6. *Alcea rosea* 'Rubra'	Hummingbirds
7. *Hesperis matronalis* 'Alba'	Lepidoptera; fragrance; edible plant
8. *Asclepias tuberosa* or	Lepidoptera, nectar source
Aster novae-angliae 'Pink Bouquet'	Lepidoptera, nectar source
9. Tree with hummingbird-feeder	Feeder birds; Bird nesting; bats
	Bird house, Bat House
10. Dipper gourd or birdhouse	Beneficial insects; male and female flowers
11. Peppergrass	Edible 10-day plant, pepper tasting
	(sulphur proteins)
12. Radishes	Edible 10-day plant, pepper tasting
	(sulphur proteins)
13 Board walkway	Amphibians, ground insects
14.Peas 'Little Marvel'	Beneficial insects,
15. Peanuts 'Early Spanish'	Beneficial insects
16. Cucumber 'Japanese Long pickling'	Beneficial insects, unusual fruit edible
17. Pumpkin 'Little Lantern'	Beneficial pollenation
18. Straw walk-way	Amphibians, ground insects
19. Entrance to tee-pee	Watchpost for children
20. Observation seats	Hummingbird viewing
21. Bowl with pine floaters	Beneficial insects drinking

Perennials

The perennial border,
a tall ship in full sail.

Perennials

 Many gardening experts consider north temperate gardens to be inferior to milder or more tropical gardens. North temperate gardens are not better or worse, but are merely different, just adding to the great diversity and variety in the world of gardens. From a plant connoisseur's point of view, a mid-summer's garden of north temperate species, well designed and cared for, in the majesty of its finely attuned blooms is like a tall ship in full sail. Its impact, color and the flowering symphony of its form is a wondrous and almost religious experience. The gardener who views and is thus part of such a garden is changed forever.

A north temperate garden exists because of the presence of a huge pool of perennials which is indigenous to the north temperate regions of the world. They are, therefore, acclimated to dormancy in harsh winters and fast and furious growth in short springs followed by flowering in hot summers. Minor climatic changes do not have a serious effect on north temperate plants, as their ability to survive enormous seasonal temperature variations is remarkable as well as surprising.

Because many of these north temperate plants have flexibility in growth characteristics combined with great beauty, they have been exposed to intensive hybridization. This has changed these flowers with a huge range of new characteristics forever. These include frost hardiness, drought resistance, vigor, color, fragrance and beauty.

Many of these plants are a repository of unique chemicals which are difficult or next to impossible to synthesize in a chemical laboratory because of their compound nature. Many of these chemicals are also changed by hybridization. In every civilization, past and present, the layman's knowledge of these naturally occurring chemicals has been identified with health. It is a great foolishness to forget or dismiss this knowledge, as in many cases of illness the route to recovery is all about us.

Perennial plants also create unique ecological niches for insects, migrating song birds, reptiles, amphibians, small mammals, and butterfly populations. For instance, the lowly dandelion releases its lysine rich pollen in spring only at a certain time of the day for foraging honey bees. Lysine is an essential amino acid which is needed for successful brood rearing. Without brood, or young, there would be no honey bees and without honey bees, no pollination. Without pollination, North America would face a severe food shortage resulting from sterile plants.

A grouping of antique plants makes an airy display in late August.

A north temperate, herbaceous perennial is a plant with a genetic target to live several successive hot and cold seasons. In that lifetime it will reproduce and set seed by means of an ingenious vehicle called flowering. In its answer to the universal call to reproduce its species, the plant will winter and live again for the same purpose in succeeding cycles.

The perennial flower is the victory of the vascular plant kingdom. The flower is the spin-off of the evolutionary process of sexual reproduction. The form of the flower evolved to attract insects to pollinate it so that reproduction of the species can proceed. So . . . it is not by luck alone that flowers are so beautiful, so fragrant, so varied so colorful and so very enticing. They are the keystone of the bioplan, filled with chemicals man has not yet learned to make even in the wildest of his dreams.

The following north temperate species will be discussed in detail: aquilegia, asclepia, aster, campanula, cornflower, delphinium, geranium, gypsophilum, hemerocallis, iris, monarda, paeony and phlox. These species form the backbone of a herbaceous, perennial border or a free form garden design. Biennials can be added to the planting scheme as can bulbs, corms, and tuberous plants to form an infinite variety in design from early spring to late fall.

My favorite flower in the big perennial border in mid-summer is black, the *Delphinium elatum* 'King Arthur.' Actually the flower itself is a deep violet, sheened with black reflections. The center of the flower, called the 'bee,' is black. The plants soar to a majesty of six to seven feet in a good year. I seem to spend July waiting for the flowers to open. When they do, it is the beginning of my orchestra of color in the border. Every plant in sight is juxtaposed at that time with my black beauties. When they are in flower, the garden sings with color. It is then that I walk around like a landlord surveying all that is mine, drinking in their beauty and wishing to share my particular corner of the planet with everyone.

My phlox collection I rescued from the jaws of a bulldozer. I was returning home from teaching at one of the local universities when I happened to notice a very big machine sitting in a very lovely garden. The two were not compatible to my mind. I hitched up my expensive skirt. (It is at times like this that my friends deny knowing me!) I asked the driver "Why?" He responded, "Orders! Take what you want!" I ran back to the lab and grabbed a handful of plastic bags. I slipped all the phlox. They survived. I am happy to say that these antique species have a new luxurious home . . . in my garden.

During the winter in Ireland gardeners chop away at hedges and shrubs, hoping and wishing that they would stop growing. I remember helping a cousin cut a piece of rose bush that decided to cross a twenty-foot span aiming for a variegated holly on the other side. It formed an arch over a gateway the horses used on the way up to the house to get their daily dose of petting. It took us most of the morning, and by the time we were finished cutting back — only a piece, mind you, of this rose — we were thoroughly exhausted and had to retire to the company of the teapot, indoors. Such are the trials of gardening in Ireland. In Canada, however, a far more refined system is in place for the ordinary gardener. We can take a rest over the winter months and dally with our gardening catalogs near a warm woodstove — mine is a 1921 Findlay Oval — and eat imported chestnuts roasted on top of it. You see, we can dream about gardening in snug comfort. The dream begins with the last flowering plant in the fall or early winter and ends with the first blossom in spring when reality takes over.

In Carrigliath *Aster novae-angliae* 'Rudelsburg', a six-foot giant with tumbles of pink reflexed flowers that smell of basswood honey blended with summer meadows, taunts the frost with a shaking of its head. I find that I daily go out into the garden to check this bank of flowers when winter is drawing close, and the chickadees pop down from the cedar limbs to reinforce this knowledge. Then I usually see a late admiral butterfly brightly skip on to the flowers for a feeding. I urge it to head south as it hovers in the air. Then I know that the garden has all been worthwhile.

By St Patrick's Day, 17th March, when the shamrock and harps are being worn on the streets of Ireland, I poke about in the beds of the raised rockery to see if I can find any surprises. In the middle of March the sun is high again on the horizon and the rays are warm enough to steam the heart out of the snow which is left, leaving a cage of delicate ice to enfold the golden tresses and green ruffed collar of the flowering aconite as it pushes its blooming way to face the rising sun. The green and gold comfort me for what I have missed and lost on this most Irish of days as I go about in my normal routine, refreshed from my long winter break and ready to start digging all over again like the eternal optimist because I know that I have all my friends to look forward to, the thousands of tips of daffodils, the red blush of the waterlilies, the shell pink colors of the shagbark hickories in the nuttery, the smells, the earth . . .

Aquilegia
COLUMBINE
Ranunculaceae
Zones 2–9

A hybrid aquilegia, Mrs. Scott-Elliot strain, with the Preston hybrid lilac 'Elinor', a late blooming lilac with a musk-like fragrance.

Columbines are hardy perennials coming from the northern temperate areas of the world. There are many fine species native to the North American continent such as *A. longissima, A. chrysantha* and *A. caerulea.* Aquilegias are planted in rock gardens and in the perennial border. The majority of the common columbines found in North American gardens are not true species but are hybrid columbines. There are hybrid strains of dwarf columbines of great beauty for the rockery and hybrid strains of exquisite pastel shades for the border. Many specie columbines flower late in the summer. If careful attention is given to planning, some of the North American species will extend flowering throughout the summer and even into September and October.

Organic Care
Most columbines like a neutral soil except for *A. caerulea* which requires an acid soil. The natural dwarf, *A. jonesii,* requires an alkaline soil. Columbines like a light, well drained sandy soil of moderate fertility. Drainage should be excellent in winter. Columbines will grow well on clay soils provided they are well drained. A rich soil will give rise to very large plants, which somewhat reduces their beauty.

Columbines can grow in full sun or half-shade. They are excellent additions to a shade garden. Columbines, especially *A. caerulea* species, grown in shade are sometimes attacked by leaf miners. Leaf miners will tunnel through the mature leaves' mesophyll leaving an ugly white track meandering through the leaf. In gardens where this becomes a severe problem, one very dilute spray of rotenone will terminate this damage. An early morning spray, just prior to flowering will be sufficient. Many columbines are very short lived, four to five years at the most, but are easily grown from seed.

Quality seeds should be purchased. *A. vulgaris* 'Nora Barlow', *A. x Helenae,* a hybrid of *A. caerulea* and *A. flabellata,* and many of the McKana giant hybrids come true from seed, as well as *A. akitensis* (syn. *A. flabellata pumila*) *A. ecalcarata,* and *A. glandulosa.*

Ecofunction

Columbines, when massed in the open, appear to be one of the favorite foods for the larva of the little sulphur butterfly (*Eurema lisa*). These butterflies are wide-spread in the eastern North American continent and can be found swarming around puddles after a summer's rain.

The columbine is also a favorite food source for hummingbirds. Red or yellow flowers are most attractive to them. A useful means of keeping these birds visiting one's garden is to hang a hummingbird feeder over a planting of columbines in the spring. The birds will return to the feeder when other nectar sources are not available.

Design

The flowers of columbines are white, yellow, blue, lavender, and red. There are also some very fine bitonal pastel shades. There are double, spurless flowers and beautiful long spurred flowers. The dwarf forms, planted in blocks, are wonderful rockery plants. Some examples are *A. akitensis* 6" (15 cm), *A. saximontana,* 2–10" (5–25 cm), *A. discolor* 4" (10 cm), *A. jonesii* 6" (15 cm), and Biedermeier or the dragonfly hybrids 15" (38 cm).

The larger columbines grow to 2.5–3' (75–90 cm) and have a spread of 12–18" (30–45 cm). The plants are covered with flowers when in bloom. The blooming time can last for up to six weeks or more if dead-headed. This makes them very useful in a border.

A. caerulea, A. chrysantha, A. longissima, A. vulgaris 'Nora Barlow', *A. v.* 'Nivera' and Mrs. Scott Elliot', and McKana' hybrids are superb mid-border plants. The blue, yellow, white, and pink flower colors combine softly with all June border flowers and bulbs, such as the late double flowered hyacinths, camassias, alliums, and the early asiatic hybrid lilies. A remarkable, identical tonal composition is that of the late flowering lilac, *Syringa prestoniae* 'Elinor', with the pink strain of the McKana hybrids. The lilac is very hardy and has a heady, spicy fragrance, completely different from other lilac species. This planting composition stays in flower for about five to six weeks.

For shade gardens, the native maiden-hair fern, *Adiantum pedatum,* combines well with the tall and dwarf versions of the native columbine *A. canadensis* and *A. c.* 'Nana'. This is a bold color composition of red-yellow and soft blue-green. The dissected foliage of both plant and fern is almost identical and acts as an additional, delicate foil for the flowers.

A. caerulea, 2.5' (75 cm), a native from the Rocky Mountains, combines naturally with another native, *Phlox divaricata,* 12" (30 cm). This fragrant composition of blue, lavender, and white is crisp, refreshing, and can fit into a shaded area. The *A. c.* 'Candidissima' and 'Alba' cultivars are good white border plants in groups of three or four.

Aquilegia Species and Cultivars

NAME	COLOR	HEIGHT	MONTH	ZONE
A. alpina	blue	2' (60 cm)	July-Aug	2-9
A. a. 'Superba'	blue	1' (30 cm)	July-Aug	2-9
A. caerulea	blue	2.5' (75 cm)	May-June	2-9
A. c. 'Alba'	white	2.5' (75 cm)	May-June	2-9
A. c. 'Candidissima'	white	2.5' (75 cm)	May-June	2-9
A. c. 'Citrina'	yellow	2.5' (75 cm)	May-June	2-9
A. canadensis	red/yellow	2.5-3' (75-90 cm)	June-July	2-9
A. c. 'Nana'	red/yellow	1' (30 cm)	June-July	2-9
A. chrysantha	yellow	2.5-3' (75-90 cm)	June-July	4-9
A. c. 'Alba Plena	double white	2.5-3' (75-90 cm)	June-July	4-9
A. c. 'Flore Pleno'	double yellow	2.52-3' (75-90 cm)	June-July	4-9
A. discolor	blue/white	4" (10 cm)	May-June	5-9
A. ecalcarata	red	12" (30 cm)N.S.	July	3-9
A. flabellata (syn. *A. Akitensis*)				
A. f. 'Pumila'	lilac/white	6" (15 cm)	July-Aug	3-9
A. f. 'Blue Angel'	purple/blue	6" (15 cm)	July-Aug	3-9
A. f. 'White Angel'	white	6" (15 cm)	July-Aug	3-9
A. x helena (*A. flabellata x A. caerulea*)	blue/white	15" (38 cm)	June-July	3-9
A. glandulosa	blue/white	8-10" (60-90 cm)	May-June	2-9
A. jonesii	blue	6" (15 cm)	June	2-9
A. longissima	yellow	2-3' (60-90 cm)	July-Oct	4-9
A. saximontana	blue/white	4" (10 cm)	June	2-9
A. vulgaris		1-2' (30-60 cm)	June-July	
A. v. 'Flore Pleno'	double white	2' (60 cm)	June-July	2-9
A. v. 'Nora Barlow'	pink/green	2' (60 cm)	June-July	2-9

DWARF HYBRID AQUILEGIAS				
Biedermeier Hybrids	Bicolors, mixed colors	15" (38 cm)	June-July	2-9
Music Dwarf Hybrids	Bicolors, mixed colors	18" (46 cm)	June-July	2-9
TALL HYBRID AQUILEGIAS				
Mrs. Scott-Elliot's Hybrids	pastels	2-3' (60-90 cm)	June-July	2-9
McKana's Giant Hybrids	pastels	2.5-3' (75-90 cm)	June-July	2-9
'Crimson Star'	red/white	(50 cm)	May-June	2-9
'Copper Queen'	red/brown	2' (60 cm)	May-June	2-9
'Rose Queen'	rose	2' (60 cm)	June-July	2-9
'Snow Queen'	white	(70 cm)	June-July	2-9
'Silver Queen '	white/yellow	(80 cm)	June-July	2-9

Asclepias are a large group of perennials found principally in North America and Africa. Two of the North American species are garden plants that are commonly known. These are *Asclepias tuberosa* and *A. incarnata*. The asclepiadaceae family is an important food and nectar source for butterflies of the North American continent, both in their wild and cultivated states.

Organic Care
Asclepias tuberosa, A. quadrifolia, A. purpurascens, and *A. syriaca* like a medium rich, dry, slightly acidic soil. The addition of rock phosphate, wood ashes, and humus in small amounts to a friable sandy soil is ideal. The soil should be well drained in both summer and winter. All of these asclepias species should be grown in full sun conditions. *A. incarnata* will grow happily in damper areas. This plant may also be planted in partial shade.

Asclepias are best grown from seed in March to May and then transplanted carefully to their final site in the garden as soon as the plants are about 6" (15 cm) tall. When mature, the plant has a most elaborate, brittle tap-root system that is easily damaged, rendering it difficult to transplant at that stage.

Ecofunction
A. tuberosa, 2' (60 cm), with its brilliant orange-red, upright, terminal umbels blooming in July and August represents party-time for butterflies. It is one of the most important flowers of a butterfly garden. Minor foliage damage due to larval feeding should be ignored. *A. incarnata,* 3' (90 cm), is also a desirable plant for a butterfly garden.

Asclepias
BUTTERFLY FLOWER, MILKWEED
Asclepiadaceae
Zones 3–9

An exceptional butterfly plant, *Asclepias tuberosa,* can be the basis of an orange-red monochrome garden.

Down from the seed capsules is used by many species of birds as nesting material. Down can also be spun with silk in a one to three ratio to make a superior yarn which is non-allergenic. This yarn can be dyed using mordants in the normal manner for silk.

Asclepias are sources of both modern and traditional medicines. The dried root was principally used as an expectorant for such respiratory tract infections as pleurisy. It was also one of the many natural compounds used as poultices on open sores. The latex-type sap of asclepias could well stand scientific investigation for some of its peculiar plastic properties.

Design

The flowers of asclepias are an attractive umbellate form in white, yellow, orange-red, or purple.

A. tuberosa flowers in July and August and becomes quite a wide bushy plant as it matures. The many flower clusters are a fluorescent orange-red and are extremely attractive. They are spectacular when massed in large numbers. They create a fine monochrome scene of hot, intense color.

A seasonal monochrome of orange-red can be created in the garden using *A. tuberosa* as its epicenter. In the May to June garden *Tulipa greigii* 'Easter Surprise', 14" (35 cm), and the late *Tulipa viridiflora* 'Artist' can be massed with *Narcissus* 'Articole' (Division XI), 20" (50 cm), against a background of the shrub, *Potentilla* 'Red Ace' and *Rosa foetida* 'Bicolor', the Austrian copper briar rose (zone 5–9). In July, *Asclepias tuberosa* can be massed with *Hemerocallis fulva,* the common tawny day-lily and *Kniphofia macowanii,* 2' (60 cm), the Torch lily. All of these species combine to make a hot color scheme so suited to city or suburban gardens. All of these species, fortunately, like similar cultural conditions.

A. tuberosa is difficult to fit into a perennial border, but it can be done using the intense blue of *Anchusa* and some white *Campanula persifolia* or *C. lactiflora* 'Alba' nearby to dilute the intensity of Asclepia's colors.

Ideal for a wild garden or a semi-wilderness area to attract butterflies are *A. quadrifolia,* 1' (30 cm), the four-leaved milkweed, whose pale pink umbels blossom in May and June. *A. purpurascens,* the purple milkweed, 3' (90 cm), whose magenta flowers bloom in June and July, and *A. syriaca,* 3–6' (90–180 cm), whose dusty rose-colored flowers are ubiquitous in North America, are both particularly good additions for a summer cottage wild garden area.

Asclepias Species

NAME	COLOR	HEIGHT	MONTH	ZONE
A. incarnata	rose-purple	3' (90 cm)	July-Aug	2-9
A. purpuracens	magenta	3' (90 cm)	July-Aug	2-9
A. quadrifolia	pink	1' (30 cm)	May-June	2-9
A. syriaca	rose	3-6' (90-180 cm)	June-Aug	2-9
A. tuberose	red-orange	2' (60 cm)	July-Aug	3-9

❦ Asters are grown mostly for their late summer and autumn display of flowers in the garden. Many North American asters have been borrowed by European breeders to develop new hybrid species. These hybrids give an explosion of color and form in the fall. The leading aster hybrids are the New York asters, *A. novi-belgii,* and the New England asters, *A. novae-angliae.* Because the parents are native to Canadian growing conditions, it appears that most of the hybrids are especially suited to north temperate gardens given their frost resistance, drought tolerance, and general plant hardiness. On the other hand, cultivars or hybrids of the Italian aster or *Aster amellus,* which are so popular in England, are not very hardy in Canada, but may be grown in zones 7–9 without winter protection.

Organic Care

Asters thrive in any neutral garden soil of medium fertility which is well drained. For maximum flowering and plant height, asters should have a reasonable supply of water throughout the growing season. The lime loving alpine asters, which grow from a crown root, can be easily grown from seed, as can the many wild asters and the hybrid, *Aster* x *frikartii.* The many new hybrids should be propagated by division as they will not come true from seed. Asters should be divided every two to three years. Many asters have rhizomous roots which form dense mats, and if they are not divided regularly, their flowering will seriously decline.

Many of the New York asters, *A. novi-belgii,* are resistant to powdery mildew. This is a fungal disease to which asters are prone in very humid summers.

The aster leafhopper is sometimes a problem. The grey nymphs, or young, are found working their way up on the older leaves. Their presence is noticed by the leaf damage they cause. They may be found in large numbers on both surfaces of the leaves. This leafhopper is a vector for aster yellows, which causes severe stunting of

Aster
**MICHAELMAS DAISY,
FROST FLOWER**
Compositae
Zones 2–9

'Alma Potschke', a *novae-angliae* aster, is a magnificent double red in September to October when few true reds are available to the gardener.

The crisp white of *Aster novae-belgii* 'White Ladies' is a fine addition to a white border in September and October.

Aster novae-angliae 'Harrington's Pink' combines very well with *Chrysanthemum rubellum* 'Clara Curtis' and *Aster ericoides* 'Chastity' (left), flowering from September into the end of October.

asters. Natural pyrethrums may be used for control.

Occasionally an aster stalk borer is busy. It is found only by the damage done to the mature flowering stalks. Should the gardener observe that the stalks have become brittle and break off readily, the borer should be suspected. Close examination of the stalks or stems will reveal a hollow dark stem. Upon discovering the presence of such a borer, it should be found and destroyed. A spring dusting of wood-ashes around the plant discourages these borers.

Ecofunction

Many asters such as *A. ericoides* accumulate selenium and are, therefore, in large amounts, poisonous to livestock. Because of this phenomena, some aster species are useful as tracer plants in finding selenium deposits for geologists.

Asters are an integral part of the butterfly garden. Shades of red and pink should be chosen for this purpose. Late butterflies will make considerable use of hardy asters in flower. Honey bees and other flying insects make asters one of their favorite stop-overs in the last pollen and nectar gathering push before winter. Considerable enjoyment can be had by watching them fill their pollen sacs with yellow pollen.

The flowering of asters coincides with the beginning of the school year in North America. Thus, these species should be part of a biological observation unit for children.

Design

A border of asters is an unforgettable spectacle in the fall. Tall asters, of any color, should be used as background material, then medium sized asters with dwarf asters in the front. A backdrop, in series, of the sweetly scented *Clematis paniculata,* which bears hundreds of clusters of small cream-colored flowers, can be used to good effect. The whole border can be underplanted with trumpet-daffodils (Division I), large cupped daffodils (Division II), or the split-corona or orchid flowering daffodils (Division XI) for a spring show. The roots of the aster will not interfere with these large bulbed daffodils which have to be so deeply planted. This concept of a fall border can be a small area or a large regular border or can be planted as a monochrome border.

Tall asters are used to great advantage at the back of a conventional flower border, where they take over from *Echinaceae purpurea,* which have, in turn, taken over from delphiniums. Of the tall strains, the author has developed two new hybrids of the New England aster, *A. novae-angliae,* *A. n-a.* 'Queen Erika' with deep rose flowers 6' (1.8 m) and an extremely long twelve-week blooming period from August into October, and a second hybrid called *A. n.* 'Comanche' 6' (1.8 m) which has an unusual, changeable flowering habit. Some flowers are white one day and change to a sky blue the following day. This aster also has a twelve-week blooming period starting in the second week of August.

The finest, by far, of all the medium height asters are the New England aster, *A. novae-angliae* 'Alma Potschke', 2' (60 cm), which is a deep true red, and the New York aster, *A. novi-belgii* 'White Ladies', 2' (60 cm), flowering for ten weeks at the end of August into September, their flowers being a clear sparkling white. This *A. novi-belgii* aster is a very good addition to a white border.

The best dwarf mounded asters are the Royal Gem Series of cultivars developed at the Royal Botanical Garden in Hamilton, Ontario. These cultivars are 18" (46 cm) and are extremely floriferous, flowering in September and October. A more dwarfed strain of cultivars has been developed from *A. dumosus* which has a more creeping habit and is a useful rock garden plant blooming in the fall.

There are a number of aster species which are good fall garden plants. *Aster x frikartii* 'Moench', (90 cm), and *A. x frikartii* 'Wonder of Staffa', (90 cm), both flower for fourteen weeks from July into October. The lavender flowers are 2" (5 cm) across with golden yellow centers. These asters are well worth growing, but are not very hardy, thriving only in zones 7–9. Planting sites in other zones should be chosen with great care to obtain the warmest microclimate in the garden.

'A. divaricatus', 18–24" (45–60 cm), the white wood aster, is a native species which has been grown in English gardens since the eighteenth century. It likes shade and dry growing conditions and has extremely attractive heart-shaped leaves which combine well with Bergenias, especially when massed. The native *A. ericoides* (the Heath Aster), 1–3' (30–90 cm), has a weeping habit. Myriads of tiny white flowers and its leaves cascade down the drooping branches. When the flowers age they become tinged with pink. The plant's form is identical to the American Elm, *Ulmus americanus*.

Aster alpinus 'Roseus' flowers in late spring.

Aster Species and Cultivars

NAME	COLOR	HEIGHT	MONTH	ZONE
A. acris	lavender-blue	36" (90 cm)	Aug-Sept	4-9
(syn. *A. Sedifolius* 'Nanus')				
A. a. 'Nanus'	lilac-blue	12" (30 cm)	Aug-Sept	4-9
A. alpinus				
A. a. 'Alba'	white	8" (20 cm)	May-June	2-9
A. a. 'Caeruleus'	blue	8" (20 cm)	May-June	2-9
A. a. 'Roseus'	rose	8" (20 cm)	May-June	2-9

NAME	COLOR	HEIGHT	MONTH	ZONE
A. a. 'Rubra'	rosy-purple	8" (20 cm)	May-June	2-9
A. amellus				
A. a. 'Rudolf Goethe'	lavender-blue	24" (60 cm)	Aug-Oct	7-9
A. a. 'Brilliant'	pink	24" (60 cm)	Aug-Oct	7-9
A. a. 'King George'	violet-blue	24" (60 cm)	Aug-Oct	7-9
A. a. 'Mauve Beauty'	mauve	24" (60 cm)	Aug-Oct	7-9
A. divaricatus	white	18-24" (45-60 cm)	July-Oct	2-9
A. dumosus				
A. d. 'Rein Richard'	pink	10" (25 cm)	Sept	2-9
A. d. 'Alert'	blue	20" (50 cm)	Sept	2-9
A. d. 'Lady-in-Blue'	blue	16" (40 cm)	Spet	2-9
A. d. 'Silverblue'	light blue	10" (25 cm)	Sept	2-9
A. ericoides				
A. e. 'Chastity'	white	40" (110 cm)	Sept-Oct	2-9
A. e. 'Blue Star'	blue	30" (80 cm)	Sept-Oct	2-9
A. e. 'Esther'	pink	24" (60 cm)	Sept-Oct	2-9
A. x Frikartii				
A. x f. 'Wonder of Staffa'	blue	28" (70 cm)	July-Oct	7-9
A. x f. 'Moench'	lavender-blue	36" (90 cm)	July-Oct	7-9
A. lateriflorus				
A. l. 'Horizontalis'	mauve	4' (120 cm)	Sept-Oct	2-9
A. linosyris	golden-yellow	20" (50 cm)	Aug-Sept	2-9
A. novae-angliae				
A. n-a. 'Barr's Blue'	purple-blue	5' (150 cm)	Sept-Oct	2-9
A. n-a. 'Barr's Pink'	pink	5' (150 cm)	Sept-Oct	2-9
A. n-a. 'Harrington's Pink'	pink	4' (120 cm)	Sept-Oct	2-9
A. n-a. 'Alma Potschke'	red	2' (60 cm)	Sept-Oct	2-9
A. n-a. 'Treasure'	lilac	3' (90 cm)	Sept-Oct	2-9
A. n-a. 'Queen Erika'	rose	6' (180 cm)	Sept-Oct	2-9
A. novae-belgii				
A. n-b. 'Blue Gown'	blue	60" (150 cm)	Sept-Oct	2-9
A. n-b. 'Mount Everest'	white	36" (90 cm)	Sept-Oct	2-9
A. n-b. 'Crimson Brocade'	red, double	20" (50 cm)	Sept-Oct	2-9
A. n-b. 'Marie Ballard'	blue, double	20" (50 cm)	Sept-Oct	2-9
A. n-b. 'Patricia Ballard'	red, double	43" (100 cm)	Sept-Oct	2-9
A. n-b. 'White Ladies'	white	24" (60 cm)	Sept-Oct	2-9
'ROYAL GEM' CULTIVARS				
A. 'Royal Amethyst'	pink	18" (46 cm)	Sept-Oct	2-9
A. 'Royal Opal'	blue	18" (46 cm)	Sept-Oct	2-9
A. 'Royal Pearl'	white	18" (46 cm)	Sept-Oct	2-9
A. 'Royal Sapphire'	dark blue	20" (50 cm)	Sept-Oct	2-9
A. 'White Opal'	white	18" (46 cm)	Sept-Oct	2-9

NAME	COLOR	HEIGHT	MONTH	ZONE
DWARF CULTIVARS				
A. 'Violet'	violet	10" (25 cm)	Sept-Oct	2-9
A. 'Snow Sprite'	white	10" (25 cm)	Sept-Oct	2-9
A. 'Ruby Mound'	red	20" (50 cm)	Sept-Oct	2-9
A. 'Pink Bouquet'	pink	12" (30 cm)	Sept-Oct	2-9
A. 'Little Boy Blue'	blue	16" (40 cm)	Sept-Oct	2-9
A. 'Little Boy Red'	red	12" (30 cm)	Sept-Oct	2-9
A. tongolensis	lilac-blue	12" (30 cm)	July-Aug	2-9

Campanula
BELLFLOWER
Campanulaceae
Zones 2–9

Campanula carpatica 'Blue Chips' can be used to great advantage in front of a perennial border.

All campanulas are excellent garden plants, especially for zones 2 and 3. Fortunately, campanulas consist of a huge range of plants, some of which are not so well known in Canada. They range from tiny creeping rock-plants to soaring 6' (1.8 m) spires in the August garden. As well as being hardy, they are non-demanding, very dependable, drought tolerant and, if they have good growing conditions, extremely long lived. Because they are so floriferous in northern solar conditions, few gardens should be without at least a few of these species. Care should be taken to search out the alba versions of campanulas because they lend a cool crispness to the garden on a warm summer's day.

Organic Care

Almost universally, campanulas require a moderately rich, well-drained, neutral or slightly alkaline soil, a pH of 7.1 or 7.2 being ideal. In the warmer climatic zones 7–9, a summer greenhouse effect of warm days and nights may occasionally induce flower damage caused by thrips. Increasing the soil pH to 7.3 by employing dry wood ashes will greatly help in reducing the thrip population.

In areas of great humidity and little air flow, downy mildew may be a problem for some of the campanula species, particularly *C. latifolia*. The fungus may be ignored, or the plants may be sprayed with a bicarbonate of soda spray.

Campanulas grow readily from seed. The seed is extremely fine and should be diluted with sand before sowing. Campanulas are easily divided and transplanted.

Ecofunction

The campanulas are rarely visited by butterflies when in flower. Beneficial wasps make good use of these flowers.

Design

The flowers of campanulas are mainly white and blue. There are only a few species with pink colors. Therefore, their main design use in the garden is as a visual binding flower, to bind visually other, more attractive and colorful flowering perennials into a harmonious arrangement of color and form. This, of course, is a very necessary element of design. In a northern garden, because of the sun's altitude and glare and the reflective power of the white campanula, these varieties have a better binding effect than the blue.

The almost universal bell shape of campanulas is useful in form repetition in the garden. The nodding bell form is easily repeated in the flowers of many shrubs such as *Wiegelia, Kolkwitzias amabilis,* the Beauty bush, for alkaline areas and *Enkianthus campanulatus* for zones 7 and warmer. It is also repeated in *Lilium mackliniae,* 5' (1.5 m), which has huge, white, campanula like flowers.

Campanulas can be divided into two main design groups for gardening: rock garden plants, which are low-growing, and border and special area plants, which range in height from about 1' (30 cm) to 6' (1.8 m).

Rock garden plants are *C. alliarifolia,* which can be a shade plant, *C. carpatica* species, *C. cochleariifolia, C. garganica, C. isophylla,* zones 8-9, *C. linifolia, C. persicifolia, C. portenschlagiana, C. poscharskyana,* also a shade plant, and the hybrids *C. x* 'E. H. Frost', *C. x* 'Grandor', *C. x* 'E. K. Toogood'. All of these campanulas form a carpet of nodding bells which are most attractive. These plants should not be just confined to the rock-garden. They can be tucked into steps, walls, troughs, and walk-ways for greater interest in the garden.

There are some surprise campanulas that can go into the border or special areas of the garden. One is *C. punctata* 'Burghaltii', 2' (60 cm), which is a very old garden plant and can be used as a specimen plant. This campanula has flowers which are purple in bud and dove grey when fully out. *C. punctata,* blooming in July and August, has long waxy pink bells flecked with crimson. This, too, is an old nineteenth-century specie which likes sandy soil. *C. carpatica* are very useful planted in drifts in front of the perennial border.

C. glomerata, the clustered bellflowers, are very good companion flowers to the June flowering asiatic hybrid lilies, because they stay in flower for up to eight weeks. *C. persifolia,* the peach-leaved bellflower, is a fine addition to the June border, but the flowers are somewhat fleeting, lasting only two to three weeks in full-sun and somewhat longer in light shade. *C. latifolia,* the broad leaved bellflowers, are very useful for a shade garden, where the soil is poor, or in a wild garden. This campanula, with its 2' (60 cm) raceme of blue bells, is a common sight in eastern Ontario as an escapee from earlier pioneer gardens.

C. lactiflora flowers from June well into August. This 4' (1.2 m) perennial is a breath-taking mass of star-shaped blooms on a multi-branched plant. The pink *C. l.* 'Loddon Anna', 42" (105 cm), is the finest garden cultivar. This cultivar can also tolerate some shade. There is also a dwarf cultivar C. l. 'Pouffe', 10" (25 cm), which is light blue. Blooming into August and September is the chimney bell-flower, *C. pyramidalis,* which has a tall sweeping pyramidal shaped 6' (180 cm) flowering spire. The flowers begin opening at the bottom of the flowering raceme and continue to open for six weeks. This bellflower is short-lived and in some gardens may be treated as a biennial as it sets seeds readily. For nooks and crannies in the garden, the tiny 3" (8 cm) *C. rotundifolia* 'Alaskan' with its light blue miniature bells is most useful as it blooms from July into September. *C. rotundifolia* is called bluebells of Scotland and it, too, is sometimes found in the wild.

There are a number of interesting design combinations that can be created using campanulas. *C. glomerata* 'Acaulis' or 'Superba', both dark blue flowers, can be massed with the asiatic hybrid lily L. 'Enchantment' or L. 'Connecticut King', both being vibrant yellow, for a hot color effect. Red or orange flowers can be added to this June combination to increase its intensity.

If white cultivars of *C. persicifolia* 'White Cup and Saucer' are placed near the front of a perennial border in groups of four or five, they will give an irregularity and depth to the border which is most interesting, as well as binding in the vertical forms of delphiniums at the back of the border. When the flowers are spent, they should be cut as the residual rosettes are very inconspicuous.

For a July soft tonal combination *C. lactiflora* 'Loddon Anna' can be planted to the foreground of *Clematis* 'Bees Jubilee', where the soft pink of the clematis is carried in a most refreshing way into *C. l.* 'Loddon Anna' pink. Pink is one of the most useful blending colors in the border or in any other plant grouping.

Campanula Species and Cultivars

NAME	COLOR	HEIGHT	MONTH	ZONE
C. alliarifolia	white	12-18" (30-45 cm)	June-July	2-9
C. betulifolia	white	4" (10 cm)	June	2-9
C. carpatica				
C. c. 'White Chips'	white	12" (30 cm)	June-Sept	2-9
C. c. 'Blue Chips'	blue	12" (30 cm)	June-Sept	2-9
C. c. 'Flore Pleno'	double blue	12" (30 cm)	June-Sept	2-9
C. c. 'Warley White'	double white	12" (30 cm)	June-Sept	2-9
C. c. 'Turbinata'	violet	4" (10 cm)	June-Sept	2-9
C. c. 'Turbinata Pallida'	blue	8" (20 cm)	June-Sept	2-9

NAME	COLOR	HEIGHT	MONTH	ZONE
C. cochleariifolia (syn. *C. pusilla*)				
C. c. 'Elizabeth Oliver'	blue	4" (10 cm)	June-Sept	2-9
C. c. 'Alba'	white	4" (10 cm)	June-Sept	2-9
C. collina	purple	9" (23 cm)	May-June	2-9
C. elantines var. *garganica*				
C. e. 'Hirsuta'	blue	3" (7 cm)	July	2-9
C. glomerata				
C. g. 'Acaulis'	dark blue	10" (25 cm)	June-July	2-9
C. g. 'Superba' (*C. g. dahurica*)	blue	20" (50 cm)	June-July	2-9
C. g. 'Superba Odessa'	dark blue	16" (40 cm)	June-July	2-9
C. g. 'Alba'	white	20" (50 cm)	June-July	2-9
C. g. 'Nana Alba'	white	15" (38 cm)	June-Aug	2-9
C. g. 'Nana Lilacina'	blue	15" (38 cm)	June-Aug	2-9
C. lactiflora				
C. l. 'Loddon Anna'	pink	42" (105 cm)	June-Aug	2-9
C. l. 'Prichard's Variety'	deep blue	36" (90 cm)	June-Aug	2-9
C. l. 'Alba'	white	36" (90 cm)	June-Aug	2-9
C. l. 'White Pouffe'	white	16" (40 cm)	June-Aug	2-9
C. l. 'Pouffe'	light blue	16" (40 cm)	June-Aug	2-9
C. latifolia				
C. l. 'Brantwood'	violet-purple	3' (90 cm)	June-July	2-9
C. l. 'Alba'	white	3' (90 cm)	June-July	2-9
C. l. 'Macrantha'	mauve	32" (80 cm)	June-July	2-9
C. linifolia	blue	10" (25 cm)	July-Sept	2-9
C. persifolia (syn. *C. latiloba, C. grandis*)				
C. p. 'Pride of Exmouth'	semi-double blue	2' (60 cm)	June	2-9
C. p. 'Cup and Saucer'	white	2' (60 cm)	June	2-9
C. p. 'Blue'	blue	2' (60 cm)	June	2-9
C. p. 'Alba'	white	2' (60 cm)	June	2-9
C. p. 'Telham Beauty'	china blue	2' (60 cm)	June	2-9
C. p. 'Rapunculoides'	violet	2' 8" (80 cm)	June	2-9
C. p. 'Mrs. M. Harrison'	double blue	2' 6" (75 cm)	June	2-9
C. portenschlagiana	purple-blue	4" (10 cm)	June-Aug	2-9
(syn. *C. muralis*)				
C. poscharskyana				
C. p. 'Stella'	blue	6" (15 cm)	June-Aug	2-9
C. p. 'Lisduggan'	pink	9" (23 cm)	June-Aug	2-9
C. punctata				
C. p. 'Burghaltii'	grey	2' (60 cm)	June-July	2-9
C. p. 'Rubra'	pink	12-18" (30-45 cm)	July-Aug	4-9
C. rotundifolia				
C. r. 'Olympica'	blue	12" (30 cm)	July-Sept	2-9
C. r. 'Superba'	blue	12" (30 cm)	July-Sept	2-9

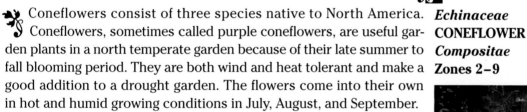

NAME	COLOR	HEIGHT	MONTH	ZONE
C. r. 'Alaskana'	blue	12" (30 cm)	July-Sept	2-9
C. takesimana	lilac-white	18" (45 cm)	July	2-9
C. thyrsoides	cream	12" (30 cm)	July-Sept	2-9
C. trachelium				
C. t. 'Bernice'	double purple	2' (60 cm)	July-Aug	2-9
CAMPANULA SPECIES FOR FLOWER BOXES AND HANGING BASKETS				
C. fragilis	blue	12" (30 cm)	July-Sept	8-9
C. isophylia				
C. i. 'Caerulea'	blue	2" (5 cm)	July-Sept	8-9
C. i. 'Alba'	white	2" (5 cm)	July-Sept	8-9
C. i. 'Mayi'	grey	2" (5 cm)	July-Sept	8-9

Coneflowers consist of three species native to North America. Coneflowers, sometimes called purple coneflowers, are useful garden plants in a north temperate garden because of their late summer to fall blooming period. They are both wind and heat tolerant and make a good addition to a drought garden. The flowers come into their own in hot and humid growing conditions in July, August, and September.

Echinaceae
CONEFLOWER
Compositae
Zones 2–9

Echinacea purpurea 'Bright Star' massed with late *Phlox paniculata* and *Monarda didyma* creates a pleasing combination which will feed many butterflies in late summer.

Organic Care

Coneflowers like a medium fertile soil that is somewhat granular in texture. The addition of sand to the planting medium will achieve this. The soil pH should be from neutral to slightly acidic. Summer and winter drainage should be excellent. Poor winter drainage will drown the dormant embrionic plant tissue. Coneflowers like full sun conditions. They are, if well drained, remarkably free of pests. They have a high wilt-point making them ideally suited to growing with a restricted water supply. In drought conditions, the leaves will not show a luxurious green color, but will turn a green-brown shade.

All coneflowers are slow to show growth in the spring and should be carefully marked. A small covering of straw during winter will help overwinter these plants in problem areas of zone 2.

Coneflowers grow well from seed. Plant divisions should be done in the beginning of June.

Ecofunction

The pink and rose-colored coneflowers, *E. purpurea* 'Bravado' and *E. p.* 'Bright Star', are indispensable for the August feeding of many migrating species of butterflies. Except for the alba cultivars, all three species are very attractive to butterflies. *E. angustifolia, E. pallida,* and

E. purpurea should always be included in a butterfly garden. Because of their late season of bloom coinciding with a school year, these species should be part of a biological observation planting for school-children.

The big seedheads filled with large seed are much loved by the goldfinches and other seed eating birds over winter.

E. angustifolia (syn. *E. pallida* var 'Angustifolia') was used by the aboriginal peoples of North America as an antivenin for the rattlesnake. An antivenin is an antidote to snake venom or poison. Such a strong antivenin from plant origin is unusual and is probably tied in with the secretory hairs which grow all over the plant's surface. It is the basis of the plant's importance as an immune booster.

Design

By happy coincidence, two groups of native plants combine wonderfully together. These are the later flowering violet-purple cultivars of *Monarda* and the quiet rose colors of coneflowers. These two groups can be used to give the back of the perennial border height in August and September. They will take over from delphiniums in flowering succession and they should be planted in between blocks of delphiniums or 12" (30 cm) to the front of this specie grouping in the border. The cultivar *E. p.* 'Bravado' flowers have wide, deep pink petals held flat, making this cultivar very handsome indeed.

A magnificent North American species *Echinacea purpurea* 'White Lustre' stays in flower for 14 weeks.

E. angustifolia, flowering in June to July, has pink flowers, the petals of which are extremely reflexed, giving this plant an interesting weeping habit, especially when massed. These plants could accentuate the weeping form of a shrub or small tree.

The *E. purpurea* 'Alba' and 'White Lustre', blooming in August to September, are a very useful addition to a white border. The white of these cultivars needs more refinement by further breeding. There is also a dwarf chance seedling *E. p.* 'Nana Alba', 12" (30 cm), in the author's garden which blooms into October and is very frost resistant. This plant is extremely useful for blocking out the stems of the August to September blooming lilies and is a very fine addition to the rock-garden.

Echinacea Species and Cultivars

NAME	COLOR	HEIGHT	MONTH	ZONE
E. angustifolia (syn. *E. pallida* var.' Angustifolia')	pale pink	2-3' (60-90 cm)	June-July	2-9
E. pallida	pink	3' (90 cm)	June-July	2-9
E. purpurea				
E. p. 'Bravado'	pink	2-4' (60-120 cm)	July-Oct	2-9
E. p. 'Bright Star'	pink	4' (120 cm)	July-Oct	2-9
E. p. 'Robert Bloom'	pink	4' (120 cm)	July-Oct	2-9
E. p. 'The King'	pink	3' (90 cm)	July-Oct	2-9
E. p. 'White Lustre'	white	2 .5" (75 cm)	July-Oct	2-9
E. p. 'Nana Alba'	white	12" (30 cm)	July-Oct	2-9

Delphinium
LARKSPUR
Ranunculaceae
Zones 2–9

Delphiniums have been part of flower gardening since the end of the sixteenth century. They have traditionally been used as background plantings for the perennial border. In that place, for majesty and sheer beauty, they are unsurpassed. Delphiniums are to the perennial border as a conductor is to a musical symphony. There are many fine delphinium species native to North America. Some delphiniums are dwarf species and others, such as *D. menziesii* and *D. zalil,* grow from a tuberous rhizome. Delphiniums are easy to grow and, if cared for properly, they can live for up to 70 years and more. The north temperate garden is ideally suited to growing this floral gem. Delphinium seeds require a deep freeze to break their dormancy. Cold winters and warm summers with early moisture are its primary growing requirements.

One specie of delphinium, *D. elatum,* has been the target of plant breeders for several decades both in Europe and North America. Cultivars of exquisite beauty have resulted from this breeding. In North America they are the Pacific Hybrid strains, the Dwarf Pacific series, and the Giant Pacific series, and, in England, the Bishop hybrids and the Blackmore and Langdon hybrids.

The delphinium, *D. elatum* 'King Arthur', with its deep violet flowers and black bee, acts as an excellent foil for lighter colors in a perennial border and becomes fluorescent in evening light.

Organic Care
Delphiniums require an alkaline soil to maintain health and longevity. A sandy or loamy soil of medium fertility that is well drained in summer with excellent drainage in winter in full sun or one-quarter shade is ideal. The soil pH should be 7.0 to 7.2. In heavy clay soils delphiniums are apt to be short-lived. These soils should be amended with sand. *D. exaltatum, D. tricorne* both require a slightly acid soil.

The addition of dolomitic limestone into the soil prior to planting will raise the soil's pH if necessary. Subsequent side-dressings of dry wood ashes will help to maintain this pH. This should be done in the spring when the new growth is about 2" (5 cm) tall.

Soils that are too rich in nitrogen will give rise to more leaf growth and a heavier plant. As a result, the mature plant will be more prone to wind and rain damage in July. Delphiniums have hollow stems which tend to add to this problem. They should be staked early in the season.

Delphiniums are sometimes prone to crown rot. This fungus will decay part of the crown in the spring and kill the growing side shoots. If it is severe, these side shoots can be removed, the root area dipped in dry woodashes and set out in a propagation bed. The remaining diseased crown should be destroyed. If brown streaking of this fungus is noticed in time, a spring side dressing of dry wood ashes will control it. Also useful in the control of this fungal disease is the practice of cutting off the flowering stalks of the plant 4" (10 cm) above the ground in November when they have died back. The flower stalk tissue is hygroscopic and acts as a wick during the winter months. The alternating dry and wet conditions, depending on the weather, will discourage fungal spore growth.

Ecofunction

Delphinium flowers are an important food source for humming birds, humming bees, honey bees, and many other flying insects. Toads love to set up house around the roots of *D. elatum* cultivars because of the shade this specie supplies. Around these species is also an excellent area in which to set up earwig traps. These insects and many more attract wrens and bluebirds who will patrol the garden and use the delphinium stakes for perching.

Young delphinium flower buds are sometimes used as a substitute for capers in caper-sauce. *D. semibarbatum* (D. zalil) yields a magnificent orange-red dye and is a useful addition to a spinner's garden.

Design

Delphiniums naturally divide into two groups of plants, the short delphiniums and the tall delphiniums. Many dwarf species of *D. grandiflorum*, which have large flowers, make fine rock-garden plants, for example *D. g.* 'Dwarf Blue Butterfly' and *D. g.* 'White Butterfly'. *D. tatiense* species are useful for the July and August rock-garden. The native *D. tricorne* 'Alba', 12" (30 cm), is a useful addition to spring bulbs, notably hyacinths and tulips. The flowers have an attractive spur and could be effectively massed with *Tulipa tarda*.

The dwarf and bushy floriferous hybrids of *D. x belladonna* are in various shades of blue and white. These hybrids are tougher and

Delphinium elatum 'King Arthur', showing the flower form, typical of the giant pacific hybrid strain of this species.

have a longer flowering period than their taller counterparts and, consequently, have greater flexibility in the June garden. They can be combined with roses, *Incarvillea delavayi* (the Chinese trumpet flower), *Fritillaria* 'Michailovskyi', *Eremurus* species, *Alliums,* or Asiatic hybrid lilies. They can also be combined with the pastel shades of Russel hybrid lupines.

D. cardinale, 3-6' (90–180 cm), the scarlet-colored delphinium can be combined with the waxy, fragrant *Lilium martagon* 'Alba' for the end of June into July gardens. This grouping is for the more patient gardener because of the difficulty in establishing *L. martagon.*

The taller delphiniums, *D. elatum* cultivars and *D. exaltatum* which blooms later into August and takes some shade, can soar to 6' (180 cm) in a good growing year. These delphiniums are used as the backdrop to the June border, *D. elatum,* and the August border, *D. exaltatum*, and, depending on the colors chosen, set the color scheme for the entire border. The cultivars of *D. elatum* range from the deepest, royal blue shades of *D. e.* 'Black Knight' to the medium blues *D. e.* 'Blue Bird' and 'Blue Jay' to the white of *D. e.* 'Galahad'. The cultivar D. e. 'Guinevere' has mauve flowers with pink slashes and a white bee. This cultivar is magnificent when massed alone, as is the dark *D. e.* 'King Arthur' which is a fluorescent, deep violet color with a black bee. The white *D. e.* 'Galahad' is stunning massed in a white border.

The two cormous delphiniums, *D. menzusii* and *D. semibarbatum,* are little known, but very useful delphiniums. They are treated in the bulb, corm, and tuber chapter. They are natural and unusual companions to lilium species.

Delphinium Species and Cultivars

NAME	COLOR	HEIGHT	MONTH	ZONE
D. x belladonna				
'Wendy'	blue with white B.	50" (125 cm)	June	2-9
'Bellamosum'	dark blue	40" (100 cm)	June	2-9
'Clivedon Beauty'	sky blue	40" (100 cm)	June	2-9
'Kleine Nacht Music'	blue	28" (70 cm)	June	2-9
'Volkerfrieden'	blue	40" (100 cm)	June	2-9
'Casablanca'	white	20" (50 cm)	June	2-9
'Moerheimii'	white	40" (100 cm)	June	2-9
D. x ruysii				
'Pink Sensation'	pink	40" (100 cm)	June	6-9
D. cardinale	scarlet	3-6' (90-180 cm)	June-July	7-9
D. carolinianum	sky-blue	2' (60 cm)	May-July	5-9
D. elatum				
D. e. 'Astolat'	lilac-pink	5' (150 cm)	June-July	2-9
D. e. 'Black Knight'	dark blue, black B.	5' (150 cm)	June-July	2-9

NAME	COLOR	HEIGHT	MONTH	ZONE
D. e. 'Blue Bird'	med. blue, white B.	5' (150 cm)	June-July	2-9
D. e. 'Blue Jay'	med blue, dark B.	5' (150 cm)	June-July	2-9
D. e. 'Galahad'	white	4.5' (135 cm)	June-July	2-9
D. e. 'Guinevere'	mauve, white B.	5' (150 cm)	June-July	2-9
D. e. 'King Arthur'	violet, dark B.	5' (150 cm)	June-July	2-9
D. e. 'Summer Skies'	blue, dark B.	5' (150 cm)	June-July	2-9
D. e. 'Green Expectations'	green	4' (120 cm)	June-July	2-9
D. exaltatum	blue	6' (180 cm)	July-Aug	6-9
D. e. 'Alba'	white	6' (180 cm)	July-Aug	6-9
D. formosum	dark blue, white B.	3' (90 cm)	June	2-9
D. grandiflorum var. chinese				
D. g. 'Dwarf Blue Butterfly'	blue	12" (30 cm)	June	2-9
D. g. 'Blue Pygmy' - gentian	blue	8:, (20 cm)	June	2-9
D. g. 'White Butterfly'	white	12" (30 cm)	June	2-9
D. g. 'Connecticut Yankees'	bitonal	1.5' (45 cm)	June	2-9
D. menziesii	blue	1.5 - 2' (45-60 cm)	June-July	4-9
	(see bulb chapter)			
D. semibarbatum	yellow	2.5 - 3' (75-90 cm)	May-Aug	4-9
(syn. D. zalil)				
D. tatsienense	blue	18" (45 cm)	July-Aug	4-9
(see bulb chapter)				
D. t. 'Album'	white	18" (45 cm)	July-Aug	4-9
D. tricorne	blue	12" (30 cm)	April-May	2-9
D. t.'Alba'	white	12" (30 cm)	April-May	2-9

Geranium
CRANESBILL
Geraniaceae
Zones 2–9

The geranium or cranesbill family is a large family of perennials which are of interest to the northern temperate gardener. The cranesbill family has strange, articulated seeds which coil upward on maturity and, once noticed, are never forgotten. Members of this family are extremely hardy and can withstand considerable cold and drought for long periods of time, making them ideal plants for rock-gardens and areas with a restricted water supply. Greenhouse geraniums are called Pelargoniums. Pelargoniums are also members of this family.

Nearly all geranium species are hardy in zones 4–9. Many are hardy in zones 2 and 3. It is suggested to gardeners in these zones, especially those with gardens that have a dependable snow cover, to attempt to grow all the geranium species except *G. palmatum* (syn. *G. anemonifolium*), zones 6–9, and *G. sylvaticum,* zones 6–9, the English mayflower, because all of the species in this family have zerophytic characteristics which enable them to withstand severe cold and drought. Zerophytic characteristics are evolutionary modifications of the plant itself in response to stress such as cold and drought. If the gardener is in doubt, the native *G. maculatum* can be used as in indicator plant. If it is found growing wild in your gardening area, then other species of cranesbill will also be successful. *G. maculatum* will be found, growing wild, along rocky roadsides with almost no soil in April to May. The plant will be about 1–2' (30–60 cm) tall and will have rose to magenta, five-petaled flowers and five lobed leaves. Crushing some of the geranium leaves will release the typical geranium scent and establish the plant's identity.

Organic Care

A good, friable, garden loam will suit all the cranesbills. The soil should be well-drained and slightly acid. Most of the cranesbills like full sun but *G. macrorrhizum* var. 'Ingwersen's Variety', *G. phaeum* species, and *G. sylvaticum* will take considerable shade. All of the cranesbills are very light feeders and require very little care.

Ecofunction

Dogs, cats, and squirrels do not like any of the cranesbill species. The oils released from the secretory hairs of the cranesbill species are irritating to these animals after having had contact with these plants. Subsequent grooming of the oily fur is distasteful. Cranesbill species can be used as 'protector plants' in a city or country garden.

    G. maculatum could be added to a herb or a pioneer garden. This geranium has been used extensively in European herbalistic medicine, including the care of periodontal disease and as an insulin substitute.

Design

There are many species of geraniums that are superior rock-garden plants. Some of these can be used for edging, either in a walk-way, near flagstones, in a wall, or planted in drifts in front of a shrubbery. If planted near flagstones or steps, the plant will mound nicely over some of the stonework in time. This gives a very attractive effect.

    For this purpose the species *G. cinereum, G. dalmaticum, G. endressii, G. sanguineum,* and particularly the variety G. s. 'Lancastriense' and the delightful little Alpine *G. farreril* (syn. *G. napuligerum),* with its compact tufts of grey foliage and pink flowers, can be used. Some of the flowers of these species are in shades of pink, others are white. Many of the flowers have very fine veining of another color with a contrasting eye or bee. These flowers stay in bloom from June into September. If these species are to be massed, cultivars with a contrasting dark bee

Geranium sanguineum 'Alpenglow' is frost, shade, and drought tolerant and blooms for most of the summer.

should be used as they are much more dramatic than the clear colors. This is why G. s. 'Lancastriense' looks so striking when massed. This plant seems to pour over a rock wall in a flowering, mounded fashion.

G. sessiliforum 'Nigrum', with its delightful brown rosettes of leaves and tiny white flowers, is thoroughly hardy and is an ideal plant for troughs. *G. himalayense* (syn. *G. grandiflorum*), *G. ibericum*, and *G. pratense* are fine plants to mass with Iris species. The tall double cultivars, especially *G. p.* 'Plenum Violaceum', 2' (60 cm), with its double deep violet flowers, combine beautifully with many of the darker colors of the tall, bearded Iris (Pogon Iris) *G. p.* 'Plenum Album', 2' (60 cm), blooming in June and July. It is a fine addition to a white border. The cultivar *G. p.* 'Mrs. Kendall Clark', with its soft pearl grey flowers marbled and veined in lighter tones, is also a lovely addition to the perennial border. Because of its height, 2' (60 cm), and unusual flowers, it should be placed somewhat to the front in the mid-region of the border. *G. psilostemon*, with its dark magenta flowers and a deep black bee, is also a fine addition to the border. The extremely hardy specie *G. wlassovianum*, 2' (60 cm), its violet flowers blooming from July into September, is a good border plant for a cold garden. These geranium species can be grouped in the border with June and July flowering alliums.

The old cultivar, available since the sixteenth century, *G. phaeum*, also called 'The Mourning Widow', probably because of its black flowers, blooming in May and June, is a very useful plant for a semi-shaded area. An unusual cultivar of *G. phaeum*, *G. p.* 'Variegatum', 2' (60 cm), has beautiful foliage, the leaves of which are streaked and splashed with pink, while the flowers have a slate-purple color. This cultivar also likes shade and can be massed to great effect with *Arisaema candidissimum* or *A. sikokianum* for a fine combination of pinks or purple.

G. macrorrhizum 'Ingwersen's Variety', 10" (25 cm), flowering from June to August, has the refreshing scent of sweet briar from the foliage. This specie could be planted with the old sixteenth-century single flowering *Rosa eglantera*, the Sweetbriar or the Eglantine Rose. The foliage of this rose smells of sweet apples in humid or rainy days. The flower forms are pink and are quite similar. This grouping is very hardy (zones 2–9) and would be a fine addition to a garden for the blind or sight impaired.

Geranium Species and Cultivars

NAME	COLOR	HEIGHT	MONTH	ZONE
G. clarkei				
G. c. 'Kashmir White'	white	15" (38 cm)	June	4-9
G. cinereum				
G. c. 'Album'	white	6' (15 cm)	June-Aug	2-9
G. c. 'Ballerina'	lilac-pink	6" (15 cm)	June-Aug	2-9
G. c. 'Splendens'	carmine-red	8" (20 cm)	June-Aug	2-9
G. c. 'Subcaulescens'	red, dark bee	8" (20 cm)	June-Aug	2-9
G. dalmaticum	lilac/pink	9" (23 cm)	June-Aug	2-9
G. endressi				
G. e. 'Wargrave Pink'	pink	15" (38 cm)	June-Sept	2-9
G. e. 'Daridge Drunce'	mauve-pink	18" (45 cm)	June-Sept	2-9
G. himalayense (syn. *G. grandiflorum*)				
G. h. 'Gravetye'	violet-blue	12" (30 cm)	June-Aug	2-9
G. h. 'Plenum'	maroon	14" (39 cm)	June-Aug	2-9
(syn. *G.h.*'Birch Double')				
G. h. 'Lily Lovell'	purple	18" (45 cm)	June-Aug	2-9
G. ibericum	violet-blue	24" (60 cm)	May-Aug	4-9
G. i. 'Album'	white	2.5' (75 cm)	June-July	4-9
G. i. 'Platypetalum'	violet-blue	2' (60 cm)	May-Aug	4-9
G. macrorrhizum (syn. *G. japonicum*)				
G. m. 'Pylzolianum'	red-purple	12" (30 cm)	June	4-9
G. m. 'Spessart'	pink	12" (30 cm)	June	4-9
G. m. 'Ingwersen's Variety'	pink	(40 cm)	June	4-9
G. maculatum				
G. m.	rose-purple	1-2' (30-6- cm)	April-June	2-9
G. m. 'Albi florum'	white	1-2' (30-60 cm)	April-June	12-9
G. farreri	pink	4" (10 cm)	May-June	2-9
(syn. *G. napuligerum*)				
G. nodosum	red	12" (30 cm)	May-June	4-9
G. oreganum				
G. o. 'Southcombe Double'	pink double	12" (30 cm)	June-Aug	4-9
G. palmatum	purple	1-2' (30-60 cm)	May	6-9
(*G. anemonifolium*)				
G. phaeum	black	2' (60 cm)	May-June	4-9
G. p. 'Album'	white	2.5' (75 cm)	May-June	4-9
G. p. 'Variegatum'	purple	2' (60 cm)	May-June	4-9
G. pratense				
G. p. 'Johnston Blue'	blue	16" (40 cm)	June-July	2-9

NAME	COLOR	HEIGHT	MONTH	ZONE
G. p. 'Striatum'	pink	12" (30 cm)	June-July	2-9
G. p. 'Tomsen'	pink	12" (30 cm)	June-July	2-9
G. p. 'Mrs. Kendall Clark'	pearl-grey	2' (60 cm)	June-July	2-9
G. p. 'Plenum Violaceum'	double, deep violet	2' (60 cm)	June-July	2-9
G. p. 'Plenum Caeruleum'	double, blue	2' (60 cm)	June-July	2-9
G. p. 'Plenum Album'	white	3' (90 cm)	June-July	2-9
G. psilostemon	magenta, black bee	20" (50 cm)	July	2-9
G. renardii	white, lavender veins	12" (30 cm)	June	4-9
G. sanguineum				
G. s. 'Album'	white	8" (20 cm)	June-Aug	2-9
G. s. 'Max Frei'	violet	6" (15 cm)	June-Aug	2-9
G. s. 'Lancastriense'	pink	10" (25 cm)	June-Aug	2-9
G. s. 'Alpenglow'	magenta	5" (12 cm)	June-Aug	2-9
G. sessiliforum 'Nigrum'	white	4" (10 cm)	June- Aug	2-9
G. sylvaticum	blue	16" (40 cm)	May-June	6-9
G. s. 'Albiflorum'	white	2' (20 cm)	May-June	6-9
G. wallichianum				
G. w. 'Buxton's Blue'	blue, white bee	6" (15 cm)	July-Sept	2-9
G. wlassovianum	violet	2' (60 cm)	July-Sept	2-9

Gypsophila
BABY'S BREATH
Caryophyllaceae
Zones 2–9

Gypsophila repens 'Alba' attracts beneficial insects into the garden

Gypsophilas are from Eurasia. They are members of the *caryophyllaceae* or Carnation family. They are specialized plants that love limestone areas, hence their name gypsophila, which comes from the Greek *gypsos* meaning chalk or gypsum and *phila*, loving. There are many famous areas of the world that have unique species of chalk-loving plants in colonies. These include, among others, the Chalk Downs in the south of England, the Burren in Co. Clare, Ireland, and in eastern Ontario from the boundary of the Gatineau Hills, including Ottawa, south to the Great Lakes. Gypsophilas will grow naturally well in these areas.

Organic Care

Gypsophilas prefer a neutral to alkaline soil, pH 7.0–7.2, of medium fertility, which is extremely well-drained in both summer and winter. Gypsophilas like a position in full sun and well spaced from other plants. An acidic soil should be well adjusted with liberal qualities of dolomitic limestone at planting. The plant will greatly benefit from yearly additions of dry wood ashes in April or May before growth commences. A light dusting, in a wide circle, 6–12" (15–30 cm), around the plant, is ample. In gardening areas where the soil is strongly acid, this dusting should be heavier and should be worked into the soil to act as an alkaline soil drench when rain comes.

Gypsophilas have a fleshy tap-root with many long, fleshy adventicious roots. This makes these plants ideally suited to dry soils. The plants are also very drought and cold resistant. Because of its root system, gypsophilas are difficult to transplant without injury. Transplanting should be done with great care. Gypsophilas are easily grown from seeds. Many gardeners seed gypsophilas into their designated spot, which eliminates transplanting. When growing seedlings, the soil surface should be kept dry at all times. Watering should be from the base of the plant container. The seedlings are prone to a disease called *Phythium de baryanum* or damp-off. This fungal disease attacks very young plants at ground level. The plant collapses on its side. This fungus needs moisture for its killing action, so a dry soil surface will eliminate this problem entirely. Mature plants, if over crowded, will be prone to fungal infections. Great care should be given to ample spacing of these species for that reason. *G. repens* should be planted 1–1.5' (30–45 cm) apart, *G. paniculata* 2' (60 cm) apart, and the hybrid *G. rosenscheier* 2.5' (75 cm) apart.

Gypsophilas should not be cut back beyond 4–6" (10–15cm) from the ground in spring or fall. Some mature stem is required for regrowth. Bushy twigs 1.5–2' (45–60 cm) can be used for staking *G. paniculata* cultivars to give a fine, fairy-like flowering effect in the border.

Ecofunction

Gypsophilas attract small, flying, beneficial insects in North America, but not honey bees, while in England and Europe, the native honey bees are very attracted to the single flowering forms of this genus.

Design

The rock-garden plant *G. cerastioides* is a tiny, creeping, matted plant having white flowers with delicate red veining. The flower form is very similar to the annual gypsophilum *G. elagans. Muscari botryoides* 'Album' or *Tulipa tarda* combine beautifully with this Alpine plant.

G. paniculata and *G. repens* have myriads of tiny, terminal, single or double flowers on plants with very small, blue-green leaves. This gives the plant, when in bloom, a billowy appearance which is most attractive and has a softening effect on all the surrounding plants in a border.

Gypsophilas are indispensable in a north temperate garden because they can be used to hide the untidy foliage of spring bulbs, such as daffodils, tulips, fritillarias, alliums, dicentras, and anchusas.

The hybrid *Gypsophila paniculata* 'Rosenscheier' forms frothy mounds of double, pink blossoms.

In the mid-summer border, when lilies are not at their peak, great clouds of G. paniculata 'Perfecta' or 'Snowflake' are splendid in between clumps of fragrant trumpet or oriental hybrid lilies. Combinations of G. paniculata 'Pink Fairy' with G. p. 'Perfect' and Lilium 'Pink Perfection' are dramatic. The pink, waxy, trumpets with their white sheen combine perfectly with the tiny pink and white flowers of gypsophilas. The oriental hybrid Lillium 'Rosario' and L. 'San Souci' also combine well with white or pink cultivars of gypsophilas. This combination has a strong honeysuckle fragrance.

G. paniculata, when planted with July or August flowering lilies, acts as a sun screen on the soil area around the lily clumps, keeping them damp and cool. This allows for a better and longer bloom-time for both the lilies and the gypsophilas.

Gypsophilas, when massed in large numbers, give a cloud-like, surreal effect in a garden. There are a number of other perennials which can achieve this effect also, including Crambe cordifolia, Aruncus dioicus 'Kneiftii', Artemisia 'Powis Castle', A. 'Lactiflora', Macleaya cordata, M. microcarpa, Limonium latifolium, L. dumosa, Thalictrum delavayi, T. dipterocarpum, Petrovskia 'Atriplicifolia', P. abrotanoides, Alchemilla mollis.

None of them, however, are quite so effective in airyness as G. paniculata or its hybrid G. p. 'Rosenscheier' when massed.

G. repens is extremely cold hardy, the pink cultivars being a little less so, and are useful edging plants in colder gardening zones. The blooming time is eight to nine weeks in June to July, and, if the plants are dead-headed, they will bloom again in August and September. The trailing habit of the plant is very attractive when used with stonework, wall-edging in a dry area, lining a walk-way or in between steps.

Gypsophila Species and Cultivars

NAME	COLOR	HEIGHT	MONTH	ZONE
G. acutifolia	white	6' (180 cm)	July-Sept	3-9
G. cerastrioides	white	4-10" (10-25 cm)	May-June	7-9
G. repens (syn. G. dubia)				
G. r. 'Alba'	white	8" (20 cm)	June-July	3-9
G. r. 'Rosea'	pink	6" (15 cm)	June-July	3-9
G. r. 'Bodgeri'	double pink	8" (20 cm)	June-July	3-9
G. r. 'Pink Baby'	rose	8" (20 cm)	June-July	3-9
G. oldhamiana				
G. o. 'Flamingo'	double pink	24" (60 cm)	June-Aug	2-9
G. paniculata				
G. p. 'Bristol Fairy'	double white	2 .5' (75 cm)	June-Aug	2-9

NAME	COLOR	HEIGHT	MONTH	ZONE
G. p. 'Perfecta'	double white	40" (100 cm)	June-Aug	2-9
G. p. 'Snowflake'	double white	40" (100 cm)	June-Aug	2-9
G. p. 'Pink Fairy'	pink	24" (60 cm)	June-Aug	2-9
G. p. 'Pink Star'	double pink	20" (50 cm)	June-Aug	2-9
G. p. 'Red Sea'	reddish pink	20" (50 cm)	June-Aug	2-9
HYBRID				
G. p. 'Rosenscheier'	rosy veil double pink	24" (60 cm)	June-Sept	2-9

Hemerocallis
DAYLILY
Liliaceae
Zones 2–9

Probably one of the best kept secrets in North America is that of the intense hybridization of the *hemerocallis* species that is taking place on this continent. The absolute explosion of diversity of these cultivars is incredible in every single way to the modern gardener. Investigating the possibilities of these new cultivars for the home garden is almost a science in itself, because fragrance, flower color, heights, and timing of bloom all come into consideration.

Some of the more spectacular cultivars are called tetraploids, meaning that the cells of the plant contain twice the normal numbers of chromosomes in the nucleus. Tetraploidy in itself is not new to plant breeders, but what is new is that this ploidy characteristic seems to confer traits of extreme hardiness, drought resistance, flower beauty, winter dormancy, form, color and in many instances a highly refined fragrance into that particular hybrid or cultivar. This is good gardening news for cold gardens in zones 2–4 and for world gardeners in general whose gardens undergo climatic stress. Gardens that are frost-bound in winter zones 2–7 have to grow daylily cultivars that go dormant in the winter. These daylilies are called dormant type daylilies. Gardeners in warmer gardening zones 8–10 are exposed to growing two other types of daylilies that keep their foliage all year round. These daylilies are called semi-evergreen and evergreen daylilies. Winter in warmer gardens sees just a green tonal change in the foliage. Coastal gardens of the western seaboard of the continent are well-suited to these daylilies. It should be noted, also, that hemerocallis ship well and can, therefore, be available to even the most remote gardens.

Flowering at the end of July, *Hemerocallis* 'Meadow mist' is a fragrant tetraploid.

Organic Care

Provided there is good drainage, daylilies will do well on a wide range of soils. A heavy clay soil should be lightened with the addition of sand to induce better drainage. A soil of medium fertility is preferred, with an annual side dressing of aged manure. A position in full sun or one-half shade is ideal. A summer mulch over the roots benefits the length of flowering. Daylilies should be planted with the crown even with or slightly below the soil surface. The orange-colored feeder roots should be spread out in a downward direction.

Some of the more valuable cultivars are very expensive and many sell for hundreds of dollars, so it is wise for the gardener to do a little home propagation. Some of the more expensive cultivars are viparious once they have reached maturity. Vipariousness is a phenomenon whereby a plant will produce little plantlets for vegetative propagation of itself. As the cultivar is finishing its flowering phase, the flowering scapes should be examined for plantlets which will be about 1" (2.5 cm) long and will resemble a tiny hemerocallis. These should be gently picked off about five days after termination of flowering and placed on a dampened paper-towel until the basal roots emerge. This will take three to four days. The plantlet is ready to be planted in a well protected propagation bed. Within two years this plantlet will be ready to flower. Vipariousness can also be induced by a lanolin indole acetic acid cream. Indole acetic acid is a natural plant hormone.

Some of the cultivars also produce seeds. The seed pod should be allowed to go brown and crack open very slightly. The shiny, large, black seeds should be collected, labelled, and stored dry at room temperature over winter. For four to six weeks prior to planting, the seeds should be refrigerated but not frozen. This chilling period will break the dormancy of the seeds. The seeds will grow into miniature plants. Flowering can be expected in two to three years.

Ecofunction

Many of the new cultivars are fragrant and attract a large number of flying insects, including honey bees. This makes the flowers a favorite place for ambush bugs and tree-frogs to forage. The leaf and leaf base are designed in such a way to catch any available dew. These damp areas attract foraging insects, which in turn attract a good toad and frog population which feed on the insects. Hemerocallis, especially the tall and intermediate types, are good companion plants to a garden toadhouse. Hummingbirds will use the nectaries of some cultivars, _H._ 'Meadowmist' being an excellent example.

All parts of _H. fulva_ are edible. Young shoots are cooked in a similar fashion to asparagus and the flowers can be cooked as fritters. The plant's flavor is not unlike mature asparagus. The flower buds of _H. middendorffii_ are a delicacy in Japan.

Design

As the name suggests in Greek, hemerocallis flowers only for one day and each flower is succeeded by another for a period of four to six weeks. The flowers are produced on long leafless stalks which are called scapes. It is the varying height of these scapes that defines the overall height of a cultivar which can vary from tall, 3' 6" (105 cm) types, to intermediate height, 30" (75 cm), to dwarf, 18–24" (45–60 cm), and midget forms of 12–18" (30–45 cm) with slender grass like foliage with an attractive weeping habit.

Three August blooming hybrid daylily species massed together and pleasingly fragrant: red *Hemerocallis* 'Oriental Gem', pink *H.* 'Kitten's Paw' and apricot *H.* 'Evening Gown'.

The hemerocallis flowering period begins in early spring, continues throughout the summer and into the fall. To assist the gardening community, specialized nurseries have coded the flowering periods. These periods are E for early, EM for early mid-season, M for mid-season, ML for mid to late season, and L for late season. These times can be related to the blooming periods of other flowers as follows: the E or early group blooms a little before and with the common garden paeony; the M or mid-season group flowers with the delphiniums in June into the end of July; the L or late season group flowers with and slightly before the late fall asters in September.

Gardeners in zones 4–9 can grow all the cultivars very successfully. Gardeners in zones 2–3 can grow the EM, M, and ML groupings to great advantage. Frost damage will limit or eliminate flowering of the other groups.

The design function of the new daylily cultivars in the garden seems almost endless. There are variants with huge flowers. These variants are called spiders and have flowers up to 10" (25 cm) across. Some flowers are open during the day and others are nocturnal. *H.* 'Mynelle's Starfish', 24" (60 cm), with spectacular 10" (25 cm) ivory flowers that are open in the evening, is one such example. Some cultivars have deeper or lighter mid-flower regions called eyezones. *H.* 'Siloam Virginia Henson', 18" (45 cm), has 4" (10 cm) pink flowers with a ruby red eyezone, and *H.* 'Siloam Bo-peep', 18" (46 cm), has fragrant 4.5" (12 cm) buff-cream flowers with a purple eye zone. Flowers with a dark eyezone mass particularly well. Many of the double cultivars are also fragrant and bloom in July, for example,

H. 'King Alfred', 20" (50 cm). They are ideal border plants. The miniature daylilies are colorful and graceful rock-garden plants. An example such as *H.* 'Pardon Me', 16" (40 cm), has fine cranberry-colored,
fragrant blooms in July.

The *Hemerocallis* 'Starling', a
tetraploid, shows fine black markings.

The foliage of all daylilies is extremely graceful and
acts as an excellent counterfoil to conifers, lawns, walk-
ways, and streams. This weeping habit which connects
and moves the eye from detail to detail within a garden
plan, yet combines all forms into a whole view, has been
used by Japanese gardeners for centuries with many
plants, including daylilies. If a blooming succession is
carefully planned with attention to height, a dramatic
herbaceous border of only these cultivars can be created.
When massed, it looks particularly graceful, especially
when planted by a walkway or lawn area. It has the additional benefit of being a low maintenance group of plants.

When designing with the black cultivars such as *H.* 'Starling', *H.*
'Prelude to Love', or *H.* 'Voodoo Doll', which are a deep chocolate red
and look black at a distance, care should be taken to set off the
blooms by planting against a contrasting light background. Otherwise
these flowers disappear. A light background would be a specimen
grouping against white trellising, a house, or grey-foliaged plants such
as *Artemisia* 'Powis Castle'. A dark background for hemerocallis
should be chosen with great care. Hedging of *Thuya* 'Nigra', the dark
green form of eastern white cedar, or *Tsuga canadensis,* Canadian
hemlock, can be used for lemon, ivory, yellow, pink, and rose hemerocallis cultivars. The deeper shades of red get absorbed by the
masked rhodopsin pigments in the leaves of the hedging and therefore do not contrast well.

Daylilies like some shade and, indeed, some cultivars can withstand considerable shade. This is very useful for a city or suburban
gardener who has to cope with the shade of surrounding buildings.
If one can arrange the garden plan in such a way that the hemerocallis gets morning full sun and afternoon shade, the flowers will stay
fresh looking for a longer period.

There are even a number of cultivars for the busy "5–9" gardener
or evening gardener. These are tall, almost 4' (120 cm) in height with
huge 4" (10 cm) blooms that fluoresce in the evening light. They are also
fragrant at that time. A splendid cultivar of this type is *H.* 'Rilla Reingold'.

Pioneer gardens should certainly grow the old triploid *H. fulva*
and its sterile double flowering cultivar *H.* 'Kwanso'. They also should
have the two fragrant *H. lilioasphodelus* and *H. middendorffii* species.
All of these plants are delightful for massing to give an informal effect,
in both small and large landscaping projects. They can be massed to

line a driveway, to give graceful lines to a garage or out-building, or can be used as a foundation planting by a house.

Hemerocallis fulva is the orange or tawny daylily that was brought to North America by the pioneers and it has naturalized extensively. There are a number of interesting hardy cultivars of this species, one of which is *H. f.* 'Longituba' with a very long tubular flower. *H. fulva* and its cultivars flower in July, except for the double flowering *H. f.* 'Kwanso' which flowers in August. This cultivar has a fine, long scape and is also excellent for naturalizing. *H. lilioasphodelus,* the lemon lily, and *H. middendorffii,* an orange daylily, are both delightfully fragrant, are ideal plants for the spring garden, and bloom with paeonies. The lemon lily *H. lilioasphodelus* flowers four to five days earlier than *H. middendorftii* and is not quite as hardy in zone 4. The flowers are frost damaged once in every six or so years in this zone.

Hemerocallis Species and Cultivars

NAME	COLOR	HEIGHT	MONTH	ZONE
H. fulva	red-orange	4' (120 cm)	July	2-9
H. f. 'Cypriana'	brown	3.5' (105 cm)	July	2-9
H. f. 'Kwanso'	red-orange	4' (120 cm)	Aug	3-9
H. f. 'Maculata'	red-purple	3.5' (105 cm)	July	3-9
H. f. 'Rosea'	rose	3.5' (105 cm)	July	3-9
H. f. 'Virginica'	double, rose	3.5' (105 cm)	July	3-9
H. f. 'Longituba'	orange	3.5' (105 cm)	July	3-9
H. lilioasphodelus	lemon	3' (90 cm)	May-June	4-9
H. l. 'Major'	yellow	3' (90 cm)	May-June	4-9
H. l. 'Rosea'	rose	4' (120 cm)	May-June	4-9
H. middendorffii	orange	3' (90 cm)	June	4-9
H. minor	yellow	18" (45 cm)	May-June	4-9
H. multiflora	lemon	3' (90 cm)	Aug-Sept	2-9

Hemerocallis Cultivars (Winter Dormant)

DWARF

NAME	COLOR	HEIGHT	MONTH	ZONE
H. 'Siloam Byelo'	rose	16" (40 cm)	July	2-9
H. 'Pardon Me'	cranberry	16" (40 cm)	July	2-9
H. 'Stella d'Oro'	yellow	18" (45 cm)	June-Sept	2-9
H. 'Mini Stella'	yellow	14" (35 cm)	June-Sept	2-9

TALL

NAME	COLOR	HEIGHT	MONTH	ZONE
H. 'Screech Owl'	rose, white trim	27" (70 cm)	July	2-9
H. 'Starling'	black	27" (70 cm)	Aug	2-9

NAME	COLOR	HEIGHT	MONTH	ZONE
H. 'King Alfred'	double, yellow	28" (70 cm)	July	2-9
H. 'Evening Gown'	peach-pink	28" (70 cm)	Aug	2-9
H. 'Silver Trumpet'	lavender	26" (65 cm)	Aug-Sept	2-9
H. 'Rilla Reingold'	yellow	42" (105 cm)	July-Aug	2-9
H. 'Firestorm'	red-yellow	31" (78 cm)	July	2-9

Hemerocallis Cultivars (Evergreen)

DWARF

H. 'Little Katie'	purple	18" (45 cm)	May-June	8-10
H. 'Courtney Vallien'	pink	18" (45 cm)	May-June	8-10

TALL

H. 'Tovarich'	red	28" (70 cm)	June	8-10
H. 'Mamie Schulze'	pink	24" (60 cm)	May-June	8-10
H. 'Pink Storm'	pink	26" (65 cm)	May-June	8-10
H. 'Grape Soda'	purple	26" (65 cm)	May-June	8-10
H. 'Little Melissa'	white	20" (50 cm)	May-June	8-10
H. 'Black Plush'	black	32" (80 cm)	June	8-10

Author's note:
There are hundreds of cultivars available and many more coming into the market each year, all with new parameters. The author's interests are hardiness and fragrance.

Iris
FLAG, FLEUR-DE-LIS
Iridaceae
Zones 2–9

The iris is the aristocrat of the gardening world. In temperament it is regal and unbending. The beauty and line of the flower is pure and wonderfully symmetrical. It is interesting for the modern gardener to know that the iris was well known to the ancient Greeks and Romans. In mythology, Iris was the goddess of the rainbow, and in the *Iliad* she is the messenger of the gods. In the scientific world of today, iridescence comes from the word iris, and, strangely, iridescence is found within the *Iridaceae* or Iris family. Iridescence is a photo-chemical phenomenon which involves incident or incoming light from an outside source to cause an object to be come self-illuminating or shimmering. Cathodoluminesence is also related to this phenomenon where columnated incident light causes an electron to become excited and give off excess energy in the form of light. The yellow and violet-purple color range of flowers of this family will be observed to exhibit these phenomena with angled incident light of the sun either in the morning or evening. This play of light is amplified by water reflection or reflecting garden mirrors. Thus the iris is well named.

The world of the iris is expanding rapidly due to clever hybridization of many of the iris species. Gardening interest in the various groups of iris is enormous and that, too, is increasing rapidly as the gardening communities of the world are exposed to more new and exciting cultivars, many of which have been developed on the North American continent.

The species of iris that can be grown can match almost every gardening situation imaginable, from water-gardens and bog gardens, to acid, neutral or alkaline soils, to dry gardens and rock gardens. The stature of the plant can vary from extremely dwarfed plants to 5' (150 cm) giants such as *I. giganticaerulea.*

To plan for many of these irises within a garden scheme, it is important to know the soil preference, the root structure, and the flowering time of the iris in question to ensure success.

The following is an approximate flowering succession time of the common garden iris groups from spring to fall.

A late blooming hybrid of *Iris germanica* exhibiting unusual yellow fluorescence.

Flowering Succession of Iris Species

SPECIE	SEASON	ZONE
I. danfordiae	March	3-9
I. histroides	March	3-9
I. reticulata	March-April	3-9
I. hollandica	April	3-9
I. aucheri	April-May	3-9
I. bucharica	April-May	3-9
I. magnifica	April-May	3-9
I. winogradowii	April-May	3-9
I. germanica (dwarf forms)	May-June	2-9
I. germanica (intermediate forms)	June	2-9
I. germanica (tall forms)	June	2-9
I. germanica (antique diploid)	June	2-9
I. siberica group	June	2-9
I. spuria	June	2-9
I. louisiana	June-July	6-9
I. pseudoacorus	June-July	4-9
I. kaempferi (Japanese Iris)	June-July	4-9
I. dichotoma (Vesper Iris)	July-Aug	3-9
Remontant Iris	Sept-Oct	2-9

The Bulbous Iris

This group of iris grow from a corm-type bulb and are, in fact, as hardy as tulips. They are mostly a spring flowering bulb, and, of course, are members of the *Iridaceae* or iris family. They are very winter hardy but are very exacting bulbs. They must have a warm and dry dormancy period after flowering. It is quite often a lack of this dormancy period which leads to the bulb's demise.

Organic Care

The iris corms *I. danfordiae, I. histroides, I. reticulata, I. aucheri, I. bucharica, I. magnifica, I. persica* like a neutral to alkaline soil of medium fertility which is high in potassium and phosphate. Dolomitic limestone can be used to adjust an acidic soil. The soil should be sandy and well drained in both summer and winter. *Iris winogradowii* needs an acidic, peaty soil which should never be allowed to dry out. The plentiful addition of milled peat moss to the soil at planting will achieve this. The corms should be planted 2–3" (5–8 cm) deep and 2–3" (5–8 cm) apart. The Juno group of iris should be planted deeper, 3–3.5" (8–9 cm) deep and spaced 4–5" (10–12 cm) apart. The root structure of *I. persica* has both corm and rhizome and should be planted with 2.5–3" (6–7 cm) of soil above the top of the corm root structure.

After flowering in early to mid spring these corms will go dormant. The corms should then stay dry and should receive considerable heat prior to fall rains. These conditions should be met for the successful yearly maintenance of these bulbs within the garden. These conditions are generally found in a dry, sandy garden or in a rockery. For maritime areas, both east and west coast, where heavy summer rains are part of a weather pattern, these bulbs may be lifted, dried, put into a paper-bag with some dry, milled peat moss and placed in the warmest part of the house where it will be hot and dry. They should be replanted in October for spring flowering.

Ecofunction

The bulbous iris are important because their early flowers provide a food source for bees and early flying insects.

Design

For flowering succession with other bulbs, corms, and tubers, the cormous iris are included in the flowering succession chart for bulbs, corms, and tubers.

In early spring, the dainty *Iris danfordiae* blooms through the snow. This iris can be planted to flower with the early crocii. The antique form of *I. reticulata* with its purple-black flowers has a refreshingly sweet scent. Its cultivar, *I. r. 'J. S.* Dijt', with its red-purple flowers has a sweet violet smell and the Juno iris *I. aucheri* with its turquoise blue flowers has a vanilla like fragrance. The Juno irises have substantial leek-like foliage making them ideal massing companions for narcissi, principally the cyclamineus *Narcissi* 'Jack Snipe', *Tulipa tarda,* or the Fosteriana or Kaufmanniana tulip groups. The rare *I. persica*, with its white and purple flowers, is a fine rock-garden plant with leaves expanding to 6" (15 cm) after flowering.

Bulbous Iris and Cultivars

NAME	COLOR	HEIGHT	MONTH	ZONE
I. danfordiae	yellow with spots	5" (13 cm)	March-April	3-9
I. histroides				
I. h. 'George'	violet, white	9" (22 cm)	March-May	3-9
I. reticulata				
old form	purple-black	8-10" (20-25 cms)	March-May	3-9
I. r. 'Cantab'	pale blue	8-10" (20-25 cm)	March-May	3-9
I. r. 'J. S. Dijt'	red-purple	8-10" (20-25 cm)	March-May	3-9
I. r. 'Natascha'	ivory	8-10" (20-25 cm)	March-May	3-9
I. r. 'Royal Blue'	violet-blue	8-10" (20-25 cm)	March-May	3-9

Pogon or Bearded Iris Group

I. xiphium hybrids (syn. *I. hollandica*, Dutch bulbous Iris)

NAME	COLOR	HEIGHT	MONTH	ZONE
I. x. 'Blue Ribbon'	lavender	1.5-2' (45-60 cm)	May-June	5-9
I. x. 'White Excelsior'	white	1.5-2' (45-60 cm)	May-June	5-9
I. x. 'Angel Wings'	white yellow	1.5-2' (45-60 cm)	May-June	5-9
I. x. 'Covent Garden'	yellow	1.5-2' (45-60 cm)	May-June	5-9
I. winogradowii	yellow	8" (20 cm)	March-April	3-9

Juno Group

NAME	COLOR	HEIGHT	MONTH	ZONE
I. aucheri	turquoise	12" (30 cm)	April-May	3-9
I. bucharica	yellow	18" (45 cm)	April-May	3-9
I. magnifica	violet	12" (30 cms)	April-May	3-9
I. persica	white, purple	4" (10 cm)	April-May	3-9
(syn. *I. rosenbachiana*)				

The Bearded or Pogon Iris

The bearded iris group consists of iris plants that are dwarfed, of intermediate, and tall garden plants. They are classified naturally into groups as such. The bearded iris is of interest to gardeners from zones 2 to 9, inclusive. All these plants are extremely cold hardy and drought tolerant as well as being world-class garden plants that can be grown with ease on the North American continent.

The bearded iris gets it name from the flower form, which, when inspected closely, has a fuzzy beard on the lower drooping petals which are called falls. Iris species without this beard are called beardless iris or Apogon iris. Whether bearded or beardless, all iris flowers have a similarity in shape which enable them to be recognized instantly as iris. Even though casual examination may put this into question, the close examination reveals the plant to be yet another iris variety.

Though beautiful, the blooms themselves have a fleeting quality. They are replaced daily as long as flowering continues. The emerging iris buds have great decorative value in a garden. The range of flower colors is immense, going from a startlingly white, through pinks, yellows, biscuit colors, to purple and black. Many flowers are bicolored, or bitonal or multi-colored. Some petals are frilled and scalloped in a most interesting way.

The Dwarf & Intermediate Bearded Iris

The dwarf iris is marvelously fragrant. For some unknown reason this fact seems to go largely unnoticed in the everyday gardening world. It may be because of the plant's small stature. The whole plant is dwarfed except for the flowers, which are disproportionally large. The full spectrum of color is found in these flowers. *Iris pumilla* is the more commonly grown species with an enormous amount of dwarfed, almost sessile flowered cultivars within its group. The natural dwarfs *I. arenaria, I. chamaeiris, I. flavissima,* and *I. mellita* are also useful spring flowering irises for the garden.

Within the dwarf bearded iris group, there are now tiny dwarfed plants. These are known as the miniature dwarf bearded iris. They range in height from 6–10" (15–25 cm). There are also the standard dwarf bearded iris, which are usually multibranched with three or four flowers per stem. They range in height from 8–15" (20–38 cm).

The intermediate bearded iris have a huge range of colors and cultivars. They range in height from 15–27" (38–69 cm).

Organic Care

The dwarf and intermediate irises like a well-drained, medium fertile soil, in both summer and winter. They do well on a sandy or clay soil, if the soil is somewhat alkaline. The dwarf irises appear to have a shorter life, however, on dense clay soils. Such soils should be lightened by a sand and dolomitic limestone mixture. Full sun is important for this plant. The rhizome or fleshy root should be .75" (2 cm) out of the soil with the adventitious roots feeding straight down into the soil. The ultra-violet rays of the sun act as a bacteria sterilant on the rhizome and keeps it healthy.

Sometimes, especially in damp or overcrowded conditions, the dwarf iris becomes susceptible to a leaf spot disease. This is found on the leaves in mid-summer after flowering. A thorough dusting of the entire plant with dry wood ashes corrects this. In late August, dwarf and intermediate iris leaves should be trimmed to about 2" (5 cm) to foil the iris borer. Tidy the plants by removing dead leaves and burning all the leaf material.

Ecofunction

As the dwarf and intermediate forms spill their exquisite fragrance into the air, they are one of the heralds of spring for the insect and human world alike.

Design

The miniature dwarf bearded iris flower in early spring after winter aconites and with aubretias and *Tulipa tarda*. The slightly taller standard dwarf bearded iris blooms next, followed by the intermediate bearded iris.

The dwarf iris are very useful rock garden plants and are also quite lovely when used for edging. The intermediate dwarf irises are fine plants for the perennial border and can be planted in association with the tall bearded iris for a four to six week succession of bloom in May into June. The tall bearded iris group blooms after the intermediate irises.

For special color effects, the dwarf and intermediate irises should be massed in groups of a single color. Both dwarf forms and intermediate forms stay in flower for ten days to two weeks. They can be grouped with *Crocus, Phlox divaricata, P. douglasii,* or one of the many *P. subulata* species. When the dwarf irises are used in a rockery, they make a magnificent spring show using a backdrop of deep green mugo pines or large round stones.

A tiny black cultivar of *Iris pumila* with yellow *Tulipa batalini* 'Bright Gem' in the rockery backgound.

Miniature Dwarf Bearded Iris Cultivars

NAME	COLOR	HEIGHT	MONTH	ZONE
Iris germanica				
I. g. 'Bees Wings'	yellow	7" (18 cm)	May	2-9
I. g. 'Marc'	blue	4" (10 cm)	May	2-9
I. g. 'Red Pixie'	red	5" (13 cm)	May	2-9
I. g. 'Lemon Puff'	lemon	7" (18 cm)	May	2-9

Standard Dwarf Bearded Iris Cultivars

NAME	COLOR	HEIGHT	MONTH	ZONE
I. g. 'Black Veil'	black-white	12" (30 cm)	May	2-9
I. g. 'Bright Vision'	apricot	12" (30 cm)	May	2-9
I. g. 'Candy Apple'	cherry	12" (30 cm)	May	2-9
I. g. 'Sarah Taylor'	yellow-violet	9" (23 cm)	May	2-9

Intermediate Bearded Iris Cultivars

NAME	COLOR	HEIGHT	MONTH	ZONE
I. g. 'Azap'	blue	18" (45 cm)	June	2-9
I. g. 'Cumquat'	orange-pink	15" (38 cm)	June	2-9
I. g. 'Viola'	violet purple	15" (38 cm)	June	2-9
I. g. 'Listowell'	yellow	15" (38 cm)	June	2-9
I. g. 'Rare Edition'	white	24" (60 cm)	June	2-9

The Tall Bearded Iris Group

The tall bearded iris in full flower gives an entirely new meaning to a flowering perennial. The tall bearded iris can grow from 2–3$\frac{1}{2}$' (60–105 cm) in height in the June garden. These cultivars and tetraploid cultivars, obtained by crossing *Iris germanica* with *I. pallida, I. cypriana* and other species of iris, are even more beautiful and sometimes as fragrant as their ancestors.

Organic Care

Although the tall bearded iris cultivars are extremely hardy, they can at times be frustratingly temperamental. This is due to the genetic call of one or other parent within the cross of the particular hybrid or cultivar. Sometimes the plant requires a higher soil pH, sometimes the plant requires more moisture at flowering, and sometimes the plant should be relocated to a much dryer spot.

Tall bearded iris like a dry, fertile, well-drained, alkaline soil with a pH of 7.2. They like full sun conditions. Drought, while not hurting them, just reduces the amount of foliage and speeds the rhizome into dormancy until conditions improve. Again, it is important that the rhizome be seen above the ground. It should be placed with 3/4" (2 cm) of the rhizome above the soil surface. The feeder roots around the rhizome appreciate a spring side-dressing of bonemeal and compost. The surface sterilizing effect of the sun's ultra-violet light is important for these rhizomes to keep disease at bay.

Some cultivars are particularly prone to soft rot, which is a bacterial disease of the rhizome. Indeed, it seems the more beautiful the flower, the greater the threat of this disease. Soft rot is a bacterial disease caused by *Erwinia carotovara* bacterium, which is very prevalent in North America. One is alerted to this disease by the truly foul smell of the Iris. In bad cases, the plant should be completely dug up and, as cleanly as possible, the soft pulpy area of the rhizome scraped off and carefully disposed of. Hands should be carefully washed three times. Then the plant should be placed in a dry area with the newly exposed, hard rhizome surface placed in 12–24 hours of direct sunlight. The full root structure should then be dipped into dry wood ashes and placed in full sunshine for a further few hours. The iris can be planted with a minimal watering and the plant will be found to make a remarkable recovery. For a less severe case of soft rot or other fungal diseases to which the iris is sometimes prone in damp weather, one or two dustings of dry wood ashes, at ten day intervals, will keep the rhizome and leaves healthy.

Areas with intense acid rain and acid snow, such as eastern North America and most of Great Britain and northern Europe, should dust the iris with dry wood ashes in April to May to increase the soil pH around the plant and thereby negate the effect of acid rain. This practice will be found to have a two-fold benefit, in that it will increase both the health and the vigor of the specimen irises.

When planting irises in a large group, the rhizomes should all point in the same direction for a more elegant display. This serves to align the leaf structure in the same plane which enhances the visual impact of the iris family.

An old diploid *Iris germanica* possibly 'Helen McGregor' echoing the identical sky blue tones of the fragrant *Phlox divaricata* in the background.

Ecofunction

While there are a few iris species, such as *I. dichotoma, I. foetidissima,* and the scarlet seeded iris, which are extremely attractive to the insect world and to the hummingbird population, the tall bearded iris is only visited by bumble bees. Apart from some species of antique iris, under normal garden conditions, the tall bearded iris do not set seed commonly. This stems from the fact that the flower is self-sterile. In other words, the flower is designed in such a way that it will not pollinate itself without some mechanical aid. This aid can be supplied by insects or by the human hand. This fact makes the iris the darling of the hybridizer.

The tall bearded iris, *I. germanica*, *I. pallida*, and *I. florentina*, are an important source of orris, which is the violet scented, powdered root stock of this group of iris. Orris powder has been used in perfumery since the Egyptians and early Greeks. It is also used as a fixative in potpourri manufacture. It is now widely used and is becoming increasingly popular in these industries. Orris powder together with powdered cinnamon bark make the delightful fragrance in the old fashioned pomanders.

Design

The bearded iris has very strong vertical planes which makes it a somewhat difficult plant to fit into a garden design in large numbers. Some thought must be given to the form of the neighboring plants before it will fit in. This is perhaps why the amateur gardener finds the iris a difficult plant to deal with. The neighboring plants should have tiny or dissected foliage. *Geranium pratense* species combine beautifully with the tall bearded iris, as does the biennial *Hesperis matronalis* or *Alchemilla mollis.* The tall bearded iris are very attractive as part of a foundation planting or when used as single specimen plants.

Bearded iris should be planted toward the front of the border in a position to increase the perceived depth of the entire border. This also allows more sun to shine on the rhizomes which increases both the flowering and vigor of the plant.

The flower stalk should be cut back after flowering and, later on in the summer, the foliage trimmed back to 4" (10 cm) above the rhizome.

In the border, the tall bearded iris succeeds the late tulips and daffodils and blooms prior to and with the paeonies.

Tall Bearded Iris Cultivars

NAME	COLOR	HEIGHT	MONTH	ZONE
Iris germanica				
I. g. 'Ming Dynasty'	orange-gold	36" (90 cm)	June	2-9
I. g. 'Beverley Sills'	coral-pink	36" (90 cm)	June	2-9
I. g. 'East Hurrah'	blue	40" (100 cm)	June	2-9
I. g. 'Vanity'	pink	38" (95 cm)	June	2-9
I. g. 'Interpol'	black	37" (94 cm)	June	2-9
I. g. 'Leda's Lover'	white	37" (94 cm)	June	2-9
I. g. 'Danger'	red	35" (89 cm)	June	2-9
Remontant or Reblooming Iris				
I. g. 'Invitation'	white apricot	35" (89 cm)	Aug-Sept	2-9

Antique Bearded Iris

There is renewed interest in the old cottage garden diploid iris. Some of these irises are hardy and disease resistant and are well worth seeking out. There is also some concern that the genetic stock of these garden jewels is being lost. Some of the old diploid irises have a very long flowering time stretching well into June. They are more delicate in appearance and are very maintenance free.

The Siberian Apogon Iris

The Siberian iris group flowers in succession immediately after the tall bearded iris has finished its bloom. The flower of the Siberian iris does not have a beard, fall petals, or erect standard petals as does the commonly known bearded iris. The iris flower, when examined from a direct, overhead position, will have three easily distinguished, identical flower parts. This together with the tall grass-like foliage makes the plant an easily identifiable iris. Underground, the plant is also different. The roots are toughly fibrous and quite long.

The Siberian iris, with its beautiful cultivars, tetraploids, and various genetic hybrids, is an extremely hardy group of plants. These plants are naturally geared to cold climate conditions of snow and run-off. If the cultural requirements of this group are met, then the Siberian iris will be extremely long lived, and is remarkably free of pests and very easy to grow.

Organic Care

The Siberian iris likes rich, moist, neutral soil, which is well-drained but damp in summer and well-drained in winter. Waterlogged soil in winter will rapidly rot the fibrous root system. This iris requires ample moisture from early spring growth to flowering. In normal years for zones 2–5, this is adequately supplied by winter snow, its melting and subsequent run-off. Dry conditions following flowering will not affect the plant. In areas of continual and heavy rainfall, such as the North American west coast, care should be taken that the iris is in a very well-drained spot in the garden. A terraced area would be ideal for this purpose.

When caring for cuttings of the new and extremely expensive cultivars of Siberian iris, some thought should be given to the overwintering of these small plant slips. This iris is usually slipped in September for maximum spring growth potential. These slips are usually received by post or from elsewhere at that time. For zones 2–5 the slips do not have sufficient fibrous rooting area to overwinter successfully in the open. They could be heeled into a coldframe or near a basement wall, or alternatively treated as a houseplant for that first winter. Once well established, the iris will be perfectly winter hardy.

Ecofunction

The Siberian iris is remarkable within the garden because it does not appear to be regularly visited by birds or insects.

Because some cultivars of the Siberian iris are moisture loving plants, this iris is both useful and beautiful if used as an edging plant for small ponds and water-gardens. In its shading capacity it reduces water temperature and evaporation from the pond surface. Both are important aspects of water-gardening on the North American continent.

Design

The Siberian iris flower has color of a more startling quality than all the other irises. The deep midnight blues, the wine reds, and the buttery yellows are particularly gorgeous. The colors positively sing with delphiniums, Madonna lilies, Asiatic lilies, and columbines in the June-July border.

The foliage is especially resplendent in the border all year. Early and late blooming daffodils can be planted near clumps of Siberian iris. As the daffodil foliage becomes unsightly, the beautiful weeping foliage of the Siberian iris masks it. There is an interesting group of Siberian iris hybrids called the Sino-Siberian irises which bloom after the Siberian iris group. These irises are good bog-garden plants.

The use of still water surfaces for flower amplification and reflection works marvelously well with all the Siberian iris cultivars. This design technique is particularly useful in a small garden and gives the feeling of space. Some of the deep blue iris show a strong iridescence which is also wonderfully magnified by water-systems, especially in evening light.

Siberian Iris Cultivars

NAME	COLOR	HEIGHT	MONTH	ZONE
Iris siberica				
I. s. 'Butter and Sugar'	yellow and white, early	28" (70 cm)	June	2-9
I. s. 'Lady Vanessa'	wine, late	36" (90 cm)	June	2-9
I. s. 'Cleve Dodge'	midnight blue iridescent	30" (92 cm)	June	2-9
I. s. 'Orville Fay'	royal blue	26" (66 cm)	June	2-9
I. s. 'Rigugi-sakura'	pink	28" (70 cm)	June	2-9
I. s. 'Sultan's Ruby'	red-violet	28" (70 cm)	June	2-9
I. s. nana alba	white	6-8" (15-20 cm)	June	2-9
I. chrysographes	black	18" (45 cm)	June	2-9

The Spuria Iris

The tall Spuria iris is a mid-summer iris group blooming at the end of June. It overlaps in time with the later blooming Siberian iris hybrids, blooms with its swamp sisters the Louisiana iris group, and overlaps a little with the early blooming Japanese iris. The Spuria iris cultivars are very tall, 2.5–4' (75–120 cm), and have attractive grass-like foliage. The plants have a fibrous root system. The flowers are more delicate in form and closely resemble the flowers of the bulbous iris, both in structure and color. The flower resembles a butterfly alighting and hence the common name, the Butterfly iris.

Organic Care

The Spuria iris group is the least demanding of all the iris family. It will grow in rich acid, neutral, or alkaline soils, in heavy or light soils, and will even withstand a long period of drought after flowering in June. The Spuria iris is extremely hardy and disease free and is practically maintenance free and long lived.

Ecofunction

The Spuria iris is visited by many beneficial flying insects which help the flower to set seeds, which it does readily.

Design

The Spuria iris will grow in full sun, but it is more useful to gardeners who have semi-shaded gardens, blooming extremely well under attenuated light conditions. This iris will also grow in very damp areas which makes it a useful subject to grow in a problem spot in a garden or for use in a bog garden or bordering a stream. The graceful foliage is attractive all summer.

Spuria Iris Cultivars

NAME	COLOR	HEIGHT	MONTH	ZONE
Iris spuria				
I. s. 'Protégé'	mauve-gold	3.5' (105 cm)	June-July	4-9
I. s. 'Red Oak'	maroon-yellow	3.5' (105 cm)	June-July	4-9
I. s. 'Sunny Day'	yellow	3.5' (105 cm)	June-July	4-9
I. s. 'Wadi Zem Zem'	yellow	3.5' (105 cm)	June-July	4-9
I. s. 'Border Town'	chocolate brown	3.5' (105 cm)	June-July	4-9
I. s. 'Pink Candles'	pink	3.5' (105 cm)	June-July	4-9
I. s. 'Premier'	blue-violet	3.5' (105 cm)	June-July	4-9
I. s. 'Imperial Bronze'	bronze	3.5' (105 cm)	June-July	4-9

The Japanese Iris

The tall, stunningly beautiful Japanese iris group is rapidly becoming a much sought after perennial by discriminating gardeners throughout the world. The Japanese iris blooms from the end of June into July, and, if given sufficient moisture, blooms for most of that month. The Japanese iris group succeeds the Spuria iris group in flowering times. The Japanese iris is unfortunately only hardy to zone 4, and even sometimes in zone 4 it needs winter protection.

Organic Care

The Japanese iris flourishes in acid, moist, and rich soil. This is an acid loving plant which will go into rapid decline if planted in alkaline soil. The soil should be liberally enhanced with milled peatmoss and well-rotted cow manure for some two to four months before the iris is planted. This gives the planting pocket time to compost and begin the decomposing process of acid rich media in which the Japanese iris will luxuriate. The peat moss will considerably increase the water-holding capacity of the soil, which will, in turn, considerably enhance flowering of this species.

Iris kaempferi 'Plenum', a magnificent double form of the Japanese Iris developed in Carrigliath.

In Japan this iris is often grown in rice paddies, which are artificially irrigated by flooding during the rice growing season and then drained and left high, yet damp, during the winter. These are the ideal growing conditions for the Japanese iris. If a mulch is being used around the Japanese iris, care should be taken to ensure that it is an acid mulch.

The root system of the Japanese iris consists of a slender rhizome from which many fibrous roots grow. The leaf growth fans out from the rhizome. These rhizomes should be planted at lease 2" (5 cm) deep. This sometimes means that the fibrous auxiliary roots, which can grow quite long, will have to be trimmed. Care should be taken to orient all the rhizomes in the same direction if a mass planting is desired. They should be spaced 2' (60 cm) apart. To transplant, slips of the Japanese iris should be overwintered similarly to the Spuria iris or considerable losses will be encountered due to the lack of sufficient roots to overwinter adequately.

Ecofunction

The Japanese iris *I. kaempferi* has a definite place near a watergarden or bog garden area. Its function is shading the water and producing dampness which amphibians need. Frogs, newts, and many species of snakes will use these moist root areas. Foraging insects, especially honey bees, will use the moisture around the leaf bases. They will pump this water and transport it to their hives. Moisture in the garden also helps the butterfly population considerably.

Design

The Japanese iris stands in the garden as a flower of great majesty. The horizontal lines of the blossom makes an interesting play with morning and evening light, and for that reason it makes an excellent specimen as a focal point.

The range of colors is rich and growing from mahogany-red through wine colors to pinks and deep imperial purple colors. There are also some double flowering forms of the Japanese iris. Attention should be given to the tapestry like quality of these flowers. Colors of creams, pastel pinks, violets, and full, rich greens should be used in the flowering material nearby. If garish colors are used, then the jewel-like quality of these Japanese irises will be lost.

I. kaemferi is sometimes sold as *I. ensata. I. ensata,* or the sword leaf iris, is a different specie.

Japanese Iris Cultivars

NAME	COLOR	HEIGHT	MONTH	ZONE
Iris kaempferi				
I. k. 'Activity'	blue	32-44" (80-100 cm)	June-July	4-9
I. k. 'Prairie Peace'	violet	32-44" (80-100 cm)	June-July	4-9
I. k. 'Taga Soda'	maroon	32-44" (80-100 cm)	June-July	4-9
I. k. 'Light at Dawn'	white	32-44" (80-100 cm)	June-July	4-9
I. k. 'Dace'	blue, double	32-44" (80-100 cm)	June-July	4-9
I. k. 'Variegata'	blue	32-44" (80-100 cm)	June-July	4-9
I. k. 'Summer Storm'	purple	32-44" (80-100 cm)	June-July	4-9
I. k. 'Sakurajishi'	pink	32-44" (80-100 cm)	June-July	4-9
I. k. 'Swirling Waves'	light violet	32-44" (80-100 cm)	June-July	4-9

The Louisiana Iris Group

The Louisiana iris group is derived from four southern native iris species, *I. fulva, I. brevicaulis, I. giganticaerulea,* and *I. nelsonii.* These native irises differ widely in size, flower color, and growing habit, but the hybrid cultivars which they have produced are magnificent plants. They are the western world's equivalent to the Japanese iris, *I. kaempferi*, and overlap in flowering time with them. The size of the flower itself can vary tremendously from 3–8" (7–20 cm) wide as can the flowering stalk from 1.5–5' (45–150 cm). All of this depends on which parents' traits are dominant. The blooming time lasts for eight weeks. There are, to date, a small number of interesting tetraploids which are slowly increasing. These tetraplolids are being actively used in new cultivar breeding programs.

Organic Care

The Louisiana iris likes acidic to neutral, rich, garden soil, which is well supplied with organic material in the form of aged manure and milled peat moss well worked into the soil prior to planting. The rhizomes should be planted 1" (2.5 cm) deep. During early growth and active blooming time, all the Louisiana cultivars should have an adequate supply of moisture and should not be allowed to dry out. The Louisiana iris require a minimum of four hours of direct sunlight which make these cultivars useful shade plants. Because the rhizomes of the Louisiana iris have a habit of creeping out of the soil when the plant is mature, they are prone to sunscald. To avoid this, all cultivars should be mulched to a depth of 3" (7.5 cm).

Cultivars of *I. fulva* appear to require more alkaline conditions, as they are sometimes prone to rust fungi. A liberal dusting of dry woodashes around the plant in spring or fall will kill the germinating rust spores.

Cultivars of *I. fulva* appear to be as hardy as the tall bearded iris *I. germanica,* which is hardy to zone 2. This would bring exciting new plant material into these zones for testing. All the cultivars of this group which have *I. fulva* parentage should be tested for cold-hardiness. To date, the Louisiana iris hybrids are definitely known to be hardy from zones 4–9. The author's trials of the Louisiana iris in her zone 4 garden have proven the hardiness of this species in colder regions. Gardeners in these zones have a huge range of new cultivars to choose from. Problem areas with high humidity should seek out the fungal resistant *I. giganticaerula* hybrids, or crosses with this parent dominant for resistance to rust and fungal disease.

Ecofunction

Many cultivars of Louisiana iris can be used as water or bog plants. They provide shade and moisture availability in the garden for both insects and amphibians alike.

Design

Since the range of color, form, and heights of the Louisiana iris exceeds that of the *I. kaempferi* or Japanese iris, the possibilities within the garden are almost endless. The tall and small cultivars make fine additions into the mid-summer border where the single and double cultivar forms also excel. Cultivars of *I. fulva,* such as *I. f.* 'Bronze Red', *I. f.* 'Chocolate', *I. f.* 'Lutea', and *l. f.* 'Maringouin Pink' should be sought out by the discriminating gardener and used in the border when splashes of red are most useful with delphiniums in June and July.

The old, well known cultivar *I.* 'Dorothea K. Williamson', which is an *I. fulva-foliosa* hybrid, could well bear testing in a north temperate garden because this cultivar is as hardy as it is beautiful. This cultivar is in high demand all over the world.

There are early, mid-season, and late blooming cultivars of Louisiana iris. There is also some re-blooming in the fall. Early blooming Louisiana iris can be used to great advantage with rhododendron and azelias in warmer gardens. The mid season bloomers blooming in June-July, such as *I.* 'Bayou Rouge', 3' (90 cm), which is tetraploid with 8" (20 cm) wide dark wine-red and red-violet flowers with eight or more blooms per scape, and *I.* 'Counterpoise', 3' (90 cm), which is a cadmium-orange and mauve bicolored, flat topped flower, could be marvelous additions to the perennial border. *I.* 'Professor Ike' 4' (120 cm), a huge tetraploid with reddish-purple, flat, flaring 6.5" (17 cm) flowers, which blooms late, would be another fine addition to a perennial border.

Louisiana Iris Cultivars

NAME	COLOR	HEIGHT	MONTH	ZONE
I. fulva	red-copper	3' (90 cm)	June-July	2-9
I. f. 'Bronze Red'	bronzy-red	3' (90 cm)	June-July	2-9
I. f. 'Chololate'	chocolate-red	3' (90 cm)	June-July	2-9
I. f. 'Lutea'	yellow	3' (90 cm)	June-July	2-9
I. f. 'Maringouin Pink'	pink	3' (90 cm)	June-July	2-9
I. 'Bayou Rouge'	wine-red	3' (90 cm)	June-July	6-9
I. 'Counterpoise'	cadmium orange mauve	3' (90 cm)	June-July	6-9
I. 'Freddie Boy'	pink orange	3' (90 cm)	June-July	6-9
I. 'Godzilla'	violet	3' (90 cm)	June-July	6-9
I. 'Professor Ike'	red-purple	4' (120 cm)	June-July	6-9
I. 'Queen o'Queens'	white	3' (90 cm)	June-July	6-9

The Vesper Iris

This beautiful, fragrant, native iris of Siberia and China is open for evening prayers, hence the name the Vesper iris. This iris has been renamed *Pardanthopsis dichotoma*.

Organic Care
The Vesper iris likes a humus rich, garden soil with a good water holding capacity to enhance blooming. The soil can be slightly acidic, neutral, or slightly alkaline. This iris is treated as a biennial by many

The Vesper iris or *Pardanthopsis dichotoma* opens around four o'clock spilling a heady fragrance into the evening air.

gardeners because it is so short lived. However, it consistently sets a full crop of viable seeds which germinate immediately in August to replace the mother plants. The fibrous root system of this iris enables the young plants to be transplanted with ease.

Ecofunction

The Vesper iris is extremely attractive to hummingbirds and honeybees. Seeds set readily because cross-pollination has been carried out. The Vesper iris is a good nectar source for hummingbirds in July and August.

Design

This is the latest blooming iris species apart from the Remontant iris cultivars, in which fall flowering has been induced. The Vesper iris succeeds the Japanese iris and the Louisiana iris cultivars blooming in late July into August. This 3' (90 cm) iris is multi-branched and has dozens of blossoms open simultaneously on one plant. The blooms open in the afternoon and into the evening. The bluish-white blooms have attractive brown-purple or red-purple spots. The petals also have white blotching.

The Vesper iris can be combined with any July blooming alliums, with trumpet lilies, or with *Galtonia candicans* in a white garden.

The Vesper Iris *(Pardanthopsis dichotoma)*

NAME	COLOR	HEIGHT	MONTH	ZONE
I. dichotoma	light blue, mottled	3' (90 cm)	July-Aug	3-9
I. dichotoma 'Alba'	white	3' (90 cm)	July-Aug	3-9

Remontant Iris Cultivars

NAME	COLOR	HEIGHT	MONTH	ZONE
I. 'Invitation'	white-apricot	36" (89 cm)	Sept	5-9

Iris Cristata Cultivars

NAME	COLOR	HEIGHT	MONTH	ZONE
I. cristata	blue-navy	4-8" (10-20 cm)	June	4-9
I. c. 'Alba'	white	4-8" (10-20 cm)	June	4-9

The Remontant Iris

Hybridization, principally of the tall bearded irises *I. germanica*, the Siberian, and the Louisiana irises, has produced a new population of irises that bloom predominantly in the fall. Some of these species might also have a light bloom in the spring followed by a heavier blooming in the shortening days of the fall.

Unfortunately, at present, the Remontant iris species are of little use to gardening zones 2–5 because early frosts seriously damage flowering. This, of course, does not preclude tetraploid cultivars of the future being extremely frost hardy. Care should be taken to maintain the fall flowering Iris in prime condition over the summer months to induce maximum flowering.

Specie Irises

Apart from the more commonly known irises, there are a number of other irises which can be grown as single specimens in the perennial border or elsewhere in the garden. These irises are hardy, beautiful and make a fine show in the June garden. Some of these irises are antique, some are little known, but for all of that, they offer a new challenge to create greater interest in the gardens of iris lovers.

Iris Cristata

Iris cristata, the crested iris, is a dwarf native iris of the eastern and southern U.S.A. This iris is 4–8" (10–20 cm) tall and has attractive pale blue flowers with a navy halo. A well-drained soil, high in humus, with partial shade is ideal. This iris should have a winter leaf mulch. *Iris cristata* is a magnificent specie iris for the rock garden. The unusual 'Alba' cultivar has a white flower with golden crests. *I. c.* 'Alba' prefers morning sun and afternoon shade.

The Pacific Coast Irises

This large group of irises are classified as the series *Californicae* of the Apogon or beardless iris group. These irises are a native, dryland iris which have been found growing along the dry regions of the Pacific coast. It appears that these plants have an unusual, ancient history which can be time checked by a study of its chromosomes. Apparently, the nearest relative of these irises are the chrysographes of Siberia. Both these iris groups, the Pacific Coast irises and the chrysographes, have 40 chromosomes per nucleus per cell. It would appear that the ancestral forms of the Pacific iris originated in Siberia, crossed the Bering Strait and made their way southward along the coast. Their route eastward was blocked by mountains, so their present day natural habitat is the west coast of California. *Iris tenax, I. douglasiana, I. innominata, I. bracteata, I. munzii,* all connoiseur plants in English gardens, are members of the Pacific Coast iris group.

The Pacific Coast irises are generally small and compact plants with slender but wiry rhizomes and narrow grass-like foliage similar to the Siberian iris. *I. douglasiana* and *I. munzii* are an exception, growing to 1.5' (45 cm). The Pacific Coast irises like a rich, neutral, well-drained soil, in both summer and winter. Winter waterlogging will kill the fibrous root system. These irises are very salt (sodium chloride) tolerant and for that reason are useful in coastal gardens. The flower colors are from red through purples to white. These irises are hardy to zone 4.

Pacific Coast Iris Species and Cultivars

NAME	COLOR	HEIGHT	MONTH	ZONE
I. douglasiana	lilac	2.5' (75 cm)	June	4-9
I. d. 'Alba'	white	2.5' (75 cm)	June	4-9
I. innominata 'Lilacina'	lilac	8" (20 cm)	June	4-9
I. i. 'Lutea'	yellow	8" (20 cm)	June	4-9
I. 'Banbury Beauty'	lavender	12" (30 cm)	June	5-9
I. 'Banbury Velvet'	violet	12" (30 cm)	June	5-9

Iris Florentina Cultivar

NAME	COLOR	HEIGHT	MONTH	ZONE
I. g.'Florentina'	blue-white	2.5' (75 cm)	June	3-9

Iris Pallida Cultivar

NAME	COLOR	HEIGHT	MONTH	ZONE
I.p. 'Aureo Variegata'	lavender	3' (90 cm)	May-June	3-9

Iris Setosa Specie

NAME	COLOR	HEIGHT	MONTH	ZONE
I. setosa	blue-purple	2' (60 cm)	May-June	2-9

Iris Tectorum Specie and Cultivar

NAME	COLOR	HEIGHT	MONTH	ZONE
I. tectorum	lilac	8-12" (20-30 cm)	June	5-9
I. t. 'Alba'	white	8-12" (20-30 cm)	June	5-9

Iris germanica 'Florentina'

This is a very old variety of iris which was grown in olden times primarily for the orris powder, which was extracted from the plant's dried root system. It is an interesting and useful addition to the herb garden.

Iris Pallida 'Aureo Variegata'

This is an iris with striking foliage. It was also used for orris powder production. The lavender flowers have a strong scent of crushed grapes.

Iris Setosa

This Alaskan coastal native is a useful specie iris for gardening in zones 2–4 as it is extremely hardy and drought resistant. The flower color is a blue-purple. Some fall petals have a white spot at their base. There are some dwarf hybrids of this iris 9" (23 cm) tall, and the foliage sometimes has an interesting basal purple color.

Iris Tectorum

This is the famous roof iris of Japan. The flowers are deep lilac to blue. The plant is compact 8–12" (20–30 cm). The plant prefers rich, moist soil which is well drained in summer and winter. The growing area should be sheltered from the wind. There is also an exquisite 'Alba' cultivar. *I. tectorum* blooms at the same time as *I. germanica*, the Tall Bearded Iris.

Iris pseudoacorus 'Floraplena' flowering in June.

 **Water Garden or Bog Irises**

Water garden or Bog irises for north temperate gardens are *Iris acorus gramineus variegatus, I. laevigata, I. pseudoacorus,* and *I. versicolor.* In the colder zones 2–5, *I. pseudoacorus* and *I. versicolor* and their many cultivars can be used. The warmer zones 6–9 have a large array of iris species which can be used for the bog or water garden, as well as the two iris specie groups for the colder gardens, *I. laevigata,* the Water Iris *I. virginica,* the blue flag iris, and many species of the Louisiana iris group.

Organic Care

A good garden soil of medium fertility, which is high in phosphate and potash is ideal for either the bog or the water garden iris. Manures, when used in the planting mixture, should be at least one year old and well composted. Fresh manures will release ammonia into the water-system which will become toxic to fish life and make an excess growth of the unicellular algae *Chlorella* and many other algal forms, an excess of which is undesirable for equilibrium in pools or bog areas. Non-draining containers are often used for planting iris species within the water garden. These containers are then placed on pond shelves. The iris soil should be topped with large pea-gravel of a limestone base, if possible. Iris plants should have the rhizomes planted in such a way that they are all oriented in the same direction. This gives a uniformity to their appearance which is most desirable.

Iris laevigata, I. pseudoacorus, and *I. versicolor* like an acid soil. Milled peat moss added to the planting mixture will achieve this. All the iris species except for *I. versicolor* like full sun. *I. versicolor* can grow and flower quite well in partial shade.

Ecofunction

All iris species significantly add to the gaseous balance of bog or water gardens. Their shading at the edges of pools and within bog areas considerably reduces water evaporation in sunny weather.

Iris acorus gramineus variegatus, the dwarf Japanese variegated sweet flag iris, has a fresh sweet smell of lime when the leaves are crushed. The leaves of *Iris versicolor* have been used in aboriginal medicine as a poultice for open wounds. This specie and its cultivars may cause contact dermatitis in some people.

Design

Iris laevigata, the Japanese water iris, is a very fine addition to a water garden. The cultivar with variegated foliage is particularly fine and provides year-round interest. *Iris versicolor* is a native eastern and mid-western iris of the North American continent. The white cultivar of this iris has lovely delicate lavender veining in the flower and is a particularly fine addition to any water garden. *Iris versicolor* has crossed with the southern native, *I. virginica.* The hybrids from this cross are also useful hardy water garden and bog plants. The double form of the *I. pseudoacorus* or yellow flag are a bright rich yellow and the foliage is particularly disease free all year.

When irises are used as part of a design in a water garden, they should be massed, if possible, and the color should be uniform for a more dramatic display of the flower form against a background of water.

Iris, when used in a bog garden, on the other hand, can be massed with different colors and different species for a gay, festive effect which is always beautiful.

Water Garden or Bog Irises and Cultivars

NAME	COLOR	HEIGHT	MONTH	ZONE
Iris acorus gramineus variegatus	blue	8" (20 cm)	June	4-9
Iris laevigata				
I. l. 'Alba'	white	2.5' (75 cm)	June	6-9
I. l. 'Albopurpurea'	white, purple	2.5' (75 cm)	June	6-9
'Colchesterensis'	blue, white	2.5' (75 cm)	June	6-9
I. l. 'Altipurpurea'	white, violet	2.5' (75 cm)	June	6-9
I. l. 'Regal'	rose-magenta	2.5 (75 cm)	June	6-9
I. l. 'Royal Cartwheel'	navy	1.5' (45 cm)	June	6-9
I. l. 'Semperflorens'	blue-violet	2.5' (75 cm)	June	6-9
I. l. 'Violet Parasol'	double blue	2.5' (75 cm)	June	6-9
I. l. 'Variegated'	violet	2.5' (75 cm)	June	6-9
Iris pseudoacorus				
I. p. 'Alba'	yellow-white	3' (90 cm)	June	2-9
I. p. 'Floraplena'	double gold	4' (120 cm)	June	2-9
I. p. 'Tall Yellow'	yellow	5-6' (150-180 cm)	June	2-9
I. p. 'Gigantea'	large yellow	3' (92 cm)	June	2-9
I. p. 'Variegated'	yellow	3' (90 cm)	June	2-9
I. versicolor				
I. v. 'White'	white-lavender	2.5-3' (75-90 cm)	June	2-9
I. v. 'Pink'	pink	2.5-3' (75-90 cm)	June	2-9
I. v. 'Rosea'	rose-white	2.5-3' (75-90 cm)	June	2-9
I. v. 'Claret Cup'	red-violet, white	2.5-3' (75-90 cm)	June	2-9
I. v. 'Kermisiana'	purple-white	2.5-3' (75-90 cm)	June	2-9
I. v. 'Illinois'	blue, hardy	2.5-3' (75-90 cm)	June	2-9
I. versicolor x I. virginica cultivars				
'Medium Violet'	violet	2.5-3' (75-90 cm)	June	2-9
'Mountain Brook'	lavender	2.5-3' (75-90 cm)	June	2-9
'Gerald Darby'	deep violet	3.5' (105 cm)	June	2-9

❧ Monarda species represent a small number of species of aromatic perennials native to North America and Mexico. Monardas are also called wild bergamot because the aroma from the plants very closely resembles that of the bergamot orange. This orange is a pear-shaped, smooth-skinned orange which is grown in southern Italy for its oil, bergamot oil, which is used extensively in the perfume industry. The oil extracted from the secretory hairs of monarda, which is

Monarda
WILD BERGAMOT
Labiatae
Zones 2–9

Monarda didyma 'Snow White' surrounded by *Phlox carolina* 'Miss Lingard' and *Echinacea purpurea* 'White Lustre'. This combination stays in flower for about eight weeks into the middle of September.

called thymol and is chemically related to bergamot oil, is now under considerable investigation as a natural flavoring compound in the fast food industry. Thymol is also used in the perfume industry, and, interestingly, monarda species also have a number of useful medicinal parameters.

All monarda species, when grown in a small amount, are quite coarse. Their real beauty comes when they are massed in large numbers because the clumps, when viewed at a distance, have a fine homogeneous, rounded aspect, which lends considerable refinement to a mid-summer or autumn border.

Organic Care

Monardas, like many members of the *Labiatae* or mint family, will grow well on poor soils and give a remarkable flowering. Monardas like a sandy, slightly alkaline soil which is well supplied with humus, phosphate, and potash. As most of the monarda species' native habitat are limestone areas, maintaining the alkalinity of the soil mixture at planting time, at pH 7.1 to 7.2 will considerably invigorate the plant. The soil should be well drained in summer and winter. Monardas will grow well in half shade, but the red and pink cultivars will be more prone to powdery mildew in humid conditions if grown in shade. A dusting of wood ashes in spring will considerably reduce powdery mildew. If the plants are grown and being used from the herb garden, a spray of bicarbonate of soda will reduce powdery mildew without affecting the plants oil glands. If powdery mildew is becoming unsightly in the border, a mild lime-sulphur spray will check the white mycelial growth on the plant's leaves in severely humid August weather. The following cultivars are resistant to this fungus: *Monarda didyma* 'Snow White', *M. d.* 'Prairie Night', *Monarda fistulosa, M. f.* 'Albescens', and *Monarda media* 'Erika'.

All monardas grow by means of a matted root system which grows either on or near the soil surface. These square roots have a system of fine feeder roots which are produced over the summer in increasing amounts as the plant flowers. A small 6–12" (15–30 cm) section of this square root will give rise to a 1–2' (30–60 cm) matted clump in two to three years. Because monardas are surface feeders, they should be divided every three years to maintain flower vigor.

Ecofunction

Hummingbirds, all bees, and butterflies love all the monarda species. They are particularly useful nectar sources in August and September. If used in a butterfly garden, *Monarda didyma* 'Adam', *M. d.* 'Cambridge

Scarlet,' *M.d.* 'Croftway Pink', and *M. media* 'Erika' are particularly good cultivars to use.

The aromatic foliage of all the Monardas make them fine plants for a blind person's garden. Because *Monarda media* 'Erika' flowers in September to October and is so attractive to butterflies, it is a useful plant for a children's observation area in a school setting.

Monardas make fine tisanes which have been greatly loved by aboriginal peoples. After the famous Boston Tea Party in 1773, "Oswego" tea or monarda tea replaced Indian tea in many homes in North America. It does to this day in the form of Earl Grey tea.

The tea from monardas may be used to relieve nausea, flatulence, menstrual pain, and vomiting. If inhaled, the water vapor containing thymol and many other volatile oils will act as an efficient expectorant. Indeed, many gardeners who have worked around monarda species are instantly aware of the refreshing mental clearing effect these plants have.

Design

Monarda species bloom in August into September and some species into October. Flowers which have dependable fall bloom are very useful in a perennial border.

The flowers of all the monarda species have dainty mop-like heads of terminal flowers with a collar of bracts of various colors enhancing the color tone of the flower. Apart from the fine, dwarf *Monarda didyma* 'Granite Pink', 10" (25 cm), all the species and cultivars range from 3–3.5' (90–105 cm). *M. media* 'Erika' grows to 6' (150 cm) and is a particularly useful red-purple flower for the back of the fall border, which combines well with the taller fall asters. Some monardas can be placed in the mid-region of the border. *M. d.* 'Adam' and *M. d.* 'Cambridge Scarlet' are true reds and can be placed in front of purple coneflowers *Echinacea purpurea* 'Bright Star' and with July and August blooming hemerocallis daylilies. *H.* 'King Alfred', a buttery, fragrant, double daylily, is a particularly fine companion to these monardas.

M. d. 'Snow White' is a particularly long blooming addition to the white border, blooming for ten weeks or more. It blooms with August lilies, *Galtonia candensis,* and August blooming alliums.

Monarda fistulosa is a slightly more refined plant than *Monarda didyma* and is a fine addition to a herb or pioneer garden. In this species, the peculiar flowering habit of a second flowering, terminal mop-like head of flowers growing through the parent head, is more

Two unnamed *Monarda didyma* cultivars, a deep rose and a light pink, soften the bright yellow of *Lysimachia punctata* in a perennial border.

pronounced and very attractive. Dotted horsemint or *M. punctata* is also a beautiful addition to a herb garden.

Monarda Species and Cultivars

NAME	COLOR	HEIGHT	MONTH	ZONE
Monarda clinopodia	pink	4' (120 cm)	July-Aug.	2-9
Monarda didyma				
M. d. 'Granite Pink'	pink	3' (90 cm)	July-Aug.	2-9
M. d. 'Adam'	red	3' (90 cm)	July-Aug.	2-9
M. d. 'Cambridge Scarlet'	red	3' (90 cm)	July-Aug.	2-9
M. d. 'Croftways Pink'	pink	3' (90 cm)	July-Aug.	2-9
M. d. 'Prairie Night'	purple	3' (90 cm)	July-Aug.	2-9
M. d. 'Souris'	violet	2.5' (75 cm)	July-Aug.	2-9
M. d. 'Thundercloud'	purple-red	3' (90 cm)	July-Aug.	2-9
M. d. 'Snow White'	white	2-3' (60-90 cm)	July-Aug.	2-9
M. fistulosa	lavender	4' (120 cm)	July-Aug.	2-9
M. f. 'Albescens'	white	4' (120 cm)	July-Aug..	2-9
M. f. 'Menthifolia'	lavender	4' (120 cm)	July-Aug.	2-9
M. media 'Erika'	purple-red	5' (150 cm)	Aug.-Oct.	2-9
M. punctata	yellow, purple dots	3' (90 cm)	July-Aug.	2-9

Paeonia
PAEONY
Paeoniaceae
Zones 2–9

The tranquil gardens of Japan and China were hallowed spots for religion, reflection, and the seeking of truth through beauty. The epicenter of this beauty in form was the paeony.

In the last century in western gardens the paeony became a popular Victorian garden flower. It is again becoming a favorite in gardens because new hybrids of various paeony species are being introduced to the public gardening arena in a range of colorful cultivars which have never been seen before. A breakthrough by the famous Japanese plantsman, the late Toichi Itoh, has introduced a buttery yellow color into the new gene pool creating the distinctive Itoh hybrids.

Paeonies have been traditionally difficult to hybridize and the resultant hybrids, difficult to propagate. A new propagation technique has recently changed all of this. A meristem propagation method has been developed in England. The meristem is the apical, cambial dome-shaped region of a plant which is genetically fine tuned for growing. With this new scientific technique there should not be too much delay from the development of a new hybrid species to its marketing.

Paeonies flower from late spring to early summer, ranging in height from about 2' (60 cm) to 7' (2.1 m) for the *P. suffruticosa* or tree paeonies. The flowers have an enormous range of color and are somewhat fleeting, lasting only two to three weeks. One of the aims of the new breeding programs is to increase the length of the flowering time, with an increase in hardiness, fragrance, and color range.

The paeony flower has a considerable range in its morphology or description. To aid in the description, the American Paeony Society has divided the paeony flower into eight different forms:

Single: The flower consists of a ring of outside petals. The male and female flower parts are in the central area.

An heirloom specie, *Paeonia lactiflora* hybrid, thought to be almost a hundred years old.

Japanese: The flower is beginning to show doubling. A ring of petals are on the outside, but some of the male parts, or stamens, are becoming petaloid. Anthers must be present.

Anemone: The anthers have gone. The central petaloids are uniformly short and narrow.

Semidouble: The stamenoid petaloids are in all stages of transformation. The formation is loose.

Crown: The carpels, or female flower parts, are nearly or fully transformed into petaloids. These petaloids differ from the guard or outer petals and the stamenoid petals.

Bomb: The central transformed petaloids are wider and differ to the outer or guard petals. There are no anthers and no collar or crown to be found.

Semirose: The carpels are fully transformed and the occasional pollen bearing stamen is found.

Rose: This is the fully doubled form, in which the stamens and the carpels are completely transformed to evenly arranged petaloids which are not distinguishable from the outside or guard petals. If this distinction is not clearly apparent, the flower is classified as a Bomb form.

Organic Care

To grow any paeony successfully a rigorous site selection must be done for excellent drainage. If in doubt, an experimental hole should be dug and a percolation test done as follows: fill the newly dug hole 2' x 2' (60 cms x 60 cm) and 2' (60 cm) deep with water. If the water takes from three to ten hours to drain completely, then your garden drainage is just right for paeonies. If the water does not drain away or takes a much longer time, then building a terraced area should be contemplated. If the soil drains too rapidly, it can be amended with aged manure and milled peat moss. Drainage should be excellent in both summer and winter.

Paeonies like a good, friable garden soil of medium fertility. The soil's pH should be from neutral to slightly alkaline, pH 7.0–7.2. A generous quantity of well-aged manure, steamed bonemeal, potash in the form of dried wood ashes, and a small amount of dolomitic limestone should be added to the planting mixture at planting time. The aeration of the soil must be excellent. The root tissue needs an abundant supply of oxygen to maintain health. Paeonies can live for an extremely long time, often 50 to 100 years or more, and will continue to benefit greatly from a rich planting medium.

The tuberous roots of the paeony are extremely brittle and easy to break. The root epidermal or surface tissue is a pink or red color and is easy to bruise. They are modified tuberous roots of some considerable size, 18" (45 cm) and up to 2" (5 cm) in diameter, fanning out from the plant underground in all directions and occupying considerable space. The tuberous roots of the paeony enables the plant to put on its considerable growth spurt in the spring followed by blooming in May or June.

After flowering, the plant likes a hot dry spell, at which time the plant goes dormant and the root tubers cure. The dormant plant is evergreen and requires no watering. Massive watering of paeonies in July and August during this dormancy phase is injurious to the paeony. The cool temperature of the fall initiates some growth activity. Paeonies are therefore planted or transplanted in the fall, from August into early September. Tree paeonies, *P. suffruticosa*, are planted in October or November, with a mulch, into a well prepared hole.

All paeonies, except the tree paeony, are planted 2" (5 cm) below the soil surface. Some growers plant the paeony level with the soil surface and mound the soil over the growing tips. Within a year or two this mound will have flattened out. Tree paeonies, *P. suffruticosa*, should be planted 6" (15 cm) below the soil surface. Tree paeonies are grafted and this depth of soil is needed to protect the graft union and grafted scion tissue above which will be responsible for flowering in the years to come. If the tree paeony is not planted to 6" (15 cm), the soil can also be mounded around the base of the plant for winter protection in the same manner that hybrid tea roses are treated in colder gardening areas. This, too, is a protective method for treating the dormant buds against desiccation. A tree paeony can get killed back in a cold winter and will set out new growth in the spring. All paeonies should also have some protection from the wind. A tree paeony will benefit from wind-protection by a house, a wall, or some other artificial structure.

Paeonies, except for tree paeonies, like full sun conditions and can withstand some high light shading from tall, overhanging trees. The tree paeony likes morning full sun and some afternoon shade. It is thought by some experts that a glacial moraine is the perfect site for a tree paeony.

If paeonies are used for hedging, they should be planted 2–3' (60–90 cm) apart. Staking by means of a metal hoop adjusted to about two-thirds of the height of the plant will help support the flowers against both wind and rain damage, especially with the new large flowered hybrids.

The *Paeonia lactiflora* 'Chocolate Soldier', long lost from Canada, blooms, in black splendor, in the garden at Carrigliath. The chocolate fragrance comes in the evening.

Paeonies are sometimes prone to botrytis blight, a fungal disease which attacks the plant in humid or rainy weather. A spring dusting of wood ashes around the plant is a good preventative measure. If this fungus is found on the paeony in late spring just prior to flowering, the areas of blight can be cut off and burned. Unfortunately, sometimes it also includes bud petioles, which abort. These, too, should be burned. Dry wood ashes or a lime sulphur spray will kill the germinating, asexual spores of this fungus.

Ecofunction

From a medical point of view, the paeony *P. officinalis* has a long and interesting history. The eminent Roman naturalist Pliny the Elder (23–79 A.D.) used extracts of the paeony to dissolve calculi or calcium rich stones in the kidneys and bladders of his patients. Ultrasound does this for us today. Paeonies also have an alkaloid which is strongly vasoconstrictive and appears to increase the coagulation or clotting time of blood.

Apart from the fact that all parts of the beautiful paeony flower are extremely poisonous, an interesting symbiosis exists between the ant and this flower. Ants assist in the blooming of paeonies. When the flower buds are ready to open, ants and other flying insects such as wasps eat the sugar secretions which tie together the outer petals of the rounded flower bud. In the act of eating this sugar, the closed

The bomb form of the paeony is useful in garden design because of its interesting spherical shape.

petals are released to open the flower.

The paeony flower is visited by honeybees, bumblebees, and hummingbirds. The flowers are also a favorite haunt of ambush bugs.

Design

Paeonies bloom from May to the end of June. The blooms are somewhat fleeting but are beautiful while they last. *P. mlokosewitschii* blooms in May, followed by *P. tenuifolia, P. japonica* and cultivars, *P. suffruticosa,* the tree paeony and its cultivars, the *P. lactiflora* with early, mid-season, and late blooming cultivars, and *P. officinalis* blooming in late June, sometimes into early July.

From a garden design perspective the most singularly different paeony flower forms are the single and Japanese, which are large dish-shaped shallow blooms, and the rose form, which is a true double, rounded, somewhat fluffy and spherical in shape.

Blooming in the late spring garden is *P. mlokosewitschii,* 2' (60 cm), with its beautiful bowl shaped lemon-yellow flowers not unlike an enlarged version of the Lenten or Christmas rose, *Helleborus niger.* This paeony is beautiful in combination with daffodils, mid-season tulips, and *Tulipa tarda.*

P. tenuifolia, 2' (60 cm), or the fern leafed paeony, has beautiful, deep red flowers and delicate fern like foliage which makes a striking companion to *T.* 'Schoonord', a double white paeony-like tulip.

In beauty, the tree paeony *P. suffruticosa* stands alone. Tree paeonies are ideal suburban plants which can benefit greatly from the protection offered by surrounding buildings. The tree paeony should be used as a single specimen 'shrub' in any garden, the sole focal point of beauty in a selected area in June. The huge flowers of the tree paeony range from the most delicate of the pastels through golden yellows to pinks and raspberry to red and deep maroons to purples. Many flowers have bitonal effects with the base of the petals being darker in color. The petal texture has a crepe like quality and the flowers have photoluminescence not often found in the plant kingdom. *P. suffruticosa* 'Marchioness' is a beautiful bitonal mauve and raspberry single flowered paeony. *P. s.* 'Kamada Nishiki' combines the royalty of an age into its imperial semi-double royal purple flowers.

The new hybrids of *P. lactiflora* make beautiful border plants. For smaller gardens there are now some dwarfed hybrids. Of these *P. l.* 'Rosedale', 19" (48 cm), an early blooming semidouble red, is probably the most interesting.

Two outstanding mid-border plants are *P. l.* 'Krinkled White', an early blooming single white flower with an interesting texture, and the late blooming *P. l.* 'Tom Eckhardt', which is late, blooming in June, and has fragrant plum-colored, single flowers.

The old *P. lactiflora* hybrids 'Jules Elie', pink, *P. l.* 'Festiva Maxima', pure white with crimson flecks, and *P. l.* 'Sarah Bernhardt', pink, are particularly beautiful when used in mass plantings or as an informal hedge.

Blooming at the end of June into July are *P. officinalis* species, which, because of their late blooming, are sometimes very useful in a border *P. o.* 'Molis' is a fine single flowered pink and *P. o.* 'Rubra Plena' is a dark red, double-flowered paeony. This paeony is particularly useful for hiding the fading foliage of daffodils and tulips in the border.

Paeonia Species and Cultivars

NAME	COLOR	HEIGHT	MONTH	ZONE
P. japonica				
P. j. 'Bowl of Beauty'	pink, white	2' (60 cm)	June	2-9
P. j. 'Isani-gidni'	white buff	2' (60 cm)	June	2-9
P. j. 'Mikado'	red, golden	2' (60 cm)	June	2-9
P. j. 'Yokohama'	pink, single	2' (60 cm)	June	2-9
P. lactiflora				
P. l. 'Tom Eckhardt'	plum golden	2' 8" (80 cm)	June	2-9
P. l. 'Krinkled White'	white yellow	2' 8" (80 cm)	June	2-9
P. l. 'Coral Charm'	coral	36" (90 cm)	June	2-9
P. l. 'Flame'	red	26" (65 cm)	June	2-9
P. l. 'Pink Lemonade'	yellow, pink cream	36" (90 cm)	June	2-9
P. l. 'Rosedale'	red	19" (48 cm)	June	2-9

NAME	COLOR	HEIGHT	MONTH	ZONE
P. mlokosewitschii	lemon yellow	2' (60 cm)	April-May	2-9
P. obovata				
P. o. 'Lutea'	yellow	2' (60 cm)	June	2-9
P. officinalis				
P. o. 'Molis'	pink single	2' (60 cm)	June	2-9
P. o. 'Rubra Plena'	red, double	2' (60 cm)	June	2-9
P. peregrina				
P. p. 'Fire King'	orange carmine	2' (60 cm)	June	2-9
P. p. 'Sunshine'	yellow	2' (60 cm)	June	2-9
P. suffruticosa				
P. s. 'Harvest'	golden	5' (150 cm)	June	2-9
P. s. 'Kamada Nishiki'	purple	5' (150 cm)	June	2-9
P. s. 'Marchioness'	mauve	5' (150 cm)	June	2-9
P. tenuifolia				
P. t. 'Rosea'	rose-pink	1-2' (30-60 cm)	May	2-9
P. t. 'Rubra Plena'	red, double	1-2' (30-60 cm)	May	2-9

Phlox
PHLOX
Polemoniaceae
Zones 2–9

Phlox are the crowning glory of the mid-summer border. Phlox are, except for one Siberian specie, native plants to the North American landscape. The range of phlox species is very large. Phlox are environmentally attuned to cold winters and warm summers. They appear to need the cold dormancy of winter for full vigor. Warm, southern gardening areas do not appear to grow phlox very well. Canada is thus a unique north temperate zone ideally suited to the growing of these species. This fact should be recognized in the form of a national collection of new and antique species of phlox somewhere in the country as a repository of these species for future generations.

Various species of phlox bloom from April into October. From a gardening point of view, phlox can be divided into spring and summer flowering species. The spring flowering species are, for the most part, low-growing or trailing species, and the summer phlox are tall plants which are excellent mid-border specimens, blooming from July into October.

Phlox paniculata 'Bright Eyes' is a most desirable phlox for the summer border because of its vigor and the clarity of its colors.

Organic Care

The spring flowering phlox like a soil of medium fertility, slightly acidic, neutral or alkaline, which is well drained in both summer and winter. All of the spring flowering phlox make excellent and rugged rock-garden plants that are remarkably hardy and drought and mildew resistant. *Phlox subulata* cultivars *P. amoena, P. bifida, P. borealis, P. douglassii, P. hoodii, P. nivalis,* and *P. unamensis* like full sun conditions. *P. adsurgens, P. divaricata, P. stolonifera,* and *P. x procumbens* are shade loving plants. In the winter months, spring flowering phlox go dormant but maintain evergreen characteristics. If there is not sufficient snow cover or if the plants have a due south, full sun exposure during the winter months, then some desiccation of the foliage will be found in zones 2–4. Depending on the winter's solar conditions, this desiccation might be severe. Although it will not harm flowering, it is unsightly. If a small amount of evergreen boughs or some other loose and stiff material is used for winter shading, these phlox will come through the winter a magnificent lush green color.

Spring flowering phlox will come into the peak of its bloom in the second year after transplanting. If the gardener desires to grow these plants in large mats, they will bloom yearly for up to 15 years and longer without further care albeit with some reduction in flowering. All spring flowering phlox can be divided and transplanted readily in March or April and again in July.

The tall, summer flowering phlox, *P. carolina* and *P. paniculata* especially, like a rich soil which is high in humus, potassium, and phosphorus. The soil should be neutral to slightly alkaline, pH 7–7.2. Phlox should not dry out between spring growth and flowering in summer as this will reduce flowering. The soil should be well drained but moist during the summer, and drainage should be excellent in winter. Phlox like full sun conditions. In more humid gardening areas, phlox can be planted with full morning sun on the plant and one to two hours of high afternoon shade to prevent bleaching of the flowers' colors. Then both plant vigor and bloom will be excellent.

Phlox subulata 'Brilliant', magenta colored, and *P. subulata* 'Eventide', pale blue, flow with the deeper blue cultivar of *Arabis caucasica* into a sea of color in the spring.

The direct ancestors of the tall flowering phlox come from areas of Canada and the United States where the soil is extremely rich in potash. If potash or potassium in liberal quantities is added to the soil at planting time and yearly thereafter, many of the so-called problems with *Phlox paniculata* cultivars will disappear.

If phlox are not faithfully divided every two or three years, they may become prone to crown rot. Since it is not always possible to divide these plants at such regular intervals, a circle of wood ashes worked into the soil around the plants in early April will help to reduce or eliminate crown rot and phlox blight as well. Phlox blight is a leaf spot fungus to which certain cultivars of *P. paniculata* are prone in humid summers. The fungal spores of both these diseases will not germinate in the harsh alkaline soil surface environment around the plant after it has been dusted with wood ashes. The wood ashes, in the meantime, will invigorate the plant by increasing the potassium content of the soil. *Phlox paniculata* 'Prospero', *P. carolina* 'Miss Lingard', *P. c.* 'Reine du jour', *P. glaberrima* 'Buckleyi', *P. ovata,* and *P. ovata* var. 'Pulcra' are all mildew resistant species of phlox.

Tall phlox should be divided in early April while the soil is cool. The central older core of the clump should be discarded.

Ecofunction

Spring flowering phlox are visited in great numbers by small, flying, beneficial insects.

P. subulata used in combination with stones or stonework makes an ideal ecological epicenter for the overwintering of lady bugs, *Hippodamia convergens.* These beneficial insects can overwinter in enormous numbers if conditions are ideal for them to do so. Leaves from deciduous trees should not be cleared up in autumn around this little ecological grouping, and, if possible, the grouping should also include the bases of large, living trees. These trees should also have leaf debris left at their southern exposures.

Lady bugs together with birds make the first line of defense for the gardener. Both adult and larval forms of the lady bugs are predaceous on aphids, scale insects, mites, and many other small garden pests. These insects are altogether necessary for the fine ecological balance within a garden. These silent partners are now being bought and used in great numbers by large scale nursery people and greenhouse operations alike. The summer flowering phlox are a favorite haunt of many species of butterflies.

Design

The spring flowering phlox, in particular both *P. subulata* and the *P. douglassi* cultivars, make ideal plants for a rock-garden, can line a walk-way, may be employed as part of a foundation planting group, and look beautiful when used as part of an evergreen garden or in planting pockets in a wall or garden steps. They are particularly beautiful when used in front of a border, but are most magnificent when used as a basis for a spring garden.

In the spring, if early daffodils are being used, *Phlox subulata* 'The Bride', which is a white cultivar, and *P. s.* 'Eventide', a pale blue cultivar, can be massed with the daffodils for a fine spring crisping effect. Gardens in zone 2 might find *P. s.* 'The Bride' a little delicate to grow and can substitute another cultivar. This beautiful white phlox cultivar is not as rugged as the other cultivars of *Phlox subulata.*

Early tulips, *T. kaufmanianna* and *T. fosteriana,* combine beautifully with great splashes of scarlet *P. s.* 'Scarlet Flame', *P. s.* 'Brittonii Rosea', pink, and *P. s.* 'Brilliant', a hot magenta color. The latter is the hardiest and toughest of the *Phlox subulata* species. *P. bifida* has very attractive flowers with bisected petals, and *P. amoena* 'Variegata' has fine variegated foliage. Both may be used with early tulips for a colorful effect. *P. nivalis,* which is similar to *P. subulata,* the flowers being more compact, can be used in zones 6 –9 for flower succession to the *Phlox subulata* species in June.

Flowering with the later tulips and daffodils are the *Phlox douglassii* cultivars. Some of these cultivars have a bitonal eye area common in many phlox species. If cultivars with a dark contrasting eye are chosen, the massing of these species is more dramatic. *P. d.* 'Appleblossom' with large, fragrant, light pink blossoms, is probably the finest cultivar that can be used with flowering, weeping apples, to mimic its flower display in a trailing form.

Phlox divaricata is the magnificent and intensely fragrant blue phlox of the North American woodlands. The rose *P. d.* 'Spring Delight' and the white *P. d.* 'Fuller's White' stay in bloom for four to five weeks in May and June. When massed with the intermediate or tall bearded iris, they make a memorable late spring display of color and fragrance.

The various hybrid cultivars obtained by crossing the super hardy *Phlox subulata* with *Phlox stolonifera* are good spring shade plants. *Phlox x procumbens* 'Folio Variegata' has pink flowers and variegated foliage. Flowering in May, it can be used with early tulips to great advantage. The tall varieties of phlox have a flowering succession which starts in June and goes into October. Some of these species are not commonly known to gardeners. Flowering begins in June with *Phlox pilosa* and *P. ovata,* the mountain phlox. In July, *P. glaberrima,* the smooth phlox, is in bloom followed by the *P. maculata* cultivars, *P. carolina (P. suffruticosa),* and the enormous group of cultivars of the *P. paniculata (P. decussata),* most of which bloom in July and August. A number of late cultivars of this specie bloom into October.

The flowers of all phlox are similar, but in the tall phlox, these flowers occur in large-headed terminal clusters called terminal cymes or panicles. The color range of the flowers is very great going from white to sparkling red to orange-red to glowing crimson to magenta to some beautiful violet shades. Some of the cultivars have eye zones of different colors. Some eye zones are similar but darker colors to the petals and some eye zones are white or a lighter color contrasting with the petals. The combined, multicolored tonal effect of this is very pleasing. In addition to this, the flowers have an interesting, spicy fragrance.

In the June border, *P. pilosa* and *P. ovata* combine well with many of the summer flowering bulbs and corms. In particular, these phlox combine well with the flowering alliums, *A. christophii* and *A. moly.*

In the July border *P. glaberrima* 'Buckleyi', rose purple, *P. maculata* 'Alpha', rose, *P. m.* 'Omega', white and violet, and the beautiful, white, sterile, *P. carolina* 'Miss Lingard', which flowers from July into October, are attractive. This old cultivar is extremely hardy and disease free. These July flowering phlox combine extremely well with Asiatic, martagon, and trumpet lilies and also with the giant alliums. These phlox should have a position in the mid-border, set slightly to the front.

Blooming in July and August are the *Phlox paniculata* cultivars. These cultivars can be dwarfed, such as *P. p.* 'Otley Ideal', 12" (30 cm), or medium height 36" (90 cm), and can soar to 4' (120 cm). Using these height variables, a stunning summer border can be designed. These phlox borders were fashionable in Edwardian gardens, but with the new cultivars available to us today, they can be even more colorful. *P. p.* 'White Admiral' and *P. p.* 'Bright Eyes' are superior mid-border cultivars, and *P. p.* 'Russian Violet', 4' (120 cm), is a valuable later blooming, tall cultivar which is useful for good color in the mid-August border.

Phlox paniculata cultivars combine well with July and August blooming oriental hybrid lilies. The mixed fragrance of both groups of plants is essential for the heady summer fragrance which underlies and augments the keen appreciation of the colorful display of the July and August border.

Phlox carolina 'Miss Lingard' flowering with the trumpet lily, *Lilium regale* 'Album', in a white border.

Phlox Species and Cultivars

SPRING FLOWERING PHLOX SPECIES AND CULTIVARS

NAME	COLOR	HEIGHT	MONTH	ZONE
P. adsurgens	lilac	12" (30 cm)	April-May	2-9
P. amoena	pink	12" (30 cm)	April-May	2-9
P. a. 'Alba'	white	12" (30 cm)	May	2-9
P. a. 'Variegata'	pink	12" (30 cm)	May	2-9
P. bifida	lavender	8" (20 cm)	May	2-9
P. b. 'Alba'	white	8" (20 cm)	May	2-9
P. borealis	lilac	6" (15 cm)	May	2-9
P. b. 'Alba'	white	6" (15 cm)	May	2-9

SPRING FLOWERING PHLOX SPECIES AND CULTIVARS

NAME	COLOR	HEIGHT	MONTH	ZONE
P. divaricata (syn. P. canadensis)				
P. d. 'Dirigo Ice'	blue	12" (30 cm)	May-June	2-9
P. d. 'Spring Delight'	pink	12" (30 cm)	May-June	2-9
P. d. 'Fuller's White'	white	12" (30 cm)	May-June	2-9
P. d. 'Laphami'	blue	12" (30 cm)	May-June	3-9
(syn. *P. pilosa* 'Fulgida')				
P. douglassii				
P. d. 'May Snow'	white	8" (20 cm)	May-June	2-9
P. d. 'Apple Blossom'	pink	6" (15 cm)	May-June	2-9
P. d. 'CrackerJack'	crimson	8" (20 cm)	May-June	2-9
P. d. 'Precious'	pink with red eye	8" (20 cm)	May-June	2-9
P. hoodii				
(syn. *P. diffusa*)	white	2" (5 cm)	May-June	2-9
P. nivalis				
P. n. 'Azurea'	blue	10" (25 cm)	June	6-9
P. n. 'Camla'	pink	10" (25 cm)	June	6-9
P. n. 'Sylvestris'	rose	10" (25 cm)	June	6-9
P. x procumbens				
'Millstream'	rose	10" (25 cm)	May	2-9
'Folio Variegata'	pink	10" (25 cm)	May	2-9
P. stolonifera				
P. s. 'Blue Ridge'	blue	9" (23 cm)	April-May	2-9
P. s. 'Grandiflora'	blue	9" (23 cm)	April-May	2-9
P. s. 'Rosea'	rose	9" (23 cm)	April-May	2-9
P. s. 'Violacea'	violet	9" (23 cm)	April-May	2-9
P. subulata				
P. s. 'The Bride'	white	6" (15 cm)	May	2-9
P. s. 'Scarlet Flame'	scarlet	6" (15 cm)	May	2-9
P. s. 'Child's Pink'	pink	6" (15 cm)	May	2-9
P. s. 'Eventide'	pale blue	6" (15 cm)	May	2-9
P. s. 'Brilliant'	magenta	6" (15 cm)	May	2-9
P. s. 'Brittonii rosea'	pink	6" (15 cm)	May	2-9
P. s. 'Model'	pink	6" (15 cm)	May	2-9

TALL SUMMER PHLOX SPECIES AND CULTIVARS

NAME	COLOR	HEIGHT	MONTH	ZONE
P. carolina				
P. s. 'Miss Lingard'	white	42" (105 cm)	July-Oct	2-9
P. s. 'Reine du jour'	white with red eye	36" (90 cm)	July-Aug	2-9
P. glaberrima	pink	2-3' (60-90 cm)	July-Aug	2-9

NAME	COLOR	HEIGHT	MONTH	ZONE
P. g. 'Alba'	white	2-3' (60-90 cm)	July-Aug	2-9
P. g. 'Buckleyii'	rose	18" (45 cm)	July-Aug	2-9
P. maculata				
P. m. 'Alpha'	rose with dark eye	32" (80 cm)	June-July	2-9
P. m. 'Omega'	white with lilac eye	32" (80 cm)	June-July	2-9
P. ovata				
P. o. 'Latifolia'	rose	15" (38 cm)	June-July	2-9
P. o. 'var. Pulchra'	pink	12" (30 cm)	June-July	2-9
P. paniculata				
P. p. 'Otley Ideal'	orange-scarlet	12" (30 cm)	July-Aug	2-9
P. p. 'Gnome'	red with dark eye	18" (46 cm)	July-Aug	2-9
P. p. 'Aida'	red with purple eye	20" (50 cm)	July-Aug	2-9
P. p. 'Prince of Orange'	pink orange	36" (90 cm)	July-Aug	2-9
P. p. 'July Glow'	rose	42" (105 cm)	July-Aug	2-9
P. p. 'White Admiral'	white	36" (90 cm)	July-Aug	2-9
P. p. 'Prospero'	rose with white eye	35" (90 cm)	July-Aug	2-9
P. p. 'Rijnstroom'	rose	40" (100 cm)	July-Aug	2-9
P. p. 'Brigadier'	orange-red	42" (105 cm)	July-Aug	2-9
P. p. 'Bright Eyes'	pink with red eye	42" (105 cm)	July-Sept	2-9
P. p. 'Russian Violet	violet purple	48" (120 cm)	Aug.-Sept	2-9
P. pilosa	pink	18" (45 cm)	May-July	3-9
P. p. 'Alba'	white	18" (45 cm)	May-July	3-9

Biennials

Introduction

Species

Organic Care

Ecofunction

Design

Species and

Cultivar List

An unusual but pleasing combination of biennials, *Verbascum olympicum* 'Silver Spire' with *Cheiranthus allionii* 'Orange' in the May and June garden.

Biennials

Biennials are a group of plants that share many similar characteristics. For the north temperate gardener, these characteristics make them very useful flowers for instant design.

A biennial plant grows vegetatively from seed the first year, subsequently blooms, sets seeds, and dies in its second year. Biennials are very easy to grow, have a six to eight week period of bloom, except for Canterbury bells which have two to three weeks, have a repeat fall bloom, and are very disease resistant. Most are extremely easy to transplant or to move, even when in flower. Biennial seeds have a germination rate which is naturally high and they self-sew readily. A number of them are very frost resistant and are useful in zones 2-4. Once flowering is over many can be removed and their place taken by summer flowering tender bulbs such as gladioli or galtonias.

An exceptional feature of biennials is their drought resistance. In their first year of growth, moisture from snow run-off is sufficient to give them a large growth boost in the spring and early summer. If the remainder of the season is dry, the young plants will stay static and flowering the following year will be slightly reduced. This is very important for dry gardening areas.

Canadian gardeners could make considerably more use of biennials in their gardens. The following are among the finest biennials for the north temperate gardener:

Alcaea rosea	hollyhocks
Anchusa azurea	bugloss
Bellis perennis	English daisy
Campanula medium	Canterbury bells
Cheiranthus	wall flowers
Dianthus barbatus	sweet williams
Digitalis	foxgloves
Hesperis matronalis	dame's rocket
Lychnis coronaria	rose champion
Myosotis sylvatica	forget-me-not
Papaver nudicaule	Icelandic poppy
Verbascum	mullein

Anchusa azurea
(syn. *A. italica, Brunnera*)
**BUGLOSS OR
ALKANET**
Boraginaceae
Zones 4–9

Anchusa is a perennial which is treated as a biennial. It is magnificent when planted in bold clumps of three or five in the center of a large, mid-summer border. Anchusa comes in a variety of blues, grows to about 2–3' (60–90 cm) tall, and is coarse, hairy, and bushy. Because of this anchusa should be viewed from a distance to obtain value from the deep color tone which is a winning aspect of this biennial.

Anchusa is very like viper's bugloss or blue weed, *Echium vulgare,* and is sometimes confused with this plant. *E. vulgare* flowers later on in the season, in July to September, and is commonly found growing all over eastern North America's derelict limestone pastures.

Organic Care

Anchusa likes a gritty or sandy, alkaline, pH 7.0–7.2, soil to which organic materials have been added in moderate amounts. The soil should be extremely well drained in both summer and winter. Anchusa grows well on poor soils.

Anchusa is not a biennial for a busy gardener, as it is difficult to keep growing from year to year. Unlike other biennials, it is propagated by root cuttings. These should be made cleanly with a sterile knife in early June and set out in a propagation bed to make sufficient vegetative growth to flower the following year. The fleshy taproot system is easily prone to injury. Cuts become sap filled immediately, which make an easy entry for bacteria or fungi into the root giving rise to crown rot. Reduced hoeing and walking around the mature plants reduces this possibility. The high water content in the taproot system is responsible for its marginal hardiness in zone 4 without adequate snow cover in severe winters.

Ecofunction

Like many members of the *Boraginaceae* family, anchusa is very attractive to honey bees. All anchusas are an extremely good nectar source for both honey bees and the larger butterflies. The nectar is secreted at the base of the ovary in such an ingenious way as to be protected from rain. Anchusas are a handsome addition to a butterfly garden.

Design

Anchusa, in clumps, carries the blue color of delphiniums, *D. elatum*, throughout the mid-summer border in a very forceful way, so that it becomes a backbone blue into which other colors can be designed to blend. The cultivar *Anchusa azurea* 'Royal Blue' is a little known but striking plant in the border.

Anchusa Cultivars

NAME	COLOR	HEIGHT	MONTH	ZONE
A. azurea (syn. *A. italica*)				
A. a. 'Loddon Royalist'	gentian blue	36" (90 cm)	May-Aug	4-9
A. a. 'Italica Opal'	sky-blue	48" (120 cm)	May-Aug	4-9
A. a. 'Dropmore'	blue	3' (60 cm)	May-Aug	4-9
A. capensis				
A. c. 'Blue Bird'	blue	1-2' (30-60 cm)	July-Sept	7-9
A. c. 'Pink Bird'	pink	1-2' (30-60 cm)	July-Sept	7-9
A. myosotidiflora	blue	16" (40 cm)	May-Aug	4-9
(syn. *Brunnera macrophylla*)				
A. officinalis				
A. o. 'Angustifolia'	blue	2' (60 cm)	July-Sept	4-9
A. o. 'Incarnata'	pink	2' (60 cm)	July-Sept	4-9

Hollyhocks flourish in all parts of North America. They were a distinct favorite of the pioneer settlers in this country and remain today as a memory of the farming community's gardens. The individual flowers of the hollyhock can be double or single and come in a wide range of colors, including white, yellow, rose, pink, and deep scarlet to black. Some flowers are richly ruffled and some are striped. If a select strain of hollyhock seed is grown, the second generation seeds will produce a bounty of colorful surprises for the gardener.

Alcea rosea
HOLLYHOCK
Malvaceae
Zones 2–9

Organic Care

Hollyhocks like a good, friable soil of medium fertility which is well drained both in summer and winter. The soil's pH should be alkaline, pH 7.0–7.1. This can be achieved by the addition of small amounts of ground dolomitic limestone and dry wood ashes to the planting mixture. A small addition of well-aged cow or sheep manure together with steamed bonemeal will reap dividends of enormous 6–7' (2–2.5 m) spires of flowers. Hollyhocks are true biennials. Although they will sometimes have a second year of flowering, these flowers are inferior in height and vigor.

The seeds of hollyhocks will germinate naturally in the garden from April to May. These self-sewn seeds should be transplanted to their final spot in the garden after the first true leaf stage when they are about 1.5" (4 cm) high. When transplanting care should be taken not to damage the long taproot they develop, even at this early stage of growth, as injury will seriously affect the plant's ability to produce quality flowers the following year. The largest, most vigorous, and best quality flowers are obtained in this manner.

In some humid years hollyhocks are bothered by rust fungi. As the name suggests, rust-colored, round spots appear mostly on the undersides of the leaves and can also occur on the stems. While it is unsightly on the plant, it will not significantly affect the flowering stage. A mild spray of lime-sulphur can be used for mature plants. Alternatively, in springtime, the ground may be dusted with wood ashes as a deterrent to this fungus where rusts have been found to be a persistent problem.

Ecofunction

The single flowered heritage hollyhocks in colors of red, buff, maroon, scarlet, and black are more attractive to humming birds and honey bees for nectar than are the double strains of this biennial. The pollen of hollyhock is very large, and is much in demand by honey bees in August and September, probably partly because of the distinct medicinal properties of this plant. It is used in the reduction of inflammation of mucous membranes. *Althaea officinalis*, and possibly *Alcea rosea,* has a high content of a chemical which can be used as a substitute for Rennet. Rennet was and is used in cheese making and also as a Victorian health dessert called junket. Interestingly, Rennet contains rennin, which is one of the universal gastric coagulating enzymes of the digestive system of humans and animals alike. The knowledge that this plant has such a sophisticated chemical system is centuries old, but it is perhaps of greater interest scientifically and medicinally in this era than it was in ancient times.

A strain of *Alcea rosea* 'Nigra'.

Design

Hollyhocks may be planted in between delphiniums, or slightly, 8" (20 cm), behind them. Hollyhocks will begin to flower after the delphiniums fade. This arrangement gives a nice, high flowering back border throughout mid-summer to late summer. It should be noted that single hollyhocks are an integral part of a traditional cottage style border.

The dwarf powderpuff strain has mixed colors and delightful ruffling on the flowers. These flowers fit well into a smaller garden.

Alcea Rosea Cultivars

NAME	COLOR	HEIGHT	MONTH	ZONE
A. r. 'Charters Double Triumph' strain double flower	mixed	7' (2.1 m)	July-Oct	2-9
A. r. 'Powderpuff' strain double flower	mixed	4-5' (1-1.5 m)	July-Oct	2-9
A. r. 'Newport'	pink	7' (2.1 m)	July-Oct	2-9
A. r. 'Pallida'	white	7' (2.1 m)	July-Oct	2-9
A. r. 'Sulphurea'	yellow	7' (2.1 m)	July-Oct	2-9
A. r. 'Scarlet'	red	7' (2.1 m)	July-Oct	2-9
A. r. 'Nigra'	black	7' (2.1 m)	July-Oct	2-9

Bellis perennis, the common English 6" (15 cm) white biennial daisy, infests lawns in the British Isles, much to children's great joy because these daisies make the yardage of flower chains for busy little hands in spring. The common daisy has been greatly improved over the years. The strain called the monstrosa super giants have very large flowers in white, crimson, and rose. These flowers rise from a dainty rosette of leaves which is in itself very attractive. There is also a miniature double flowering strain, 'Miniature Double Button', 5" (12 cm), with fully double flowers of white, red, or rose colors.

Bellis perennis
ENGLISH DAISY
Compositae
Zones 4–9

Organic Care

Bellis perennis like a medium rich, slightly acid soil. They like damp but not waterlogged growing conditions in the spring. A high clay component in the soil is much to their advantage. Gardeners in zones 8–9 will not have any trouble overwintering this daisy. Gardeners in zones 5–7 will have to provide some winter protection in areas where a snow cover is not dependable. Gardeners in zones 2–4 will have to provide protection to *Bellis perennis* plants such as a cold-frame or evergreen boughs or straw. All *Bellis perennis* are remarkably free of disease.

Ecofunction

These little daisies are visited by honey bees in the spring and summer. The leaves of *Bellis perennis* are covered with glandular hairs, the bases of which have complex oils. These oils have a very soothing and restorative action on epidermal tissue or skin. An extract of the leaves has been used for centuries as a spring skin tonic in many European countries.

Design

All of the *Bellis perennis* cultivars have a unique, strong scent. These daisies are much beloved by gardeners. They make very pert planting companions to pansies or a simple but beautiful edging to a small lawn and a delicate flower border. Their tiny, compact, rosette form is beautiful in a rockery. They may be used to great advantage in nooks and crannies in even the smallest of gardens.

Bellis Perennis Cultivars

NAME	COLOR	HEIGHT	MONTH	ZONE
B. p. 'Monstrosa Super Giant' strain	crimson, rose white	6" (15 cm)	Apr.-June	4-9
B. p. 'Miniature Double Button' strain	crimson, rose white	5" (13 cm)	April-June	4-9
B. p. 'Tubulosa'	rose	6" (15 cm)	April-June	4-9
B. p. 'Dresden China'	pink	3" (7.5 cm)	June-July	4-9
B. p. 'Robert'	white	3" (7.5 cm)	June-July	4-9

Campanula medium
(syn. *C. grandiflora*)
CANTERBURY BELLS
Campanulaceae
Zones 2–9

Campanula medium is called Canterbury Bells, and is a true biennial. The flowers resemble rounded cups on saucers and are rose, white, and blue. The flowers are large 2" (5 cm) and are abundant on the plant, which can grow to 3' (90 cm) tall.

Organic Care

Canterbury bells like a sandy soil which is high in humus, phosphate, and potash. The soil should be neutral or slightly alkaline. Small additions of dolomitic limestone to the soil greatly enhance flowering in this species. The soil should have excellent drainage in winter to avoid the fungal disease, crown rot, to which Canterbury bells are prone if grown in wet soil. Crown rot in Canterbury bells will be found to be a dark brown, damaged area at the base of the plant. It may include all of the growing crown and the roots. In all instances, the fibrous root system of the plant is damaged, which will seriously affect subsequent flowering. Infected plants should be discarded.

Canterbury bells will self seed readily and the plants may be transplanted at any stage of growth up to flowering. The plants should be watered well two hours prior to transplanting to induce full vigor as they are particularly susceptible to desiccation. A reasonably sized root-ball should be lifted with the plant. It should be well watered after transplanting.

It is a wise practise to maintain a small stock of Canterbury Bells to replace those which may be winter-killed.

Ecofunction

Campanula medium is an excellent source of pollen and nectar for bumble bees and honey bees and sometimes butterflies.

Design

Canterbury bells are traditionally used in front of delphiniums in a flowering border, especially the 3" (7.5 cm) flowered cultivar C.*m.* 'Calycanthema'. They are excellent companions as the color tones and flower forms complement one another beautifully. Canterbury bells stay in flower for two weeks in hot weather. In the milder west coastal regions they will stay in flower for three weeks or longer with a good flower repeat in August or September. In the prairies and eastern Canada, this repeat bloom is not worth while; hence, plants should be removed from the border at the end of June and be replaced with tender flowering bulbs such as gladioli or dwarf Canna lilies in pastel shades.

The unopened flowers of *Campanula medium* reflect an interesting repetition of shape with the Russell hybrid lupine 'Limelight'.

Campanula Medium Cultivars

NAME	COLOR	HEIGHT	MONTH	ZONE
C. *m.* 'Cup and Saucer Special' mixture	mixed	30" (75 cm)	June	2-9
C. *m.* 'Bells of Holland' strain	mixed	15" (38 cm)	June	2-9
C. *m.* 'Alba'	white	3' (90 cm)	June	2-9
C. *m.* 'Caerulea'	blue	3' (90 cm)	June	2-9
C. *m.* 'Rosea'	pink	3' (90 cm)	June	2-9
C. *m.* 'Nana'	blue	10" (25 cm)	June	2-9
C. *m.* 'Calycanthema'	mixed	20" (50 cm)	June	2-9

Cheiranthus
WALLFLOWERS
Cruciferae
Zones 2–9

There are two species of biennial wallflowers that can be grown in north temperate gardens, *Cheiranthis cheiri* or the English wallflower, and *Cheiranthis allionii* or the Russian wallflower. In European gardens *Cheiranthus* species are commonly known as *Erysimum,* even though there is a small technical variation in the ovaries of both species. The English wallflower needs some overwintering protection in zones 5 and 6. The Siberian wallflower can be grown in any gardening zone that has a dependable snow cover over winter. These plants and their flowers are very frost tolerant. Both species of wallflowers have a delightfully pleasant fragrance, the fragrance of the Russian wallflower being stronger and sweeter.

The individual flowers of Russian wallflowers are a bright yellow-orange color. The plant grows in a gradual way into a 30" (80 cm) bushy form from a spring rosette of foliage. English wallflowers are yellow, yellow-brown, or red to red-black in color. There are also double flowering and variegated cultivars. The bushy habit is more pronounced in the English wallflowers, which can grow up to 3' (90 cm) or more. In milder climates, zones 9 and 10, they make a valuable late fall and winter flower. Some good dwarf cultivars of English wallflowers are also available.

Cheiranthus allionii 'Orange' with *Verbascum phoenecium* in the children's secret garden.

It is likely that cold hardy cultivars or hybrids of English wallflowers crossed with Himalayan species would emerge for colder northern gardens if trials were to be conducted, as cold hardiness lies within the genetic possibility of the *Cruciferae* family.

Ecofunction

All single flowered cultivar forms of both English and Russian wallflowers have a plentiful supply of nectar and pollen. They are thus useful food sources for honey bees and hummingbirds alike.

Wallflowers contain the cardiac glycoside, Cheiranthin. Cheiranthin, when ingested by butterflies, acts as a chemical protective compound. Species of prey digest the butterfly and get violently ill. They will not feed again on that particular butterfly. Thus wallflowers act as beneficial plants in a butterfly garden. Wallflowers are an essential ingredient of potpourri.

Organic Care

Both Russian and English wallflowers like a neutral soil of medium fertility. These plants also grow remarkable well on lean soil. Good drainage in both summer and winter is essential for healthy plants. They are excellent plants for maritime gardens. Russian wallflowers benefit from some shade, especially in the colder growing zones where shade reduces desiccation of the overwintering foliage. Both species are extremely easy to grow from seed. Some strains of English wallflowers may be treated as annuals. If seeded in very early spring they will give bloom in the fall. This is useful for the milder areas of zones 8 and 9.

Design

Russian wallflowers are useful in zones 2–9 and English wallflowers in zones 5–9. Both can be massed with late spring bulbs to great advantage, the Russian wallflower being superior in this respect. They can be massed with the split-corona narcissi or *Narcissus* 'Articole'. Because they have such a long flowering time, eight to ten weeks, they can also be used with late tulips. A splendid combination is the viridiflora tulip 'Artist' or 'Golden Artist', which are burning orange colors, mixed with Russian wallflowers, which serve to accentuate this sea of orange color.

Cheiranthus Species and Cultivars

NAME	COLOR	HEIGHT	MONTH	ZONE
C. allionii 'Gold Bedder'	yellow	12" (30 cm)	May-June	2-9
C. a 'Orange'	orange	12" (30 cm)	May-July	2-9
C. cheiri 'Harper's Crewe'	double yellow	15" (40 cm)	May-July	5-9
C. c. 'Bowles Mauve'	mauve-blue	3' (90 cm)	July-Aug.	5-9
C. c. 'Butterscotch'	orange	12" (30 cm)	May-June	5-9
C. c. 'Jacob's Jacket'	amber	12" (30 cm)	May-June	5-9
C. c. linifolium 'Variegatum'	mauve	18" (45 cm)	May-June	8-9

The Sweet William is a biennial member of the carnation or *Caryophyllaceae* family. They are exquisitely fragrant and extremely colorful. Colors of white, red, rose, crimson, carmine, and violet as well as bicolors of all of these mixed with fringed flowers and auricled petals of great beauty are available to the gardener. The flowers stay in bloom for eight to ten weeks beginning in June. The tall cultivars reach 12" (30 cm) in height. Dwarf forms are also available. The 'Ideal' series, a new hybrid of Sweet William, *Barbatus* x *chinensis*, has larger flowers and has the great advantage of being extremely frost tolerant even in zones 2 and 3. This strain is also drought tolerant.

Dianthus barbatus
SWEET WILLIAM
Caryophyllaceae
Zones 2–9

The fragrant *Dianthus barbatus* 'Atrococcineus.'

Organic Care

Sweet Williams prefer a sandy neutral soil of medium fertility that is well drained in both summer and winter and is located in full sun. When preparing a bed for Sweet Williams, the bed should be considered to be a permanent planting. A well-prepared bed will easily last for ten years without renewal. Because the area will naturally re-seed every fall, the supply of fresh plants will be plentiful. Some surprises of new variants may occur resulting from cross-pollination.

Sweet Williams are remarkably free of pests. In damp, cool spring weather a small amount of crown rot may occur. The offending plants can be discarded. The resulting empty spaces will soon fill in, naturally.

Ecofunction

Sweet Williams are visited by hummingbirds. The flowers can be used in a quick-mix potpourri.

Design

Sweet Williams are extremely fragrant and as such are an essential part of a fragrance border. They are also an integral part of a cottage-style garden. Sweet Williams are an effective ground cover for dry, sunny areas in a garden. If they are used at the front of a perennial border in repeating blocks, they have a spectacular effect. Lilies of all kinds can be grouped behind them. The Sweet Williams act as a very cooling ground cover for their roots. They may be interplanted with Carpathian harebells, *Campanula carpatica*, placed slightly to the forefront of the border. The *D. b.* 'Albus' cultivar can be used to great effect in a white border in front of regal lilies and clumps of *Monarda didyma* 'Snow White' and interspersed with *Campanula carpatica* 'White Chips'.

Dianthus barbatus Hybrids and Cultivars

NAME	COLOR	HEIGHT	MONTH	ZONE
D. barbatus 'Albus'	white	10" (25 cm)	June-July	3-9
D. b. 'Atrococcineus'	red	10" (25 cm)	June-July	3-9
D. b. 'Nigricans'	violet-purple	10" (25 cm)	June-July	3-9
D. barbatus x D. chinensis				
'Telstar' series	mixed	8" (20 cm)	June-July	2-9
'Ideal' series	mixed	10" (25 cm)	June-July	2-9

Digitalis purpurea
FOXGLOVE
Scrophulariaceae
Zones 2–9

The common foxgloves of the hedges of Ireland, England, and Europe are true biennials which grow extremely well in north temperate gardens. These biennials have been grown in medicinal gardens since the sixteenth century. The plant grows in its first year as a very large rosette. By September it can reach from 1–1½' (30–45 cm) across. In all cases, the bigger the rosette, the taller and better the flowering spire the following year. If the overwintered rosette has a snow cover in zones 2–5, this biennial will be perfectly happy. Cold gardens without a snow cover will have to resort to the use of some winter protection to reduce desiccation.

Organic Care

Foxgloves like a moderately rich, sandy, slightly acidic soil. Good drainage in both summer and winter is absolutely necessary for healthy plants. Foxgloves grow well in full sun or in half shade. In shaded areas the flowering time is delayed by a week or so. Foxgloves are very susceptible to crown rot, which is caused by soggy conditions in winter. The roots are killed and the crown areas become brown and pulpy. Infected plants should be discarded as they will not recover. Drainage should be improved.

Ecofunction

Digitalis purpurea contains cardiac glycosides, as does *D. dubia, D. ferruginea, D. grandiflora, D. lutea, D. mertonensis, D. laevigata, D. nervosa, D. subalpina, D. parviflora, D.* x *siberica,* and *D. viridiflora.* Cardiac glycosides are found in many other plants, but in *Digitalis purpurea* the numbers of different active glycosides and their concentration is high, comprising around thirty separate identifiable compounds. Cardiac glycosides are used in the treatment of heart disease as a cardiotonic. They increase the pumping action of the heart by 30 percent without a simultaneous increase in oxygen. They are therefore extremely useful in congestive heart failure and coronary heart disease treatment.

Cardiac glycosides also have an interesting protective function for the butterfly kingdom. Large butterflies, such as the monarch butterfly *Danaus plexippus*, collect these glycosides from *D. purpurea,* milkweeds, wallflowers, and many other plants they frequent. These glycosides are harmless to butterflies. However, in avian predators, such as king birds and blue jays, the ingestion of these glycoside-filled butterflies makes the birds violently ill. Thus the avian predator learns a horrible chemical lesson.

A beautiful strain of unmarked *Digitalis purpurea* 'Alba', with *Centaurea montana* 'Coerulea'.

Design

Foxgloves are stately flowers growing in ideal conditions up to 5' (1.8 m). The long spire is covered with white, cream, apricot, yellow, pink, or purple tubular flowers. The insides of the flowers have exquisite, chocolate-colored markings.

Foxgloves, especially the white and yellow cultivars, are wonderful massed in a shade garden. The groupings should be large, including at least twenty or more specimens. Foxgloves can also be seeded into pockets in a garden wall, where they give a careless flowering charm to that area. The plants will be somewhat reduced in size.

Foxgloves are remarkable when grouped under the Northern catalpa tree, *Catalpa speciosa*, zone 4–9, whose white flowers are very similar to D. *purpurea* 'Alba'.

Foxgloves, in groups of three, lend a regal aspect to the perennial border, where their long eight to nine week period of bloom, beginning in June, is very useful. Their height and graceful nodding flowering tips add a non-conflicting mass to delphiniums. The *D. p.* 'Campanulata', which has large flowers, *D. lutea,* and *D. p.* 'Sutton's Apricot' are particularly useful in this respect. Foxgloves can be removed from the border in July and replaced with white or pink canna lilies.

Gardeners in zones 4–9 have a smaller but quite respectable repeat bloom in August and September.

Digitalis Species and Cultivars

NAME	COLOR	HEIGHT	MONTH	ZONE
D. ferruginea	cream and amber	5' (150 cm)	June-July	4-9
D. grandiflora	yellow	2' (60 cm)	June-July	6-9
D. lanata	white	2' (60 cm)	June-July	6-9
D. lutea	yellow	2' (60 cm)	June-July	5-9
D. purpurea	purple	3' (90 cm)	June-July	2-9
D. p. 'Sulton's Excelsior Hybrids'	mixed	3' (90 cm)	June-July	2-9
D. p. 'Alba'	white	3' (90 cm)	June-July	2-9
D. p. 'Campanulata'	purple	3' (90 cm)	June-July	2-9
D. p. 'Isabellina'	yellow	3' (90 cm)	June-July	2-9
D. p. 'Sutton's Apricot'	apricot	3' (90 cm)	June-July	2-9
D. p. x Siberica	yellow	2' (60 cm)	June-July	4-9
D. thapsi	purple	3' (90 cm)	June-July	5-9
D. viridiflora	green	2' (60 cm)	June-July	4-9

Hesperis matronalis
DAME'S ROCKET
Cruciferae
Zones 2 – 9

A massing of fragrant *Hesperis matronalis* 'Alba' and 'Purpurea' with diploid *Iris germanica* 'Headlines', a fine, long-lasting, late spring display of blooms for butterflies in the garden.

Dame's rocket or sweet rocket is a biennial that was brought into Canada by the early pioneers. Old abandoned settlements can quite often be identified by the masses of sweet rocket and common lilac hugging the old ruins in many parts of eastern Canada and New England.

Dame's rocket can grow to 4' (1.2 m) and has a bushy habit. It is somewhat like an elongated annual stock with an equally wonderful, spicy smell. The flowers range from pure white to lilac to purple. Dame's rocket will self seed readily. As a member of the cabbage family, it is the hardiest of all the biennials, which makes it particularly useful for zones 2 and 3.

Organic Care

Dame's rocket will grow in a wide variety of soils and will put on a remarkably good flowering even on poor soils. A sandy neutral soil which is moderately high in humus and is well drained in winter is the ideal soil. Full sun to partial shade is the ideal site. Waterlogged conditions in winter will cause crown rot in the one-year-old plants, which will seriously affect their flowering in the following spring and early summer.

Dame's rocket is always remarkably free of any kind of insect damage.

Ecofunction

Dame's rocket is an extremely plentiful source of pollen and nectar for butterflies, hummingbirds, and bees. The single flowered cultivars are king-pin plants of a north temperate butterfly garden.

The plant, when it is in flower, is considered to be a gland stimulant. The early pioneers used sweet rocket as a dual purpose plant. When young, prior to flowering, it was used as a nutritious salad green as it is a member of the *Cruciferae* or cabbage family.

Design

Dame's rocket looks beautiful when planted as a back-drop to the tall bearded iris. If white, purple, wine, or violet colors are used, they complement the color variations found in Dame's rocket very nicely.

Single or double cultivars of Dame's rocket are excellent additions to a perennial border, where they should be placed slightly to the forefront, as they can be removed and replaced when flowering has ceased. *Hesperis matronalis* 'Alba' is slightly more fragrant than all the other cultivars and is an essential addition to a north temperate fragrance border. It would appear that the double forms of Dame's rocket are extremely rare if not extinct in North America.

Hesperis matronalis Cultivars

NAME	COLOR	HEIGHT	MONTH	ZONE
H. m. 'Alba'	white single	4' (120 cm)	May-July	2-9
H. m. 'Purpurea'	violet single	4' (120 cm)	May-July	2-9
H. m. 'Flore Pleno'	purple double	4' (120 cm)	May-July	2-9
H. m. 'Alba Plena'	white double	4' (120 cm)	May-July	2-9
H. m. 'Lilacina Flore Pleno'	lilac double	4' (120 cm)	May-July	2-9

Lychnis coronaria
(syn. *Agrostemma coronaria*)
Rose Champion
Caryophyllaceae
Zones 2–9

Lychnis coronaria 'Rosea' with *Monarda didyma*.

Lychnis coronaria, because it is an old cottage garden plant, has many common names, including mullein pink, rose champion, and dusty miller. In Europe, where it originates, the plant is a short-lived perennial that re-seeds easily, but in the north temperate garden it has all the characteristics of a true biennial.

The plant grows from a rosette in its second year to 20" (50 cm) tall and is completely grey-white in color. The entire plant is covered with dense white hairs, which gives the plant a surreal characteristic enhanced by the fluorescence of the magenta flowers in the *L. c.* 'Atrosanguinea' cultivar.

Organic Care

Lychnis coronaria likes a light, well-drained, neutral, sandy soil in full sun. The soil should be of medium fertility. If it is allowed to get impoverished, this biennial is prone to a virus disease which can easily be identified by albino forms of the plant in its first year stage. These should be destroyed and the soil enriched. The odd plant with crown rot can be easily identified and should also be discarded.

Ecofunction

The nectaries of this plant are at the base of the stamens making it difficult for foraging honey bees and other insects.

Design

Lychnis coronaria cultivars flower in June and July, adding much grace to the mid-summer border.

Lychnis coronaria is a garden designer's dream, as all characteristics of this plant make it remarkable in the garden. The white hairs in sunshine and glowing flowers gives it a surreal effect, especially when massed. If planted near *Verbascum olympicum* 'Silver Spire' and *Stachys byzantina* 'Silver Carpet', this surreal effect is repeated in a most interesting way. *L. c.* 'Rosea' is a fine pink cultivar for a perennial border, as

is *L. c.* 'Oculata', which is white with an attractive rose eye. The *L. c.* 'Alba' is rarely seen, but is a fine addition to a white garden.

> *Lychnis coronaria* is a garden designer's dream.

Lychnis coronnaria, especially *L. c.* 'Oculata', make splendid companions to delphiniums, notably *Delphinium elatum* 'Black Night' with its deep purple-black flowers. The lychnis should be massed to the front of the delphiniums for this dramatic color scheme.

Lychnis coronaria Cultivars

NAME	COLOR	HEIGHT	MONTH	ZONE
L. coronaria 'Alba'	white	2' (60 cm)	June	2-9
L. c. 'Rosea'	rose	2' (60 cm)	June	2-9
L. c. 'Oculata'	white, rose	2' (60 cm)	June	2-9
L. c. 'Atrosanguinea'	magenta	2' (60 cm)	June	2-9

Myosotis sylvatica
FORGET-ME-NOT
Boraginaceae
Zones 2–9

The true biennial Forget-me-not is a May flowering plant. The old, blue cultivar was a mainstay of the cottage garden. The flowers are tiny and come in various shades of blue, white, and pink. Some cultivars have a dense growing habit, but all are easy to grow.

Ecofunction

Myosotis sylvatica is a member of the borage family, the medicinal uses of which go back to early Roman times. Although this family is known to be a beneficial herb, its chemical components are extremely complex, and to date, are not well understood. One of the more unusual aspects of this plant is that it seems to increase lactation in nursing mothers. This means it has a precise target action on the pituitary gland by increasing oxytocin secretion. Further scientific investigation of the *Boraginaceae* family is needed.

Pollen of *Myosotis sylvatica* is tiny and is a bispherical shape. It gets into the nectar and subsequently the honey because the bees accidently syphon both together. Honey with a good content of this pollen is both healthy for bees and the consuming public.

Organic Care

Forget-me-nots like a neutral, average garden soil, with a higher clay component to absorb the moisture this biennial likes. Sandy soil should be amended with peatmoss to increase its waterholding capacity. Forget-me-nots will grow in full sun, but they are also an excellent semi-shade plant. Seeds should be broadcast in June onto a well-drained spot and overwintered *in situ*. They may also be seeded into a cold frame to provide extra winter protection. Damp-off of young seedlings can be prevented by a dusting of wood ashes as the young cotyledons, or first 'true leaves', emerge.

Design

When massed, forget-me-nots form an airy froth with which mid-season and late tulips of all kinds blend beautifully. For milder zones 8–9, the earlier flowering blue cultivar *M. s.* 'Oblongata Perfecta' can be used with Kaufmanniana and Fosteriana tulips. The pink cultivar *M. s.* 'Carmine King' or the large flowered pink cultivar *M. s.* 'Rosea' combines beautifully with the double late pink *Tulipa* 'Angelique' or the multiflowered *Tulipa* 'Modern Style' which has mixed tones of pastel pink. This creates a gorgeous block of pink that stands out against the verdant pea green of a northern spring. *M. s.* 'Royal Blue' acts as an ideal background to the recently introduced purple-violet shades of spring hyacinths 'Ostara' and 'Blue Delft'.

Myosotis sylvatica 'Victoria Blue' is an ideal plant for a city garden.

Myosotis sylvatica Cultivars

NAME	COLOR	HEIGHT	MONTH	ZONE
M. s. ' Victoria Blue'	blue	6" (15 cm)	May-June	2-9
M. s. 'Carmine King'	rose	8" (20 cm)	May-June	2-9
M. s. 'Royal Blue'	blue	12" (30 cm)	May-June	2-9
M. s. 'Alba'	white	12" (30 cm)	May-June	2-9
M. s. 'Oblongata Perfecta'	blue	12" (30 cm)	April-May	5-9
M. s. 'Compacta'	blue	6" (15 cm)	May-June	2-9

Papaver nudicaule
ICELAND POPPY
Papaveraceae
Zones 2–9

The Iceland poppy is a native of the Arctic regions of Canada, Greenland, and Iceland. This is an extremely hardy biennial. The plant is a dainty rosette with flowers that are a miracle of delicacy and color, in yellow, orange, pink, rose, salmon, carmine, and white. Some strains have bicolors and others have crêped petals. Depending on the strain, the plants can vary from 10" (25 cm) *P. n.* 'Wonderland' to 24" (60 cm) *P. n.* 'San Remo'.

Ecofunction

All cultivars of *Papaver nudicaule* are extremely attractive to honey bees and bumble bees. They collect the dark pollen and a small amount of nectar. They seem to also collect a small amount of opiate compound, as close examination will reveal that the honey bees are somewhat intoxicated. Doubtless these opiate compounds are extremely useful in the bees domestic routine. *Papaver nudicaule* does not have the milky, opium-laden sap of the annual *P. somniferum*. But this native of Canada could well go on a pharmacognacist's list for detailed chemical analysis, as this plant has every indicator of being a fruitful source of undiscovered drugs.

Organic Care

Icelandic poppies do well in a sandy, well-drained neutral soil which is high in phosphate and potash. The drainage should be excellent both in summer and winter. Poor drainage causes crown rot. Icelandic poppies will grow well in full sun or light shade, and will put on a remarkable show on poor soils.

Design

Icelandic poppies bloom from mid-May into the beginning of July. If the fall is cool, there will be a respectable reblooming of this specie. Icelandic poppies are magnificent massed into a late spring border in large numbers. They bloom with the later narcissi and tulips. The taller strain *P. n.* 'San Remo' or the crêped *P. n.* 'Champagne Bubbles' should be mixed with these spring bulbs. Icelandic poppies are suited to the rock garden and look splendid in that setting. The smaller strains *P. n.* 'Wonderland' are very fine when seeded into nooks and crannies of the garden.

Icelandic poppies are difficult to transplant and should be spring seeded where they are expected to bloom the following year.

Papaver nudicaule Cultivars

NAME	COLOR	HEIGHT	MONTH	ZONE
P. n. 'San Remo' strain	bicolors	24" (60 cm)	May-July	2-9
P. n. 'Unwin Giant' strain	mixed	18" (45 cm)	May-July	2-9
P. n. 'Wonderland' strain	mixed	10" (25 cm)	May-July	2-9
P. n. 'Champagne Bubbles'	mixed	20" (50 cm)	May-July	2-9

Verbascum
MULLEIN
Scrophulariaceae
Zones 2–9

The native North American *Verbascum thapsis* with fine architectural lines, used as a perching plant for a bird's water bath.

Verbascum phoeniceum and *V. thapsus,* the common mullein, are two biennials which are very hardy and grow well in most north temperate gardens. *V. pheoniceum* grows 2–3' (60–90 cm), with fine spires of rose, mauve, purple, and white. V. *thapsus* is the common native mullein of North America and grows to 6' (2 m). Its European native 3' (1 m) counterpart is now an endangered specie. Improved strains of V. *thapsus* can soar to 7' (2.1 m). These yellow spires of velvety grey-green foliage are used to great advantage in the stately gardens of Europe.

Ecofunction

V. thapsus is visited by honey bees for its pollen. This plant has a very definite place in a pioneer garden or a herb garden. It was used as a herb in the treatment of pulmonary ailments such as bronchitis and asthma in the medieval monasteries of Europe. Interestingly, many North American aboriginal peoples medicinally used this plant for identical bronchial complaints principally by smoking its leaves.

Organic Care

Both mullein species like full sun and a sandy, well-drained neutral garden soil of medium fertility. The soil should be well drained in summer and winter. Poor winter drainage occasionally causes crown rot in *V. thapsus. V. phoeniceum* is not often affected by any disease. Both mulleins form a rosette of foliage in their first year. *V. phoeniceum's* rosette is 6–8" (15–20 cm) across and is completely flat, while the V.

thapsus has a fine 12" (30 cm) rosette of velvet grey-green leaves. Both mulleins have an extensive taproot system which is extremely brittle and difficult to transplant if the rosettes are mature (one year old). Transplanting should take place to their permanent beds when the seedlings are at their second or third leaf stage. Care should be taken that the taproots remain intact. In both species the flowering spires unfurl from the center of the rosette in a manner similar to the fiddle-heads of the *Osmunda regalis* fern.

Design

V. phoeniceum is a stunning early summer flower, flowering from mid-May to July. It has a fine place in the mid-region of the border and can be used effectively with columbines in a spring setting.

V. thapsus is an architectural plant. It can be used as a background planting in the border to accentuate steps or a pathway. In both cases it instills the illusion of depth and length.

V. olympicum 'Silver Spire' grouped with *Lychnis coronaria* 'Alba' and the perennial *Verbascum chaixii* 'Album' in front of the silver leafed *Elaeagnus augustifolia,* the Russian olive, zone 3–9, creates a shimmering, iridescent garden scene at mid-day, which is most interesting.

Verbascum Species and Cultivars

NAME	COLOR	HEIGHT	MONTH	ZONE
V. blattaria 'Albiflorum'	white	1-2' (30-60 cm)	June-Sept	3-9
V. bombyciferum	yellow	4-6' (1.2-1.8m)	June-Sept	3-9
V. olympicum	yellow	6' (1.8 m)	June-Sept	2-9
V. o. 'Gainsborough'	yellow	3' (90 cm)	June-Aug	2-9
V. o. 'Silver Spire'	yellow	5' (150 cm)	June-Aug	2-9
V. o. 'Arctic Summer'	yellow	6' (175 cm)	June-Aug	2-9
V. thapsis	yellow	6' (2 m)	June-Sept	2-9
V. phoenecian	mixed	3-4' (90-120 cm)	May-July	2-9
V. p. 'Alba'	white	3' (90 cm)	May-July	2-9

Bulbs, Corms and Tubers

A host of daffodils in April.

Bulbs, Corms & Tubers

Gardens in northern temperate climates can grow a remarkable progression of flowering bulbs from early spring to late fall. All the gardening zones from 2–9 permit growth of bulbs, corms, and tubers. As a huge country in the northern hemisphere, Canada can boast enormous wealth in its native species of flowering spring and summer bulbs. The cold, dry winters induce dormancy, which is a dominant requirement of some bulbs. The hot, dry summers considerably reduce the chances of disease in those bulbs and increase flowering by inducing mild plant stress. Many parts of Canada are totally suited to the growing and propagation of bulbs. Some particularly noteworthy areas are Prince Edward Island and eastern New Brunswick. Gardeners in colder zones 2–3 have limitations resulting from temperature fluctuations in the spring. Heavily mulching bulb beds with evergreen boughs over winter will delay the warming of the soil, which will in turn delay growth and flowering in the spring. Bulbs such as narcissus, tulips, and scillas will withstand 4°F (-15°C) temperatures and colder, if they have just started to grow. The cellular material in the growing bulb will still be dense and frost injury will be minimal. Such cold temperatures will considerably slow down any further growth until the weather improves. Gardeners in zones 2–3 have to more carefully select and plan the bulbs they are able to grow in their gardens.

Trial and error of the new cultivars may well be the method by which gardeners in these zones can expand both their knowledge and collection of desirable plants. Warm spring temperatures trigger growth in bulbs. Subsequent night temperatures of 14°F (-10°C) or lower, common in northern and prairie gardens in spring, may then significantly damage emerging and elongating shoots.

The Anatomy of a Bulb

A bulb is a modified plant. The stem is reduced and the leaves become fleshy, holding considerable amounts of water. The embrionic flower is at the heart of this vegetative apparatus ready to grow as soon as the right light, temperature, and moisture switches are thrown. This is, in all likelihood, à genetic response to moisture shortages within the evolutionary life cycle of the bulb. Once a bulb has flowered, it will then proceed to pack away all kinds of provisions within itself to ensure it can repeat its life cycle and maybe, if it is lucky enough, add to its generation in the form of bulbils or bulblets. The modification in size, the reduction of leaves, the food storage, and its geographical ancestry, if cold, impose on a bulb frost resistant characteristics. Death to a bulb is either too much water or too little water, resulting in bulb rot or severe desiccation.

Bulb Guide

The typical conundrum, even for the most experienced of gardeners, is bulbs. When do they flower? What planting companions should they have? How does one hide unsightly, dying foliage? What specific requirements do these bulbs have? How should the soil be treated and how deep should bulbs be planted? The majority of these questions stem from the garden's life cycle. In the peak of its majesty a summer flower bulbous arrangement can be much admired and then subsequently desired. When the time has come for the planting of such an arrangement, it is fall or spring and the flowering landscape has dramatically changed. One is left with both a blank stare and mind, for memory is short.

The following bulb guide is meant as an aid for determining flowering succession of bulbs, corms, tubers, and some modified tuberous roots. For zones 4, 5, and 6, this guide is an exact fit for the seasons. For zones 2 and 3, the fit will be somewhat compressed because of the shorter growing season and longer days. For zones 7, 8, and 9, spring and fall are more temperate and subsequently the flowering succession will be expanded, commencing from February and sometimes from January.

Variations within the guide will also be found within the individual garden. Heavy clay soils are slower to warm up than light, friable sandy soils. A bulb planted deeper than its indicated depth will delay flowering. A shaded flower bed will delay flowering, sometimes by as much as a week. A full sun, southern exposure in the spring will force flowering ahead of schedule by more than a week. Flowering times and sequencing can be modified through skillful microclimate manipulation. These variations can be used by the clever gardener as a tool to increase the flowering succession of bulbs, corms, and tubers within the garden's framework.

Alliums are flowering members of the onion family. The flowers grow from an onion scented bulb which can vary greatly in size depending on the specie. Alliums are as important an addition to the flower garden as they are in the kitchen garden.

Allium
FLOWERING ONION
Amaryllidaceae
Zones 2–9

Ecofunction

Alliums have an important natural insecticidal function as *in situ* plant material within the garden. They have the added benefit of broad spectrum antibiotic and antifungal properties attributed to chemical compounds such as allicin, allicetoin I and II, which are antibiotic, and allyl disulphide, and allyl propyl disulphides, which are antifungal. All alliums can be crushed and used externally to treat cuts, acne, bee and wasp stings, a useful on-the-spot remedy for the gardener. As our knowledge of soil chemistry expands, we find that such plant-produced chemicals are important components of an healthy soil micro-ecology.

Knowledge of the health benefits of alliums has been in existence since before written history. It is only relatively recently that the scientific community has taken up the challenge of its investigation, with many positive results, much to our benefit. Thus, an ecologically sound garden should have some alliums and the choice, fortunately, is enormous.

Organic Care

All allium species like a moderately rich, well-drained sandy soil. Drainage should be excellent in winter. Many alliums like an alkaline soil, while a few definitely prefer acidic conditions. There are a few alliums which show preference for a high humus content in the soil and these are inclined to be North American native species.

Some native alliums thrive in dense shade and some like light shade, such as *A. karataviense, A. moly, A. triquetrum,* and *A. ursinum.* The majority prefer full sun conditions. Alliums should be planted

Allium moly, primrose, and *A. oreophilum* 'Zwanenburg', rose, have a natural insecticidal function in a rockery.

two to three times the bulb height in planting depth. The smaller bulbs should be planted three times their height and the larger bulbs should be planted twice their height. Phosphate and potash should be added in the form of bonemeal and wood ashes. Attention should be paid to the acid-base requirements of the bulb. Peatmoss with manure will give acidic conditions. Dolomitic limestone will change the balance to an alkaline pH.

Design

The vast majority of alliums are hardy from zones 4–9. Their hardiness in zones 2 and 3 are mostly untried. If gardeners in zones 2 and 3 have garden areas that are snow covered throughout the winter season without freezing and thawing, alliums hardy in zones 4 and 5 could be grown. The following are suggested species for trial: *A. azureum (A. caeruleum), A. karataviense, A. elatum, A. moly, A. odorum, A. oreophilum* 'Zwanenburg', *A. sphaerocephalon* and the wild species *A. tricoccum,* the wild leek, *A. cernuum,* the nodding onion, *A. stellatum,* the prairie onion or wild onion, *A. vineale,* field garlic, and *A. canadense,* wild garlic.

In all cases, alliums have a similar flowering form, that being a ball-head on top of a tall or short flower stalk. The planting of such a form has to be done with great care, otherwise the garden will look misshapen. The tall alliums *A. giganteum, A. elatum* (syn. *A. macleanii*), and *A. aflatunense* should be planted in groups of four or five, never singly. They should act as a focal point within a border or near weeping-form shrubbery. The alliums of medium height, 1.5 –2' (45–60 cm), should be planted near flowers of insubstantial foliage, such as *Gypsophila paniculata* and *Perovskia atriplicifolia*, to act as a foil. The smaller alliums are very dainty and look well in nooks and crannies or in a rock garden.

Allium species can be found blooming in May, June, July, and August. In May, *A. neapolitanuum* (syn. *A. cowanii*), zones 6–9, also called the daffodil garlic, has fragrant flowers, 2' (60 cm). The fragrant *A. karataviense,* zones 4–9, with its sessile, large, lilac flowers placed like a ball between blue-green foliage, is a spectacular rockery plant when massed. *A. elatum*(syn. *A. macleanii*), zones 6–9, 40" (1 m), with lilac flowers are similar and can be massed with late flowering tulips and camassias.

In the June garden a very large number of alliums can be grown. The award-winning *A. aflatunense* 'Purple Sensation', zones 3–9, has 2' (60 cm) tall purple sparkling flowers preferring lots of sun. The hardy *A. azureum (A. caeruleum)*, zones 2–9, has 2' (60 cm) tall blue flowers. *A. moly,* zones 3–9, with 12" (30 cm) dainty yellow flowers, can be used with 'Harrison's Yellow', an old fashioned rose, zones 3–9. *A. christophii,* zones 4–9, have huge mauve flower globes on 1.5'

Allium karataviense produce a spherical, lilac flowerhead to form one of the most unusual edging plants in a walkway.

(45 cm) stems. *A. oreophilum* 'Zwanenburg', zones 4–9, is a dainty, 6" (15 cm), red-flowering allium. *A. rosenbachianum* (*A. stripitatum*), zones 5–9, 30" (75 cm), with fine violet flowers, and *A. roseum,* zones 5–9, with pink flowers on 2' stems, prefer full sun. *A. triquetrum*, zones 5–9, a partial shade lover, is 18" (45 cm) with soft green flowers. *A. ursinum,* zones 4–9, has 18"(45 cm) white flowers. *A. nigrum* zones 4–9, a lime lover, has 2.5" (75 cm) green flowers. The very attractive *A. unifolium*, zones 5–9, is a miniature with 10" (25 cm) flowers.

In the July garden, flowering with the trumpet lilies and looking very fine with them, are some very attractive and useful alliums. The alkaline loving *A. narcissiflorum,* zones 6–9, has beautiful 8" (20 cm) nodding plum-colored bell-shaped flowers. *A. flavum*, zones 4–9, is fragrant and acid loving, with 12" (30 cm) lemon flowers. *A. giganteum*, zones 5–9, has huge red flowering balls on soaring 4' (120 cm) stems. *A. sphaerocephalon*, zones 4–9, has 3' (90 cm) dense cone shaped violet-red flowers. *A. odorium* (*A. ramosum*), zones 3–9, has fragrant red and white flowers, 20" (50 cm).

The August garden has a number of alliums which are probably most useful to the Canadian gardener. These alliums flower with *Galtonia candicans*, the summer hyacinth. *A. cirrhosum*, zones 4–9, being acid loving, have many violet-pink nodding umbels on 20" (50 cm) flowering stalks. There is an *album* version of this plant. Both should have moist conditions. *A. flavum puchellum album*, zones 4–9, 18" (45 cm), has nodding white flowers. Chinese chives or *A. tuberosum,* zones 3–9, 20" (50 cm), with white flowers make a fine addition to the flower border. There is also a mauve-flowered garden version of this allium.

Allium Species

NAME	COLOR	HEIGHT	MONTH	ZONE
A. aflatunense	violet (purple sensation)	2' (60 cm)	July	3-9
A. azureum (*A. Caeruleum*)	blue	2' (60 cm)	July	2-9
A. bulgaricum	blue/green	3' (90 cm)	May	5-9
(*Nectarocordum bulgaricum*) (see *Nectarocordum*)				
A. canadense	white/pink	8-24" (20-60 cm)	June	3-9
A. c. 'Mobilense'	pink	8-24" (20-60 cm)	June	3-9
A. cernuum	neu., white/pink/purple	1-2' (30-60 cm)	July	3-9
A. c. 'Album'	white	8-24" (20-60 cm)	July	3-9
A. christophii	mauve	1.5' (45 cm)	June	4-9
A. cirrhosum	violet	20" (50 cm)	June	4-9
A. cirrhosum album	white	20" (50 cm)	June	4-9
A. elatum (*A. macleanii*)	lilac	40" (100 cm)	May	6-9
A. flavum	yellow	12-20" (30-50 cm)	July	4-9
A. flavum puchellum album	white	18" (45 cm)	August	4-9

NAME	COLOR	HEIGHT	MONTH	ZONE
A. flavum puchellum roseum	rose	18" (45 cm)	August	4-9
A. giganteum, (A. ampeloprasum)	red	4' (120 cm)	June	5-9
A. karataviense	lilac	8" (20 cm)	June	4-9
A. moly	primrose yellow	12" (30 cm)	June	3-9
A. narcissiflorum	plum	7" (18 cm)	June	6-9
A. neapolitanum (A. cowanii)	white	1.5' (45 cm)	May	6-9
A. neapolitanum roseum	Rose	1.5' (45 cm)	May	6-9
A. nigrum	green and white	2.5' (75 cm)	May	4-9
A. odorum (A. ramosum)	Red	20" (50 cm)	June	3-9
A. oreophilum 'Zwanenburg'	red	20" (50 cm)	June	4-9
A. rosenbachianum, (A. stripitatum)	violet	30" (75 cm)	May	5-9
A. rosenbachianum 'album'	white	30" (75 cm)	May	5-9
A. roseum	pink	2' (60 cm)	May	5-9
A. sphaerocephalon	violet	3' (90 cm)	July	4-9
A. stellatum	lilac-pink	1-2' (30-60 cm)	July	3-9
A. stellatum 'album'	white	1-2' (30-60 cm)	July	3-9
A. tricoccum	white	12" (30 cm)	June	3-9
A. triquetrum	green	18" (45 cm)	June	5-9
A. tuberosum	white	20" (50 cm)	August	3-9
A. tuberosum 'Mauve'	mauve	20" (50 cm)	August	3-9
A. unifolium	pink	10" (25 cm)	June	5-9
A. ursinum	white	18" (45 cm)	May	4-9
A. vineale	pink, white	1-3' (30-90 cm)	June	3-9

Anemone
WINDFLOWER
Ranunculaceae
Zones 3–9

Anemones are dainty, spring flowers which have a bright and daisy-like appearance. They have showy sepals of cream, white, rose, deep reds, and purples. The flowers occur singly, often in large numbers, from finely dissected, deep-green foliage which is also very attractive.

Ecofunction

For some people skin contact with anemones may cause irritation of contact dermatitis. Aneomes contain broad spectrum antibiotics and have been used in folk medicine to treat rheumatism.

The morphology of the anemone flower makes it a prime target for the smaller of the flying beneficial insects. They are also a useful source of pollen for the honeybee which sometimes bores into the base of the flower to collect sap used to moisten the collected pollen.

Organic Care

All anemones prefer alkaline conditions. They like a good, rich sandy loam to which liberal quantities of dolomitic limestone has been added. The plants should have full sun to partial shade, the dappled shade of tall trees or shrubs being much to their liking.

Anemones have extremely irregular cormous or rhizomous roots. The cormous roots of *A. blanda* should be soaked for two hours before planting. These dark, cormous rhizomes will have a circular area from which the foliage will grow. This should face upward when planting. However, some corms are so irregular that it is impossible to tell top from bottom. Therefore, it is always advisable to order extra in the event that some are lost due to being planted upside down.

Design

Anemone blanda are the most commonly grown anemone species in zones 4–9. These charming spring flowers are blue, white, or rose. The foliage is fern-like and is most attractive. These anemones prefer some shade. The flowers are from 6–8" (15–20 cm) tall and are most colorful when planted around trees or in the foreground of a shrubbery.

Anemone apennina, zones 3–9, is a taller version of *Anemone blanda*, 10" (25cm), but has rhizomous roots. The plant forms fine mats that are very long lasting and useful in a rockery.

Anemone biflora, zones 4–9, has a tuberous rhizome and has beautiful bright crimson flowers 3–8" (7–20 cm) tall, the leaves being fern-like and sessile. It is also ideal for a rockery and should be kept dry after flowering. This anemone has the genetic possibility of being extremely cold hardy. Attempts should be made to grow it in zones 2 and 3 of the North American prairie.

A beautiful old Irish cultivar, 'Robinsoniana', of the European anemone, *A. nemorosa*, zones 7–9, could readily be used on the north-east coast of North America. The flower is powder blue and likes both shade and rain.

Anemone pavonina grows in full sun in zones 8–9, 18" (30 cm) tall. This crimson anemone has a fibrous, rhizomous root system. In zone 9, it will bloom in February to March, making a fiery companion to daffodils.

Anemone Species and Cultivars

NAME	COLOR	HEIGHT	MONTH	ZONE
Anemone blanda				
A. b. 'Blue Star'	blue	6-8" (15-20 cm)	April	4-9
A. b. 'White Splendour'	white	6-8" (15-20 cm)	April	4-9
A. b. 'Rosea'	rose	6-8" (15-20 cm)	April	4-9
A. apennina				
A. a. 'Alba'	white	4-9" (10-22 cm)	April	3-9
A. a. 'Allenii'	pale blue	4-9" (10-22 cm)	April	3-9
A. a. 'Purpurea'	mauve	4-9" (10-22 cm)	April	3-9
A. a. 'Plena'	white	4-9" (10-22 cm)	May	3-9
A. biflora	red	3-8" (8 - 20 cm)	April	3-9
A. nemorosa 'Robinsoniana'	blue	6-10" (15-20 cm)	April	7-9
A. pavonina	crimson	18" (45 cm)	March	8-9

Arisaema
JACK-IN-THE-PULPIT
Araceae
Zones 3–9

Arisaemas are also called Jack-in-the-pulpit. There are a number of very beautiful native species which are now rarely seen in the wild. There are also some species from the high mountains of China and Japan that can be grown in the North American temperate garden.

Arisaemas are plants for woodland gardens and for bog and shade gardens. All arisaemas have modified flowers which give them such an unusual appearance. Sepals and petals are modified into the outside tube-like structure called the spathe, which, in some species, has long attractive white stripes. The sexual part of the plant is on a central, club-shaped structure called the spandix. There are tiny male and female flowers on the base of this spandix. The female flowers get fertilized and give rise to the attractive red berry clusters of the fall. Some species have male flowering spandix and female flowering spandix on separate plants so only the female plants, in this case, will show colored berries in the fall.

Ecofunction

Arisaemas are natural companion plants for amphibians. The bunches of pear-shaped, red fruit clusters are a favorite food of forest animals. They are eaten with relish and the seeds dispersed throughout the forest floor. Arisaemas are also known as Indian Turnip on the North American continent. The underground rhizome was collected, cleaned, and boiled prior to eating. The rhizome was also boiled, dried, and then ground into a flour which was similar to cornstarch. The flour was used both as a food and a medicine. For medicinal purposes, the indigenous peoples applied a dusting of powdered root on the temples and head to decrease the pain of headache.

Raw arisaema rhizomes contain calcium oxalate, as does rhubarb, which is destroyed by heating. Calcium oxalate is a poison.

Organic Care

Arisemas like acid soil which is high in humus and water-holding capacity. The soil should never dry out for these species. Peat moss can be used to increase the water holding capacity of the soil. These species benefit from a summer mulch. The soil, particularly the surface soil under the mulch, should be enriched with phosphate and potash.

Arisaema corms look like swollen, Dutch crocus corms, the feeder roots coming from the top of the corm with a few coming from the corm base. As the plant grows, these roots become more numerous and, consequently, areas around arisaemas should not be walked upon. Gardening boards should be used for plant maintenance to displace the gardener's weight over a large area. The corms should be planted 3" (7 cm) deep. Berries may be fall sewn to propagate the *A. sikokianum* and the native species.

Design

The native *A. dracontium* 1–4' (30–120 cm), zones 6–9, can be combined with *A. tortuosum* 20" (50 cm), zones 6–9, an interesting flower with a wavy vertical spandix. Both species have light green-colored flowers. Early May flowering *A. ringens*, zones 5–9, 14" (35 cm), with its contorted black-purple spathe and longitudinal white and green stripes, has two interesting cultivars, *A.praecox* 'T. Koyame', which has a green spathe, and *A. sieboldii,* with a purple spathe.

June flowering species are the most commonly grown. The native *A. triphyllium*, 1–2' (30–60 cm), zones 4–9, has a beautiful spathe with white stripes on a purple or bronze background. *A. atrorubens* is very similar as is *A. stewardsonii,* which flowers a little later. *A. amurense*, 8–12" (20–30 cm), zones 3–9, has a beautiful green and purple striped spathe. The hardy *A. sikokianum*, 8" (20 cm), with its white, blunt-topped spathe and its purple-red glistening spandix, should be grown more frequently in zones 4–9.

In the mid-summer garden the fragrant *A. candidissimum* 12–15" (30–40 cm), zones 3–9, likes half-shade. It has a beautiful light rose and white-striped spathe. There is a lovely gradation of color in the spathe foliage going from white around the rim to the candy-striped area which vanishes into green at the base of the spathe. The flower pedicel continues in a deep brown. If this arisaema is massed into groups of five, it has a very light and dainty aspect. *A. consanguineum,*

12–15" (30–40 cm), zones 3–9, also has a light colored spathe of tannish purple and white longitudinal stripes.

The berries of arisaemas are extremely attractive in the fall. They can be massed with the new and exciting deciduous holly cultivars that are being bred in North America. *Ilex verticillata,* also called winter-berry, zone 3–9, has a fine red-berried garden cultivar 'Winter Red' and a beautiful orange sport 'Winter Gold'. Smaller city gardens could use 'Red Sprite', a beautiful tiny red-fringed holly. This holly and 'Hopewell Myte' are dwarf cultivars of the *I. x* sparkleberry. (*I. verticillate* x *I. serrata*). The massing of arisaemas and hollies can form the backbone of a very fine winterscape for a Canadian shade garden.

Arisaema Species and Cultivars

NAME	COLOR	HEIGHT	MONTH	ZONE
A. triphyllum	green on purple or bronze	1-2' (30-60 cm)	June	4-9
A. triphyllum zebrinum	white on purple or bronze	1-2' (30-60 cm)	June	4-9
A. atrorubens	green on purple or bronze	1-2' (30-60 cm)	June	4-9
A. stewardsonii	white on purple or bronze	1-2' (30-60 cm)	June	4-9
A. dracontium	green	1-4' (30-120 cm)	June	6-9
A. tortuosum	green	20" (50 cm)	June	6-9
A. ringens	white on green	14" (35 cm)	June	5-9
A. praecox 'T. Koyama'	green	12" (30 cm)	June	5-9
A. sieboldii	purple	12" (30 cm)	June	5-9
A. sikokianum	red-purple	8" (20 cm)	June	4-9
A. amurense	green on purple	8-12" (20-30 cm)	June	3-9
A. candidissiumum	rose on white	12-15" (30-38 cm)	July	3-9
A. consanguineum	purple fawn on white	12-15" (30-38 cm)	July	3-9

Begonia tuberhybrida
TUBEROUS BEGONIA
Begoniaceae
Zone: Tender Summer
Tuber

Tuberous begonias have been bred by the vigorous hybridization and selection of many South American begonias to produce the single, frilled, crested, daffodil-flowered, camellia, ruffled camellia, rosiflora, carnation, picotee marginata with tepals having bicolor marginal lines, marmorata with veins blotched, pendula, and multiflora types of begonias.

Modern apartment-style living of the twentieth century with its limited green spaces has given rise to a tremendous interest in plants that are easy to care for, beautiful and floriferous, shade-loving and able to withstand high temperatures. Hybrid tuberous begonias rate high in this group. Upright tuberous begonias are also excellent shade garden plants.

There are two definite strains of begonias. The European strain is being developed in Europe, while the Pacific hybrids are being developed in California.

Ecofunction

Tuberous begonias will brighten up a shaded garden with considerable sculptured charm. The red, scarlet, and pink forms of this plant can be used to entice humming birds to feed in a shady area or on a balcony. Salamanders particularly like the cooling damp conditions around this plant, especially when it has reached full growth in July or August.

A shade loving tuberous begonia in the secret garden.

Organic Care

The tubers of the hybrid begonias are large, 1–4"(3–10 cm), fleshy, and slightly concave on the upper surface. It is from this surface that one to three colored eyes emerge. The tuber should be planted with the eyes above the soil and the tuber itself barely covered with soil ¼" (5 mm).

Tuberous begonias like a somewhat acid, sandy loam which is well drained. The practice of incorporating spent coffee grounds into the soil produces some tubers of spectacular size. The soil should be high in nitrogen, potassium, and phosphate. Moisture should be supplied evenly throughout the summer for maximum size and flowering. The upright forms of begonias can grow to 2' (60 cm) by August and should have some supports as the heavily flowering branches are inclined to get top-heavy with dew or in a rain and can then easily break off just at the interface between the shoot and the tuber.

Winter Care

Hybrid begonias flower in summer until the day-length is considerably shortened in October when the leaves will show fading and signs of dormancy. The tuber will go completely dormant over the winter months and will show signs of growth at the end of February or early March.

In the coldest areas of zone 9 and in warmer zones, tuberous begonias can over winter naturally in the ground. In zones 7–8, tuberous begonias can complete their natural cycle of growth and flowering. In early or late October, tubers can be carefully dug and prepared for winter storage. For zones 2–6, when killing frosts can come from the end of August into the fall, begonias have to be treated differently. The first killing frosts will seriously damage the leaves and flowering stems, almost dissolving them. These 'wet' branches should be snapped off and discarded. The tubers should be carefully dug up. The main lateral feeder roots should not be broken but should be lifted complete with the tuber. These will shrink away during dormancy. The tubers should then be placed in a dry place and exposed to 48 hours of direct sunshine to dry, cure, and irradiate the tubers. If frost threatens, frost protection must be supplied. The tubers, at this stage, will have fragments of stem sticking up from the tuber body. Adhering garden soil can be shed from the tuber by gentle shaking or rubbing. When the tuber is clean, the stem fragments should be snapped off at a natural node as close to the tuber as possible. The tuber should be placed in the sun again until the sap from the broken nodes dries. This will take an hour or so. The tubers should be dusted with wood ashes and placed in dried, milled peat moss in layers in a cardboard box and stored cool and dark with temperatures above 32°F (0°C) during the winter months.

In the colder zones 2–6, the tubers are potted in March in a flat or individual pots indoors and are exposed to approximately one to two hours of direct sunlight. As the growing eyes come along, the plant can be placed into an area with more light. In April or May the tubers can be planted out after danger of the last killing frost. This treatment will considerably speed up flowering for the summer months.

Design
The colors of the flowers of tuberous begonias are very vibrant yellows, reds, red-oranges, pinks, roses, and whites. There are also some bicolors, tepals with clear margins of another color, and interesting splotch coloration such as *B. marmorata*, similar to that found in carnations. All of these colors are beautiful and bountiful in hanging baskets. In a garden bed, if they are to be massed, they should be massed separate from other flowers. The red leafed begonia hybrid may be planted with variegated hostas for a dappling effect in a shade garden. The daffodil begonias, which indeed do have the trumpet daffodil form, may be mixed with a careful color choice of matching caladiums and the calla pastel hybrids. The red-orange daffodil begonias could be mixed with *Caladium* 'Mrs. F. M. Joyner', which has bright scarlet leaf veins. The calla pastel hybrid 'Flame' would give a stunning plant vignette for a shade area because of the calla's corolla flower form being repeated in the begonia. The flame color would be woven in all three species against the speckled calla, the textured caladium, and the cream veining of the daffodil begonia's foliage.

Begonia Species

NAME	COLOR	HEIGHT	MONTH	ZONE
Ruffled picotee tuberous begonias				
B. 'Calypso'	cream tepals, red margins	18" (46cm)	June-Aug	9*
B. 'Santa Barbara'	yellow	18" (46cm)	June-Aug	9*
B. 'Santa Cruz'	ruby red	18" (46cm)	June-Aug	9*
Multiflora tuberous begonias				
B. 'Mrs. Helen Harms'	yellow	24" (50cm)	June-Aug	9*
B. 'Jewel of Ghent'	salmon-copper	24" (50cm)	June-Aug	9*
B. 'Switzerland'	scarlet flowers, bronze foliage	24" (60cm)	June-Aug	9*
Pendula Begonias				
B. 'San Lucas'	orange	24" (60cm)	June-Sept	9*
B. 'San Pablo'	pink	24" (60cm)	June-Sept	9*
B. 'San Ramon'	scarlet	24" (60cm)	June-Sept	9*

*Frost-free storage required in zones 2–8

Bulbocodium
BULBOCODIUM
Liliaceae
Zones 4–9

Bulbocodium is represented by two species of spring flowering corms that are very useful for dry gardens. Superficially, the corms look like crocii or colchicums, but the sexual apparatus of the plant is different.

Bulbocodium vernum is like a large, open, multi-flowering crocus with a strong magenta color, the leaves emerging after flowering in April. This is a hardy alpine plant and should be tested in zones 2 and 3, for in colder areas of its native Alps it delays flowering until June.

Bulbocodium vernum has an eastern European counterpart, *Bulbocodium versicolor*, which is a smaller plant liking drier conditions.

Ecofunction
The flowers of these early spring flowering corms represent for the honeybee an early supply of fresh pollen and perhaps a little nectar after the harsh months of winter.

Organic Care
Bulbocodium likes a well-drained, good, slightly alkaline, garden soil and full sun. The bulbs should be separated and replanted every two years for maximum flowering.

Bulbocodium Species

NAME	COLOR	HEIGHT	MONTH	ZONE
Bulbocodium vernum	magenta	6" (15 cm)	April	4-9
Bulbocodium versicolor	magenta	3" (7 cm)	April	4-9

Caladium
ELEPHANT'S EARS
Araceae
**Zone: Tender Summer
Rhizome**

Caladiums are natives of the tropical forests of South America. They are tender rhizomous plants that go dormant in the winter. Although they are shade loving plants, they tolerate dappled shade but not direct sunlight which can burn the leaves. These plants are very useful for the warmer gardening zones (6–9) that enjoy higher humidity and high summer temperatures. The summer temperatures of the maritime regions are not suited to this plant material as they require consistent temperatures greater than 75°F (24°C) to flourish. Caladiums are grown for their wonderful leaf coloring of red, white, and green and the texturing of the leaf surfaces which are used as colorful foils in a shade garden.

Ecofunction

If caladiums are grown in dappled shade, they themselves will form an effective shaded under-story for most amphibians, including salamanders and newts, if grown near water. This double shade in the garden will protect these creatures from the damaging effect of increased U.V. light penetration, and will protect, to some extent, the immune systems of these species.

Organic Care

Caladiums like a rich, well-drained soil. Gardeners in zones 2–6 should pot caladiums early in March or April. The growing temperatures should be 5–10°F (3–5°), higher than for begonias. They should be planted in the early summer garden one or two weeks later than begonias.

In the fall, after the first mild frost, dig the rhizome and leave dry and cure at 70°F (21°C). When the curing process is finished, the leaves will fall off the plant. Winter storage should be in dry milled peat moss at 70°F (21°C) or above, which are normal household temperatures.

Caladium Cultivars

NAME	COLOR	HEIGHT	MONTH	ZONE
C. x hortulanum 'Canadidum'	white leaves veined with dark green	20" (50 cm)	June-Aug	7-9
C. x h. 'White Green'	white leaves veined with red	20" (50 cm)	June-Aug	7-9
C. x h. 'Rosebud'	pink leaves with a green centre	20' (50cm)	June-Aug	7-9*
C. x h. 'Mrs. F. M. Joyner'	green with scarlet veining and bright green leaf margins	20" (50 cm)	June-Aug	7-9*
C. x h. 'Red Frill'	ruffled red leaves with a green margin	20" (50 cm)	June-Aug	7-9*

*Frost free storage required in zones 2-6

Camassias are a group of spring flowering bulbs native to North America. They are very hardy bulbs (zones 3–9) that resent being moved.

Camassia
CAMASS
Liliaceae
Zones 3–9

Ecofunction
The flowers of all the camassia species are visited by honeybees and other beneficial flying insects for early fresh pollen.

The bulbs of *C. scilloides*, which resemble an onion, can be used all year round as a food source, boiled or baked, like potatoes. Bulbs of *C. scilloides* are high in natural sugars and were a favorite food of the indigenous peoples of North America.

Organic Care
The bulbs should be planted from 4–5" (10–12 cm) deep in a rich, moist, well-drained soil. The soil should not be allowed to become parched during the summer months.

C. cusickii has foul smelling bulbs which can be put to great advantage as 'protector' bulbs for other valuable bulbs against burrowing moles, voles, mice, and chipmunks in garden zones 3–4.

Design
C. cusickii flower in June. Its 3.5' (1m) tall racemes of steel-blue flowers appear with blue-green foliage. *C. leichtlinii* towers to 4' (1.2 m), bearing fine racemes of violet-blue 'Atrocaerulea' or white 'Alba' flowers. *C. quamash* has long, light blue racemes of 2.5' (75 cm), as does the wild hyacinth or *C. scilloides*.

Camassias can be massed with late tulips, the fragrant *Leucojum aestivum* 'Gravetye Grant', or *Fritillaria michailovskyi* and arisaemas in a partial shade garden. *C. leichtlinii* 'Alba' is a particularly fine border plant.

Camassia Species and Cultivars

NAME	COLOR	HEIGHT	MONTH	ZONE
C. cusickii	blue-green	3.5' (1 m)	June	3-9
C. leichtlinii				
C.l. 'Atrocaerulea'	violet-blue	4' (1.2 m)	June	3-9
C.l. 'Alba'	white	4' (1.2 m)	June	3-9
C. quamash	blue	2.5' (75 cm)	June	3-9
C. scilloides	blue	2.5' (75 cm)	June	3-9

Canna
CANNA LILY
Cannaceae
Zones: Tender Summer
Rhizome

The common garden canna hybrids *C. x generalis* are seeing a revival of interest in North American gardens. These canna hybrids are of mixed parentage, but the genetic pool has produced groups of hybrids which are of interest to the gardener because they bloom in August and September when many gardens are going into floral decline.

Ecofunction

The canna lily provides shade for the amphibian population in the summer months. Because of the monocotyledon design of the leaf bases, canna leaves catch moisture condensation and early morning exudation. Both act as drinking fountains for insects and small birds in the early morning hours.

Organic Care

Cannas are tropical, rhizomous plants and are consequently easily injured by frost. In gardening zones 8 and 9, cannas can remain in the ground over winter. In gardening zones 2–7, cannas can be stored indoors or the tubers can be planted 5–6" (12–15 cm) deep outdoors, after the last killing frost dates. Plants that have been prestarted will flower earlier and have a longer flowering period.

Cannas should be dug after the first killing frost, trimmed back and sun dried for six hours, then stored in dry, milled peatmoss over winter above 32°F (0°C).

A clean, sterile knife can be used to cut canna tubers, one eye left per piece for propagation. The cut should be allowed to air dry for one hour to callus before planting. Cannas like full sun and a well-drained, rich garden soil which has a high humus component. This component should be a mixture of well-aged, rotted manure and peat moss.

Design

Cannas can be massed in an entry-way for the home or in the garden. The pastel colors of the dwarf and semi-dwarf hybrids are very useful for the flower border. They may also be used within a garden area for August color, the bicolors being particularly useful in this respect.

There are tall and medium, 3–5' (1–1.6 m), dwarf and semi-dwarf hybrids, 2–2.5' (.6–.7 m). The stamenoid flowers are rich in color, ranging from reds, yellows, and pinks to bicolors of pink and white, crimson and yellow, apricot and orange. The foliage also can be most attractive ranging from a deep green to purple to variegated in *C.* 'Striped Beauty'.

Canna Hybrid Cultivars

TALL CULTIVARS

NAME	COLOR	HEIGHT	MONTH	ZONE
C. 'Cleopatra'	red-yellow	5' (1.5 m)	Aug-Sept	8-9*
C. 'King Humbert'	red-russet foliage	5' (1.5 m)	Aug-Sept	8-9*
C. 'Madame Butterfly'	pink-cream margins	5' (1.5 m)	Aug-Sept	8-9*

DWARF CULTIVARS

NAME	COLOR	HEIGHT	MONTH	ZONE
C. 'Lucifer'	red-yellow margins	2.5' (75 cm)	Aug-Sept	8-9*
C. 'Rosalinda'	pink-cream bitone	2.5' (75 cm)	Aug-Sept	8-9*
C. 'Stripped Beauty'	yellow variegated foliage	2.5' (75 cm)	Aug-Sept	8-9*

PFITZER'S HYBRIDS

NAME	COLOR	HEIGHT	MONTH	ZONE
C. 'Chinese Coral'	coral-pink	2.5' (75 cm)	Aug-Sept	8-9*
C. 'Primrose Yellow'	yellow	2' (60 cm)	Aug-Sept	8-9*
C. 'Salmon Pink'	rose	2.5' (75 cm)	Aug-Sept	8-9*

*Frost free storage required in zone 2–7

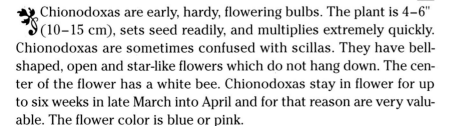

Chionodoxas are early, hardy, flowering bulbs. The plant is 4–6" (10–15 cm), sets seed readily, and multiplies extremely quickly. Chionodoxas are sometimes confused with scillas. They have bell-shaped, open and star-like flowers which do not hang down. The center of the flower has a white bee. Chionodoxas stay in flower for up to six weeks in late March into April and for that reason are very valuable. The flower color is blue or pink.

Chionodoxa
GLORY-OF-THE-SNOW
Liliaceae
Zones 2–9

Ecofunction

There are many species of chinodaxas, some of which have not made it as yet into the north temperate garden. For the most part they flower early as the snow recedes and represent for the honeybee an immediate source of fresh pollen vital to the growing brood at this time. Chionodoxas are 'frontier plants.' They live on the fringe of the impossible with snow. These plants, too, could be tested for nerve regeneration compounds.

Organic Care

Chionodoxas are planted 3" (7 cm) deep. The bulbs are very tiny. Despite this, they will compete with grass because flowering is almost over before the grass makes its growth surge. Chionodoxas like an alkaline, well-drained, good garden soil in full sun.

Design

Chionodoxas flower with scillas and snowdrops. Because of its long period in bloom, the later flowering *C. gigantea,* 6" (15 cm), can be massed with early Fosteriana tulips 'Red Emperor', a scarlet tulip *T. chrysantha* 'Tubergen's Gem', 6" (15 cm), with its red and gold cups, as an ideal companion. The rose chionodoxas *C. luciliae* 'Pink Giant' or *C. luciliae* 'Rosea' make a wonderful pink and white tonal companion for *Magnolia stellata* 'Rosea' or *Magnolia kobus*. This grouping will tolerate an alkaline soil. *C. luciliae,* 4" (10 cm), with blue and white flowers are a delightful foil to the yellow flowers of forsythia, *F.* 'Northern Gold' or *F.* 'Ovata Ottawa' for zones 3–9 or the beautiful weeping forsythia *F. suspensa* 'Sieboldii' for zones 5–9.

Chionodoxas Species and Cultivars

NAME	COLOR	HEIGHT	MONTH	ZONE
C. luciliae	blue	4" (10 cm)	April	2-9
C. luciliae 'Gigantea'	blue	6" (15 cm)	April	2-9
C. luciliae 'Pink Giant'	pink	4" (10 cm)	April	2-9
C. luciliae 'Rosea'	rose	4" (10 cm)	April	2-9
C. sardensis	blue	4" (10 cm)	April	2-9

Colchicum
AUTUMN CROCUS
Liliaceae
Zones 5–9

Colchicums are a group of plants that mainly flower in the autumn. The most commonly known of these is *Colchicum autumnale*. Colchicums are sometimes confused with crocii, to which they are related. Colchicums are hardy from zone 5–9, a few spring flowering species being hardy from zones 4–9. They are somewhat difficult to maintain in a Canadian garden over a period of years because colchicums require plenty of moisture in July and August for good root growth prior to flowering.

Ecofunction

Colchicums are extremely poisonous bulbs. Although they were used medically in ancient times, they were thought to be too toxic for use. They are an important source of the drugs colchium and colchicines in modern medicine. *C. autumnale* has one of the highest levels known of serotonin, which is an important vasoactive amine found throughout the animal kingdom. In man this amine is closely connected with migraines, schizophrenia, and Parkinson's disease, among others.

Organic Care

The bulbs require a nutrient rich, deep clay, well-drained soil which is moist in late summer. They require full sun and should be planted 3–4" (8–10 cm) deep in an area of the garden devoid of grass allocated to these bulbs alone.

Design

The rare and difficult *C. luteum,* zones 4–9, blooms in April. Its yellow 4" (10 cm) flowers are sessile and have an interesting flowering succession from the axils of the leaves. This colchicum stays in flower for about three weeks and is ideal for a rock garden. Both flower and bulb are very hardy. *C. luteum* needs to be dry after flowering to cure the corm for spring growth. The beautiful pink *C. szovitsii* flowers from March to June in zones 4–9, and the apricot-colored *C. fasciculare,* zones 4–9, a lover of alkaline soil, flowers from February to April.

Autumn brings a range of bloom beginning with the August flowering *C. aggripinum,* which is 4" (10 cm) tall and has beautiful pink flowers. In late August *C. byzantium* has lilac pink flowers and a lovely fragrance. In September the *C. autumnale*, pink, and its white cultivar 'Album', have a long flowering time, followed by the double *C. autumnale* 'Plentiflorum', a magnificent 6" (15 cm) double rose flower. *C. speciosum* 12" (30 cm), with rose-lilac flowers of immense size and attractive white throats, are magnificent when massed in large numbers, especially by a walk-way. Finally, a farewell to the tropical and hardy waterlily blooms of autumn can be made by the *C.speciosum* 'Waterlily' hybrid, which mimics the form of the waterlily by outspreading its petals to the sun.

Colchicum Species, Hybrids and Cultivars

NAME	COLOR	HEIGHT	MONTH	ZONE
C. luteum	yellow	6" (15 cm)	April	4-9
C. szovitsii	pink	5" (12 cm)	April	4-9
C. fasciculare	apricot	4" (10 cm)	March	4-9
C. aggripinum	pink	4" (10 cm)	Aug	5-9
C. byzantium	lilac pink	4" (10 cm)	Sept	5-9
C. autumnale	pink	6" (15 cm)	Sept	5-9
C.a. 'Alba'	white	6" (15 cm)	Sept	5-9
C. a. 'Pleniflorum'	amethyst	6" (15 cm)	Sept	5-9
C. Speciosum	rose	12" (30 cm)	Sept	5-9
C. s. 'Aitchisonii'	rose	12" (30 cm)	Sept	5-9
C. s. 'Cassiope'	rose	12" (30 cm)	Sept	5-9
C. s. 'Oxonican'	rose	12" (30 cm)	Sept	5-9
C. s. 'Waterlily'	rose	12" (30 cm)	Sept	5-9

Crinum
CRINUM LILY
Amaryllidaceae
Zones 7–9

Crinum lilies can be grown as garden plants in gardening zones 7–9. They are grown for their strap-like foliage, fragrance, and tropical looking flowers. These lilies like full sun and resent being moved, so should be left to form generous sized clumps.

Ecofunction

Bulbs of the crinum species are toxic. In warm gardens these species, especially when in full sun, donate a magnificent fragrance to the garden's air.

Organic Care

Crinum lilies thrive in extremely rich, especially in high-phosphate, well-drained soil in both summer and winter. Even moisture throughout the growing season promotes flowering, except for *C. americanum,* which requires more moisture, and is useful in the bog or water garden.

Design

The hardiest 5°F (-15°C) and most commonly grown is *C. bulbispermum* 3' (1 m), which blooms from early June through July. The flowers are extremely attractive pale pink with a strong pink stripe on 4" (10 cm) long corollas. Blooming in July and August is *Crinum x powellii*, a cross between *C. bulbispermum* and *C. moori.* The flowers are smaller 2' (60 cm), extremely fragrant, and a number of beautiful cultivars are available.

Crinum Species and Cultivars

NAME	COLOR	HEIGHT	MONTH	ZONE
C. americanum	white	2' (60 cm)	March	9
C. bulbispermum 'Alba'	white	3' (90 cm)	June-July	8-9
C. b. 'Roseum'	rose	3' (90 cm)	June-July	7-9
C. b. 'Gulf Pride'	pink-white	3' (90 cm)	June-July	7-9
C. x powellii				
C. x p. 'Elaine Bosauquant'	red	3-4' (90-120 cm)	July-Aug	7-9
C. x p. 'J. C. Harvey'	pink	3-4' (90-120 cm)	July-Aug	7-9
C. x p. 'St. Christopher'	white	3-4' (90-120 cm)	July-August	7-9
C. latifolium 'Zeylanicum'	pink-white	2' (60 cm)	May	9

For mass effect of early spring flowering, the crocus is the most popular spring bulb throughout the world. Crocii have been used in gardens for many centuries. The colors are white, yellows, blues, and purples. Some species are bitonal, bicolored, and striped. Crocii are divided into two groups by flowering period: spring crocii and autumn crocii.

Crocus
CROCUS
Iridaceae
Zones 4–9

Spring Crocii

Of the spring crocii there are three interesting groups for the northern temperate gardener. These are the *Crocus chrysanthus* group, the *Crocus vernus* (Dutch crocii), group and the species crocii group.

The *Crocus chrysanthus* cultivars have been developed from the extremely hardy *Crocus chrysanthus* specie. These are the earliest flowering crocii. The corms are very small, 1/3" (1 cm). The flowers are sessile with the leaves appearing after flowering. These species should be planted in nooks and crannies in the garden. They should not be planted in the lawn because the small corm cannot compete with grass roots very effectively.

The *Crocus vernus* or Dutch crocii have larger corms, 3/4" (2 cm), flower later, and both leaves and flowers appear together at flowering time. These crocii can be planted in lawns. They are slightly less hardy and robust than the *C. chrysanthus*.

The specie crocii consist of an assemblage of crocus species, some of which are extremely hardy and some of which are not. Their cultural requirements are somewhat different. Gardeners in zones 2–3 are encouraged to experiment with some members of this group.

Crocus chrysanthus 'Snow Bunting' and *C.c.* 'E.P. Bowles' defy hard frosts to bloom in March.

Autumn
Crocii

These crocii flower in the autumn from August into September and October. The corms are large, 3/4" (2 cm), similar to the Dutch crocii group. Autumn crocii should be planted in flower beds and not in lawns.

Ecofunction

The many crocus species, especially in the company of the winter aconite (*Eranthis hyemalis),* are among the best plants worth watching for school children. The pollen grains of the crocus are large and golden and are easily seen. The yellow flowered varieties also produce some nectar at the base of the flower. The honeybee is too preoccupied by her steep climb to obtain this to notice her observers. *C. satius*, also known as the saffron crocus, has a long and ancient history of use in China, the Far East, and Europe. It is used in modern medicine, in the perfume industry, as a condiment, and as a water-soluble dye for food and clothing.

Organic Care

Crocii like a well-drained sandy soil which has been enriched by phosphate and potash in the form of bone meal and wood ashes. In moisture laden soils crocii will use their contractile roots to push themselves out of the ground to higher land. In doing so, they often perish from frost injury. Crocii like full sun or light shade. New crocii corms are formed on top of the old corm. This progression leads to the corms being at or very near the soil surface in three to four years. Consequently, corms should be dug up and replanted every four years to prevent losses due to frost damage.

Spring flowering crocii can be planted any time in the fall, and fall crocii should be planted in the spring in March or April. Healthy corms should have a fine papery brown coat and be solidly plump. Diseased corms should be discarded. Small corms should be planted 2" (5 cm) deep and large corms should go 4" (10 cm) deep or a little deeper in lawns.

Design

Some of the specie crocii, *C. ancyrensis* and *C. tomasinianus,* are the first crocii to bloom, blooming with eranthus, bulbous iris, snowdrops, and scillas. A little later on in the month, the *Crocus crysanthus* group flowers are followed closely by the *Crocus vernus* group. These two groups flower with chionodoxa, double snow drops, and various cultivars of *Iris reticulata.* In the late August garden, the various species of the autumn flowering crocii begin their fall show.

Crocus Chrysanthus Hybrids

NAME	COLOR	HEIGHT	MONTH	ZONE
Crocus chrysanthus				
C.c. 'Blue Pearl'	blue	2"(5 cm)	Feb–March	3-9
C.c. 'Skyline'	blue	2" (5 cm)	March	3-9
C.c. 'E. P. Bowles'	yellow	2" (5cm)	March	3-9
C.c. 'Gypsy Girl'	gold	2" (5 cm)	March	3-9
C.c. 'Herald'	violet	2" (5 cm)	March	3-9
C.c. 'Ladykiller'	purple	2" (5 cm)	March	3-9
C.c. 'Snow Bunting'	white	2" (5 cm)	March	3-9

Crocus Vernus (Dutch Crocii)

NAME	COLOR	HEIGHT	MONTH	ZONE
Crocus vernus (Dutch Crocii)				
C.v. 'Queen of the Blues'	blue	2" (5 cm)	March-April	4-9
C.v. 'Vanguard'	blue	2" (5 cm)	March-April	4-9
C.v. 'Yellow Mammoth'	yellow	2" (5 cm)	March-April	4-9
C.v. 'Pickwick'	lilac & orange	2" (5 cm)	March-April	4-9
C.v. 'Twinborn'	purple striped	2" (5 cm)	March-April	4-9
C.v. 'Joan of Arc'	white	2" (5 cm)	March-April	4-9

Specie Crocus

NAME	COLOR	HEIGHT	MONTH	ZONE
C. ancyrensis	yellow	4: (10 cm)	Aug-Sept	3-9
C. biflorus 'Weldenii Fairy'	violet	2" (5 cm)	March-April	2-9
C. korolkowii	yellow	2' (5cm)	March-April	2-9
C. tomasinianus 'Barr's Purple'	purple	2 (5cm)	March-April	2-9
C. tomasinianus 'Ruby Giant'	purple	2" (5cm)	March-April	2-9

Autumn Crocii

NAME	COLOR	HEIGHT	MONTH	ZONE
C. laevigatus	lilac	4" (10cm)	Aug-Sept	7-9
C. longiflorus	lilac	5" (10cm)	Aug-Sept	7-9
C. sativus (saffron crocus)	violet	6" (15cm)	Aug-Sept	4-9
C. speciosus	blue	6"(15cm)	Aug-Sept	4-9
C. zonatus (*C. kotschyanus*)	orange	2" (5cm)	Aug-Sept	4-9
C. karduchorum	violet	2" (5cm)	Sept-Oct	4-9

Dahlia
DAHLIA
Compositae
Zones: Tender
Summer Tubers

Dahlias are tender, tuberous rooted flowers originating from the mountainous areas of Mexico, Central America, and Colombia. In many parts of the world dahlia flowers of superior beauty, color, and form are shown in competition. The breeding, growing, and showing of these exhibition dahlias requires great gardening expertise.

Ecofunction

Dahlias, especially the new miniature bedding dahlias which stay in bloom for most of the summer, are an important source of pollen and nectar for all beneficial insects in the garden. They also supply shade and dampness for the amphibian population, which, in turn, appreciates a well-stocked insect larder.

Organic Care

Good drainage and full sun are essential for dahlias. Dahlias like a very rich soil with a medium nitrogen and a high phosphate and potash content. The soil should be acidic. Dahlias do not do well on calcareous soils. They appear to suffer from dahlia stunt, which can be viral in origin or physiological. The transport of water and food within the plant does not seem to take place with much efficiency, resulting in a poor, stunted growth pattern.

Tall dahlia cultivars should be planted 6" (15 cm) deep into warm ground and then staked. The hole should be slowly filled in as the plant grows. Miniature dahlias should be planted 3.5 – 4.5" (9–12 cms) deep and filled in as growth commences. Fish emulsion fertilizer is an ideal summer fertilizer for increasing dahlia bloom.

Dahlias are perennials in the milder gardening zones of 8 and 9, but have to be treated as tender flowering tubers in zones 2–7. The overall genetic design of the plant, with its hollow stems and high sap content, makes the dahlia extremely susceptible to freezing. In zones 2–7 the tubers are harvested after the first killing frost.

After the first killing frost, in zones 2–7, dahlias should be carefully lifted. It is essential that the gardener not injure the tuberous roots. They should be allowed to air dry in direct sunlight for one or two hours. The tubers should be turned once or twice. Loose soil should be gently shaken from the bunch of tubers. The tubers should be planted in a plastic bucket in damp sand with shoots upright. They should have 2" (5 cm) of sand below them and about 3" (7 cm) of sand above them. The bucket should be covered loosely so the sand can breathe. This should be stored above 32° F (0°C) over winter. In zones 2–4 where the winter season is long, a light sprinkling of water in February and another in April will keep the tubers in prime condition.

Dahlias may be readily propagated. Prior to spring planting a sterilized knife should be used to cut the tubers at their connecting bridge in the area of the old stalk, leaving at least one eye per tuber group. These tubers can be started indoors or can be planted outside after the last killing frost. Earwigs like to forage in dahlias. To maintain a reasonable balance of these creatures, wrens can be attracted into the garden to feed on the earwigs.

Design

All the dahlias are technically classified into groups depending on the varied morphological features of the flowers. These are single-flowered; anemone-flowered; collarette, an open flower with a ring of ray florets and a second smaller ring of a different color forming a collar around the daisy-like central disk; decorative, being double flowered; ball; pompom, with flowers being smaller than ball and the sphere flattened; and cactus, which are doubles with floral, quill-like rays.

For garden design purposes the Dahlias may be divided into two major groups, the tall dahlias or border dahlias and the miniature dahlias or bedding dahlias.

The tall dahlias, 3–5' (1–1.5 m), are used in borders, blooming in August, and are particularly useful at this time because of their abundant bloom and color until the first frosts. These dahlias are very useful in zones 5–9, or in the colder gardening zones where some frost protection can be given to the flowers.

The miniature dahlias,10–24" (25–60 cm), are used very often as bedding dahlias, but these dahlias are also extremely useful at the front of the border. Miniature dahlias are a little hardier and they flower much earlier in July into August, and if well watered, will give a fine succession of bloom until the first frost. These dahlias are easier to grow and less demanding than the taller cultivars. In regions of Canada where there are problems growing the taller cultivars, the miniature cultivars may be more successful.

The colors of the new cultivars of dahlias have an enormous range. Single colors range from whites through yellows to pinks, reds, oranges, and flame to deep purple. There are also bicolors and multi-colors with bitonal petals and beautiful streaking on the petals. The foliage of some cultivars can also have some lovely bronze shading.

Dahlia Cultivars
Tall Dahlias

NAME	COLOR	HEIGHT	MONTH	ZONE
D. 'Gay Princess'	pink (informal) decorative	4.5' (1.4 m)	Aug-Sept	8-9*
D. 'Lady Linda'	yellow (formal) decorative	4.5' (1.4 m)	Aug-Sept	8-9*
D. 'Orchid Lace'	white brushed with mauve, cactus	5' (1.5 m)	Aug-Sept	8-9*
D. 'Juanita'	red cactus	3.5' (1.1 m)	Aug-Sept	8-9*
D. 'Kochelsee'	dark red pompom	3-4' (1-1.2 m)	Aug-Sept	8-9*
D. 'Awaikee'	red with white colar colarette	3.5' (1.1 m)	Aug-Sept	8-9*
D. 'Bishop of Llandaff'	red anemone	3' (1 m)	Aug-Sept	8-9*

Miniature Dahlias

NAME	COLOR	HEIGHT	MONTH	ZONE
D. 'Arabesque'	yellow cactus	18" (45 cm)	July-Aug	8-9*
D. 'Bambino'	white single	14" (35 cm)	July-Aug	8-9*
D. 'Bonne Esperance'	pink single	10" (25 cm)	July-Aug	8-9*

*Frost free storage required in zone 2-7

Delphinium
LARKSPUR
Ranunculaceae
Zones 4–9

Delphinium menziesii, a Canadian west coast native, flowers for two months in June and July.

There are a number of tuberous delphiniums, two of which have horticultural importance in a northern temperate garden, *D. menziesii* and *D. semibarbatum* (syn. *D. Zalil, D. sulphureum*). *D. menziesii* is a native specie of British Columbia and *D. semibarbatum,* of Iran. Both species go completely dormant after flowering, like the native trillium.

Ecofunction
Delphiniums are a useful food source for hummingbirds. *D. semibarbatum* yields a spectacular orange-red dye depending on the mordant used. All delphiniums are poisonous. They have been used as an effective control for skin parasites.

Organic Care
Tuberous delphiniums prefer neutral to alkaline, sandy or loamy soil of medium fertility which is high in potassium and phosphate for good tuber growth. A well-drained soil in summer and winter is a necessity for healthy tubers.

Design
Both tuberous delphiniums grow to 2.5' (75 cm) or more. *D. menziesii* have rich deep blue flowers in June and July which combine well with

alliums, *Nectaroscordum bulgaricum*, or the red Chinese *Lilium concolor pulchellum*. The beautiful bright yellow flowers of *D. semibarbatum* with their straight spurs are in flower from May to August. The loose racemes combine well with *Eremurus stenophyllus*, 2'–3' (.6–1 m), and the Asiatic hybrid *Lilium* 'Yellow Blaze', 4'–5' (1.3–1.7 m), *Meconopsis cambrica*, 8–24" (20–60 cm), the Welsh poppy and *Oenthera tetragonia* 'Fireworks', 20" (40 cm), and the everblooming dwarf daylily 'Stella d'Oro', 20" (40 cm). This sunny combination would be useful for a dry city garden.

Delphinium Species

NAME	COLOR	HEIGHT	MONTH	ZONE
D. menziesii,	deep blue	2.5' (75 cm)	June-July	4-9
D. Semibarbatum	yellow	2.5' (75 cm)	May-August	4-9
(syn. *D. Zalil, D. sulphureum*)				

Eranthis is a yellow flowering small tuberous plant. It flowers from January to March. The flower is sessile and the flower bud will break through the snow to flower. The flower has an extremely attractive ruff of green leaves, which is greatly enhanced by large group plantings.

Eranthis
WINTER ACONITE
Ranunculaceae
Zones 3–9

Ecofunction
In the winter aconite, nectar is produced and stored in vase-shaped containers which are, in fact, modified petals. In zone 4 gardens, these containers are well stocked for honeybees and other insects from mid-March on. On any sunny day early spring bees can be found working these flowers. Winter aconite is poisonous to cattle, horses, and people.

Organic Care
Winter aconite resent being moved. Divisions should be made after flowering, the damp tubers being planted the same day. Dry tubers from a nursery should be placed into damp peat moss, which has been dampened with lukewarm water, then wrapped in damp burlap and placed in a cool dark spot for 48 hours. The tubers should be planted 'eye' side up. There will be some losses, even with this careful approach. The growing eyes are sometimes difficult to find, as the corms vary in shape. Using a hand lens, the root area is somewhat easier to find. This will assist you in positioning the tuber for planting.

Eranthis hyemalis or the winter aconite heralds the spring in March in zone 4 despite bitterly cold weather.

Design

Flowering is from four to six weeks. Companion plants could be cro-cus, bulbous iris, snow-drops, and scillas. *Eranthis* likes a well-drained, stoney, alkaline, sloping soil. Rocks can be used to create a microclimate in zone 2. *Eranthis* prefers full sun but will flower longer in half shade. *Eranthis* can be used as carpeting for alkaline loving trees, e.g,. *Ulmus rubra,* the slippery elm, *Tillia americana,* the bass-wood, or *Ostrya virginiana,* the hop-hornbeam.

Eranthis Species and Cultivars

NAME	FLOWER FORM	COLOR	HEIGHT	MONTH	ZONE
E. hyemalis	sessile flowers	yellow	4" (10cm)	March	3-9
E. cilicicus	large flowers	yellow	4" (10cm)	March	3-9
E. c. 'Bulgarians'	large flowers	yellow	4" (10cm)	March	3-9
E. c. 'Guinea Gold'	large flowers	yellow	4" (10cm)	March	3-9
E. longistipitatus	non-sessile flowers	yellow	5" (12cm)	March	3-9

Eremurus
DESERT CANDLE
Liliaceae
Zones 4–9

Eremurus, also known as the desert-candle, comes from the mountainous deserts in central Europe. These plants are defi-nitely for the adventurous gardener. *E. stenophyllus (E. bungei)* and hybrids, the Shelford Hybrids *(E. olgae* x *E. stenophyllus),* are hardy from zones 4–9 with some protection: *E. elwesii* and *E. himalaicus, E. cristatus,* and *E. robustus* are hardy from zones 5-9.

Ecofunction

The myriads of open flowers on these desert candles makes them very attractive to the smaller wasps and other flying beneficials in the garden.

Organic Care

Eremurus have cormous tubers that are shaped like a flattened jelly-fish. These tubers are extremely brittle and should be handled with utmost care as the plant will be very prone to disease if it suffers any injury. An injured tuber will exude a reddish sap which should sun-dry for 24 hours before any attempt is made to plant it. This tuber is planted in a wide hole, 3–5" (7–12 cm) deep. The hole should have an in-fill of sharp dry sand. The planting soil should be enriched with phosphate and wood ashes. Ideally, the soil should be a sandy gar-den soil that is extremely well drained in both summer and winter. The July and August soil conditions should be quite dry, as the *Eremurus* tuber needs a hot, dry dormancy and curing period after flowering. The flowering scape fades rapidly in July.

In late winter or very early spring for zones 4 and 5, the tuber, which should be marked, needs a cone of sharp dry sand poured over it to retard spring growth. Then the area should have some evergreen boughs criss-crossed over it to shade the soil. When the very large shoots, similar to asparagus shoots, emerge, they are frost-resistant and will withstand quite cold temperatures, but when the shoot has elongated to about 12" (30 cm), it becomes very vulnerable to frost damage because the sheath of leaves protecting the bud opens, revealing a fleshy flowering tip which is high in water-content ready to elongate. If this stage can be delayed in cold gardening areas, then one is rewarded with magnificent flowers.

Gardeners in zones 4 and 5 should choose June and July flowering *Eremurus* species and cultivars as opposed to May and early June flowering ones because delays in the opening of the flower-bud in a frost-prone area considerably increase the chances of successful flowering.

Many species of *Eremurus* seed out quite readily in northern gardens and hopefully a more frost-hardy cultivar will emerge for zones 2 and 3.

Design

E. cristatus, zones 6–9, is the earliest to flower. It has a fine 2' (60 cm) spike of pink and white flowers. *E. elwesii*, zones 5–9, can soar up to 6–10' (2–3.5 m) under optimal growing conditions. The fragrant pink flowers are as novel as they are beautiful. There is an 'Alba' cultivar. The gardener who manages to grow this eremurus is lucky indeed. It can be massed with Asiatic hybrid lilies, *Nectarocordum bulgaricum* and *Allium christophii,* in the June border. The pure white 3' spires of *E. himalaicus* flower early in June as do the peach spires of *E. robustus,* 6.5–10' (2–3.5 m). *E. stenophyllus*, with 3' (1m) primrose flowers, and its hybrids and the pastel Shelford hybrids, 5–6' (2 m), which are orange-buff, pink-white, and dark yellow, are more suitable and easier to grow for the majority of gardeners.

Eremurus Species and Hybrids

NAME	COLOR	HEIGHT	MONTH	ZONE
E. cristatus	pink and white	2' (60 cm)	May	6-9
E. stenophyllus (*E. bungei*)	yellow	2-3' (60-90 cm)	June-July	4-9
E. x Shelfordii hybrids	pastels	5-6' (150-180 cm)	June-July	4-9
E. himalaicus	white	2-3' (60-90 cm)	June	5-9
E. robustus	peach	6.5-10' (200–350cm)	June	5-9
E. elwesii	pink	4' (120 cm)	May	5-9
E. elwesii 'Alba'	white	4' (120 cm)	May	5-9

Erythronium
ADDER'S TONGUE,
DOG-TOOTH VIOLET
Liliaceae
Zones 3–9

Erythronium species are found scattered throughout the world. The erythroniums are some of the most beautiful of our early spring flowering bulbs. The flowers are somewhat fleeting, lasting only from one to two weeks, but the chocolate mottling of the foliage makes them attractive for much longer. Erythronium flowers are mostly solitary, like a tiny trumpet lily, and are pink, rose, lilac, yellow, and white.

Ecofunction

All erythroniums are excellent candidates for wild shade gardens. The mottled leaves of the North American species act as an excellent foil for the frog and toad population.

Both the leaves and underground tubers of *E. americanum* are edible when cooked. It served as a root vegetable of the indigenous peoples of North America. Erythroniums are toxic to poultry, a fact which is interesting scientifically.

Organic Care

Erythroniums like a soil high in humus with some lime. Partial shade is ideal for them. In full sun the flowers will last only one week. The soil should be well drained in the winter.

Design

E. japonicum, zones 4–9, flowers after the large Dutch crocii. The flowers are a beautiful pink-lilac color, 4–6" (10–15 cm) tall, and can be massed to great effect in a shade garden.

The European *E. dens-canis,* zones 4–9, with its rose-colored flowers, 6" (15 cm), can be massed with the early Fosteriana tulip with similarly mottled foliage. The tall 16" (40 cm) white *E. revolutum* 'White Beauty', zones 4–9, and its beautiful pink hybrid *E. revolutum* 'Jeanette Brickell', zones 4–9, can be massed or grouped with smaller 6" (15 cm) Kaufmanniana tulips. *E. tuolumnense* 'Pagoda', zones 5–9, 10" (25 cm) tall, bright yellow flowers, or *E. grandiflorum* 12–24" (30-60 cm) zones 6–9, bright yellow and multiflowered are magnificent with 'Sweetheart', a Fosteriana hybrid tulip which is a white and soft-yellow combination.

There is a late flowering, June to September depending on mean temperature, native subalpine erythronium, *E. montanum,* of the west coast of Canada. Hybrids of this species might well prove to be hardy for zones 2 and 3. Gardeners in zones 2 and 3 could try planting erythroniums in a microclimatic area of their garden. The bulbs should be planted 4" (10 cm) deep, with a higher potassium and phosphorus ratio in the soil mixture to induce frost resistance in the bulb and enhance flowering.

Erythronium Species and Cultivars

NAME	COLOR	HEIGHT	MONTH	ZONE
E. americanum	yellow	4" (10 cm)	April	3-9
E. dens-canis	rose	6" (15 cm)	April	4-9
E. japonicum	lilac	6" (15 cm)	April	4-9
E. revolutum 'White Beauty'	white	16" (40 cm)	April	4-9
E. revolutum 'Jeanette Bickell'	pink	16" (40 cm)	April	4-9
E. tuolumnense 'Pagoda'	yellow	12" (30 cm)	April	5-9
E. grandiflorum	yellow	1-2' (30-60 cm)	July	6-9

Fritillaria
FRITILLARIA
Liliaceae
Zones 4–9

❧ Fritillarias rank highly as bulbs useful for beauty, design, height, massing, and in some instances, for the chemical protection of other spring and summer bulbs. Fritillarias are an enormous group of plants flowering from mid-spring to early summer with a great diversity of form, flower color, flower form, and height. They come from the northern hemisphere and occur naturally at very high altitudes. Therefore, being subalpine, fritillarias are very frost hardy. The whole range of these bulbs needs to be tested in zones 2 and 3.

Ecofunction

The bulbs of *Fritillaria imperialis* 'Aurora' (orange), 'Lutea' (yellow), 'Rubra Maxima' (red) and the variegated foliage cultivar 'Aureomarginata' (red) have a chemical which gives off a strong skunk-like odor. This chemical is extremely volatile and filters through the soil as well as in the air. This chemical is strongly deterrent to all burrowing creatures such as rabbits, mice, moles, voles, and ground squirrels. One or two bulbs placed at a distance of 20 feet apart should afford protection to the average size garden against these creatures.

The alkaloide present in all the fritillaria need to be scientifically investigated. *F. meleagris*, the favorite of Sweden, seems to have a chemical which depresses heart function.

Organic Care

All fritillarias prefer a sandy or gritty, rich, well-drained soil. The winter drainage should be excellent. Many of the fritillarias live on limestone screes in their native habitat and correspondingly respond well to additional lime with phosphate in their soil mix. All fritillarias go dormant very rapidly after flowering and the site has to be well marked if

Fritillaria imperialis 'Lutea Maxima' grouped with *Narcissus* 'King Alfred', *N.* 'Mount Hood', and *Tulipa kaufmanniana* species.

the bulbs and bulbils are to be dug up in August or September for division and replanting. This should be done every three to four years.

Design

In early April, *Fritillaria persica* 'Adiyaman' blooms. The bell-like flowers are a deep plum color and are most attractive. Massing this fritillaria with early tulips is very effective. A mixture of fritillaria with 'Juan', the orange-red and yellow Fosteriana hybrid tulip with the yellow and cream of 'Sweetheart', both being 18" (45 cm) tulips, begins the spring tapestry with rich coloring.

Fritillaria meleagris, a vanishing native of old English meadows.

F. persica 'Adiyaman' bulbs are smaller than *F. imperialis* and should be planted 4–5" (10–15 cm) deep. The bulbs should be spaced from 8–12" (20–30 cm) apart.

The next significant fritillaria to bloom occurs in the middle of April. This is the towering yellow *F. imperialis* 'Lutea', which can reach 3' (1 m) high. The red *F. imperialis* 'Rubra Maxima' flowers later. *F. imperialis* 'Lutea' flowers at exactly the same time as many of the large trumpet flowered daffodils (narcissi division number 1) such as 'King Alfred' and 'Mount Hood'. Both these daffodils are the tallest common daffodils grown and grow from 12–18" (30–45 cm). They are both very fragrant. The 'King Alfred' is buttery yellow and 'Mount Hood' is a cool white. These two daffodils are excellent companions to *F. imperialis* 'Lutea', showing off the drooping yellow flowers with their huge white anthers to perfection. This arrangement is the backbone composition for a spring bulb border.

Also flowering in April is *F. uva-vulpis*, formerly *F. assyriaca*, a delicate beauty of 8–12" (20–30 cm) with yellow-tipped, maroon flowers which are strikingly beautiful. A grouping of four or five could be used as a spring focal point in a border, rockery, or elsewhere in the garden. The bulbs should be planted 4" (10 cm) deep. The magnificent *Fritillaria imperialis* 'Rubra Maxima' flowers in May. It is similar in all respects to the *F. imperialis* 'Lutea'. However, with its striking red color one has to choose planting companions carefully to show off the flower's form properly. White narcissi make a fine contrast. Combining 'Thalia', a white fragrant 16" (40 cm) triandrus hybrid narcissus, with 'Papillon Blanc', a white split corona butterfly narccissus 18" (45 cm), and 'White Parrot', 24" (60 cm), heavily fringed tulips, makes an excellent composition. Alternatively, the viridiflora tulip 'Artist' has an identical color and tonal composition with *F. imperialis* 'Rubia Maxima' in reds, green, and purple flower bases. Then this arrangement could be set into a mass of white, late hyacinths such as 'Madame Sophie'.

Flowering also in May is *F. pontica*, 12–16" (30–40 cm), each stem carrying a beautiful green bell. The bulbs are small and should be planted 4" (10 cm) deep. The large 2.5' (75 cm) *F. verticillata* carries many cream and green bells and is most attractive. This fritillaria is a medicinal herb from Japan where it is used in cough medicines. Both these fritillarias combine very well with the long lasting viridiflora tulip 'Spring Green'.

Blooming in June are the *F. meleagris* and the *F. michailovskyi*. The *F. meleagris* are 12–18" (30–45 cm), with nodding checkered bells of white, bronze, grey and purple, on wiry stems. These flowers are ideal in a rockery or in an area under a medium-sized tree where they can be massed alone. They should be planted 4–5" (10–12 cm) deep for that reason. When dividing and replanting these tiny bulbs, some wire screening should be used over the area as protection against ground squirrels for a month or so.

The beautiful small flowers for F. *michailovskyi*, 6" (15 cm), should be used as a focal point in the garden. These graceful deep-plum-colored, bell-shaped flowers have a band of bright yellow at the flare of the bell. The bulb is like a small version of *F. imperialis* and should be planted 5" (12 cm) deep, in slightly acidic soil.

Fritillaria Species and Cultivars

NAME	COLOR	HEIGHT	MONTH	ZONE
F. persica 'Adiyaman'	plum	3' (90 cm)	Apr-May	4-9
F. imperialis 'Lutea Maxima'	yellow	3' (90 cm)	Apr-May	4-9
F. imperialis 'Rubra Maxima'	red	3' (90 cm)	May	4-9
F. imperialis 'Rubra Aureomaeginata'	red	3' (90 cm)	May	4-9
F. imperialis 'Aurora'	orange	3' (90 cm)	May	4-9
F. uva-vulpis	maroon	8-16" (20-40 cm)	May-June	4-9
F. pontica	green	12" (30 cm)	May-June	4-9
F. verticillata	cream/green	2 1/2' (75 cm)	June	4-9
F. meleagris	mixed	12-18" (20-40 cm)	June	2-9
F. m. 'Alba'	white	12-18" (20-40 cm)	June	2-9
F. michailovski	plum	6" (15 cm)	June	4-9
F. straussii	dark purple	8" (20 cm)	June	4-9

Galanthus
SNOWDROPS
Amaryllidaceae
Zones 2–9

These delightful hardy bulbs bid farewell to winter and herald spring with their dainty, nodding, white and green flowers. Sometimes these bulbs will flower through the snow. In all gardening zones, snowdrops are indicator plants for the cessation of cold and the commencement of warmer days. Their time clock has been set genetically, as they occur at the alpine snowline naturally, to flower when the snow begins to recede with the warming sun's rays.

The flowers are green and white, the inside corolla having various patterning of deep-green with the outside sepals being pure white. The various species grow from 1/2" to 6" (1 cm to 15 cm) tall.

Ecofunction

The galanthus species herald the end of the winter and the beginning of spring on the snowline of mountains and in gardens. In its solitary cold beauty, it holds the key to nerve regeneration, for which there is much excitement in the scientific world. The alkaloides are in the bulb. The bulb may be crushed and used as an external poultice for frostbite. The principal alkaloid is galanthamine, also called Nivalin, and is a cholinesterase inhibitor useful in the treatment of poliomyelitis.

Organic Care

A well-drained, neutral, good, garden soil, with full sun or light shade is considered to be ideal. The bulbs should be planted from 3–4" (7.5–10 cm) deep, though the larger specie G. ikariae should be planted a little deeper, 4^1/$_2$" (12 cm). Gardeners in zones 2 and 3 should plant snow drops at 4" (10 cm) to retard spring growth. Snow drops will create a good colony over a number of years if left undisturbed.

Design

For zones 4–6 a succession of flowering for the month of March can be obtained by the use of several species of *Galanthus*. For zones 7–9, this succession will begin from January to March. For colder areas, zones 2 and 3, the later blooming *Galanthus* might be more dependable. The large, beautifully flowered snow drop G. elwesii blooms with winter aconites, early crocii, iris, and scillas.

Later on, the common snowdrop G. nivalis and a yellow and white cultivar G. nivalis 'Alleni', a speckled cultivar G. nivalis 'Viridapicis', and the large 6"(15 cm) G. ikariae ssp latifolius, which has the largest leaves of all the galanthus species, flower with *chionodoxa* and *scilla*.

The latest flowering galanthus is the fragrant double G. nivalis 'Flore Pleno' and the late flowering cultivar of the common snowdrop G. nivalis 'Scharlockii'. These flower with *Iris reticulata*, the *Crocus chrysanthus* hybrids, and the large flowering Dutch crocus hybrids.

Galanthus Species and Cultivars

NAME	COLOR	HEIGHT	MONTH	ZONE
G. elwesii	white	7" (18cm)	March	2-9
G. nivalis	white	4" (10cm)	March	2-9
G. nivalis 'Alleni'	white/yellow	4" (10cm)	March	2-9
G. nivalis 'Viridapicis'	white	4" (10cm)	March	2-9
G. ikariae ssp. latifolius	white	6" (15cm)	March	2-9
G. nivalis 'Flor Pleno'	white	4" (10cm)	March	2-9
G. nivalis 'Sharlockii'	white	4" (10cm)	March	2-9

Galtonias are tender bulbs from South Africa. They are hardy from zones 4–9, but have to be stored over winter in zones 2–3. They are extremely useful in the garden because they flower in the beginning of August and stay in flower until well into September.

Ecofunction

Galtonias are not fragrant despite their reputation for being so. They are an important source of nectar for hummingbirds and beneficial insects who collect nectar from the six deeply set nectaries at the base of each flower. The nectar is produced in the morning and evenings during the long six-to-eight week flowering period.

Organic Care

The bulbs are about the size of a large 'King Alfred' daffodil. They should be planted 2.5–3" (6–8 cm) deep in zones 2–3 after the last killing frost. They should be planted somewhat deeper, 5" (12 cm), above the tip of the bulb, in zones 4–9, when it is the intention to overwinter them *in situ*.

The bulbs like a sandy soil which is rich in humus, phosphate, and potassium and is very well drained. The soil should be neutral to slightly acid. The bulb should be dug after the first killing frost, air-dried for six hours, the long flowering stems trimmed to 2" (5 cm), dusted with dry wood ashes to discourage fungi, and stored in dry, milled peat moss in a thick paper bag overwinter at temperatures above 32°F (0°C). The bulbs are extremely easy to overwinter and do not require any additional care.

The galtonias may be readily propagated from seed. The long seed capsule, containing a large number of black seeds, should be harvested in September and overwintered dry, in a paper bag, at room temperature. The seeds should be planted in May-June. They have a very high germination rate. They will produce small bulbs the first year and flowering bulbs the second year. These small, year-old bulbs should be stored in a similar fashion as the large bulbs.

Design

Galtonias stay in bloom for six to eight weeks in the late summer to early fall garden. The flowers of *G. candicans* are white and bell-shaped like a hyacinth but are non-fragrant. Depending on the size of the bulb, the flowering scape can be from 2–4' (60–120 cm) high. The lovely, long flowering scape continues to produce flowers from the tip down, as it grows. One large bulb may have two or three flowering scapes.

Because galtonias have such a long flowering time, they flower

Galtonia
SUMMER HYACINTH
Liliaceae
Zones 4–9

Galtonia candicans, an indispensable August to September flowering bulb.

with the fragrant trumpet lilies, a number of alliums, and the extremely fragrant, oriental hybrid lilies. Galtonias are spectacular with regal lilies, *Allium cirrhosum* 'Album' and the white oriental hybrid lily called 'Casablanca' in a white fragrant border.

G. princeps is a more compact galtonia which is very like *G. candicans* and should be treated similarly. It has pale green bell-like flowers, the scapes being a little shorter in stature.

Galtonia Species

NAME	COLOR	HEIGHT	MONTH	ZONE
G. candicans	White	2-4' (60-120 cm)	Aug-Sept	4-9
G. princeps	Green	2' (60 cm)	Aug-Sept	4-9

Gladiolus
CORN FLAG
Iridaceae
Zones: Tender Summer
Corm

A hybrid gladiolus developed at Carrigliath.

Gladioli are members of the iris family. They are tender, summer flowering corms from warmer regions of the world. There is an interesting tradition in Canadian kitchen gardens to grow some of these bulbs with vegetables. This practise is quite old and a good one because it increases cross-pollination by insect attraction into male and female vegetable flowers consequently increasing yield. These commonly grown gladioli are hybrid gladioli produced by multiple crossing of many different gladioli species such as *G. carneus, G. cardinalis, G. natalensis, G. oppositiflorus, G. primulinus, G. purpureoauratus,* and *G. Saundersii.* Work on these hybrid gladioli is continuing with great intensity to produce the spectacular crop of flowering hybrids available to gardeners. Since the gene pool for hybrid gladioli is so large, frost hardy gladioli cultivars will emerge in time. One such hardy cultivar is *Gladiolus impressive,* 2' (60 cm), which has pink and rose florets and is hardy from zones 3–9. It can be treated as a perennial corm in these gardening zones.

Ecofunction

The hybrid gladioli have been used in the vegetable gardens of North America for generations. They are an essential part of the bioplan, particularly in the edible landscape, in that they attract all manner of pollinating species to the garden in the hottest and driest times of summer. These pollinators include the hummingbird and a great variety of flying insects.

Organic Care

Gladioli like full sun and a well-drained, rich garden soil. They do particularly well in sandy loams or in clay loams. The richer the soil is in available nitrogen, potassium, and phosphate, the larger the corms will be for the following year's garden.

Gladioli should be planted 3–4" (8–10 cm) deep and 6" (15 cm) apart. Hilling up the soil as the flowering stalk reaches 4–5" (10–12 cm) in height will produce a very upright plant which is wind-stable.

Thrips can be a serious problem for gladioli. Thrips feed on the leaves, buds, and young flowers of gladioli causing the flowers to collapse. However, the yellow cultivars of gladioli seem to be quite immune to thrips. Proper cool winter storage and a second dusting with wood ashes of the overwintered corms or new corms just prior to planting considerably reduces the thrip population.

Gladioli should be left in the garden until the first killing frost. The plants should be dug and dried in direct sun for three to four days. They should subsequently be allowed to air dry for an additional two weeks if possible. If frost threatens, they should be protected. This will cure the corms by drying and the ultra-violet irradiation of the sunlight will sterilize the corm's surface. After drying, the foliage may be cut back, leaving a stub of about 1.5" (4 cm) which will protect the growing tissue. The corms should be dusted with dry wood ashes as a fungicide and insecticide. Any hard, dry corms should be discarded. The corms can be stored dry by hanging them in a mesh bag or placing them in fine milled, dry peat in a cool dry place which does not go below 32° F (0°C).

Design

The hybrid cultivars of gladioli are particularly useful in garden design and are noteworthy for new variety in flower size, shape, markings, and textures. The new hybrid gladioli are magnificent border and garden flowers. They can be used to follow narcissi, tulips, and paeonies in a summer flowering succession, but more useful, however, is the fact that these new hybrids can flower in early, mid, or late summer to continue this succession of flowering. The VE or very early hybrids will flower under 80 days following planting, E 90 days, EM 100 days, M 110 days, and the LM will flower 120 days following planting.

There is also a dwarf strain of hybrids called *Gladiolus nanus,* the butterfly gladiolii, 2' (60 cm) tall, and these are becoming extremely popular plants for city gardening where space is more limited. They are the product of *G. cardinalis* crossed with *G. tristis.* Miniature varieties, 1.5–3' (45–90 cm), are also becoming popular.

There are several species of gladioli which are interesting perennial corms that may be grown in the milder climates of zones 8 and 9. These are *G. italicus,* magenta, and *G. atroviolaceus,* whose black-red flowers come from one side of the flowering spike which has a weeping form. *G. byzantinus,* 3' (90 cm), has magenta-colored flowers with a white central line. This perennial corm is hardy from zones 4–9. There is an 'Alba' and a 'Rubra' cultivar of this specie also.

Gladiolii Hybrid Cultivars and Species

NAME	COLOR	BLOOMING TIME
GRAND HYBRID GLADIOLUS 3–7' (1–2.5 M)		
'Morning Mist'	blue	EM
'Greenland'	green	M
'Peach Melba'	orange	EM
'Cavalcade'	pink	M
'América'	cream & white	E
'Red Ribbon'	red	EM
'Sunray'	yellow	LM
'Lilac Festival'	purple	EM
'Brownstone'	smokies	EM
'Green Beret'	green	VE
'Candy Apple'	rose	VE
MINIATURE HYBRID GLADIOLUS 1.5–3' (60–90 CM)		
'Bluebird'	blue	E
'Mexican Girl'	bright orange, yellow centre	EM
'Littlest Angel'	white and cream	M
SPECIE GLADIOLUS 3' (90 CM)		
G. italicus	magenta	8-9
G. atroviolaceus	black-red	8-9
G. byzantinus	red-magenta	4-9
G. byzantinus 'Alba'	white	4-9
G. byzantinus 'Rubra'	red	4-9

Hyacinthus
HYACINTH
Liliaceae
Zones 4–9

❧ *Hyacinthus orientalis* is the source of the many cultivars of the common garden hyacinth which is used both for indoor and outdoor culture. The color range of these cultivars is enormous and all are exquisitely fragrant. There is now a new interest in hyacinths because cultivars have been bred which are early, mid-season, and late flowering. The 'Flore Pleno' or double cultivars flower later in the season; the smaller, wild forms, *H. orientalis* 'Roman Hyacinth', blue, white, and pink, flower earlier in March or April depending on zones, as do the multiflora cultivars.

Ecofunction

Hyacinths should be grown for their fragrance alone which enhances the airspaces within the garden. It is also an important early source of pollen and nectar for the insect population. A very important aspect of this species is that the nectar is available to all because it is secreted as three, large, sugar-rich beads at the top of the flower's ovary for easy consumption.

Organic Care

Hyacinths are not quite as hardy as daffodils or tulips and there are more losses due to bulb rot. However, a grouping of hyacinths can flower faithfully in the same spot for 15–20 years. The first year of bloom the bulb will produce a thick strong flowering spike packed with flowers, but the subsequent flowers will be multi-spiked and the flowers will be looser. The whole general appearance of the flower will almost revert to the wild form.

Hyacinthus orientalis reverting to a more pleasing form after several years in the ground.

Hyacinths like a rich sandy or gritty, well-drained soil which is high in potash and phosphate. The soil pH should be neutral; acid soils should be adjusted with dolomitic limestone to neutrality. A high humus content in the soil or dense, water retaining soils will induce bulb rot, and for that reason clay soils are poor candidates for hyacinths. Clay soils should have a high component of sand added to them before planting these bulbs. Hyacinths like full sun conditions, but will flower quite well in 25 to 50 percent shade, although a little later and with less flower. It is important for the hyacinth to be tip dead-headed and for the foliage to be allowed to die back naturally. This process takes longer with hyacinths than other spring bulbs. This is unsightly, so thought should be given to this in the general garden plan.

In sandy loam, hyacinths should be planted with 4–5" (10–12 cm) of soil above the top of the bulb. In extremely sandy soils or in sod, hyacinths should be planted 6" (15 cm) deep. For clay-loams hyacinths should be planted 3.5–4" (8–10 cm) deep.

Design

Hyacinths are difficult bulbs to fit into a garden design because of their strong vertical growth and the lack of grace in the foliage at all times. As can be seen from the bulb guide, early, mid-season, and late hyacinths flower with the small cup narcissus group, the single and double early tulips, and the triumph and the Darwin hybrid tulips. The double hyacinths flower with the double narcissus group, the double and single late tulips, and the Greigii, Rembrant, fringed, lily, and parrot flower tulips. However, unless the garden is extremely large, small groups of hyacinths do not combine well with narcissi or tulips.

For a small garden area, single red-purple hyacinths can be grouped with *Trillium sessile* or, for a more sunny effect, primrose yellow hyacinths. 'City of Haarlem' may be grouped with *T. s.* 'Luteum'. These two groupings combine the beautiful flowering cones of both hyacinths and trilliums, while the mottling of the trillium foliage is echoed in the light reflections of the hyacinth flower.

Hyacinths complement shrubbery. For zones 2–9 *Syringa vulgaris x hyacinthiflora* 'Maiden's Blush', a wonderful new lilac cultivar from Manitoba, Canada, with pink hyacinth like flowers, combines with the super fragrant double pink hyacinth 'Chestnut Flower' and 'Madame Haubensak', both excellent late blooming hyacinths.

For zones 5–8, the intensely fragrant *Viburnum farreri,* pink and white flowering, or the 'Album' cultivar can be used as a fragrance screen with 'L'innocence', a white hyacinth, and 'Violet Pearl', a pink-lilac hyacinth cultivar. These hyacinths completely complement the viburnum flowers both in color and their unbelievable fragrance.

For zones 8–9, the California lilac *Ceanothus impressus* 'A. T. Johnson' can have a massing of the late flowering 'Blue Giant' hyacinth. Both this lilac and the hyacinth have similar cultural requirements.

Hyacinth Cultivars

NAME	COLOR	FLOWERING TIME
'Roman Hyacinth'	white, blue, pink	VE
'Bismark'	blue	VE
'L'Innocence'	white	E
'Jan Bos'	rose	E
'Anne Marie'	pink	E
'Madame Sophie'	white	E
'Carnegie'	white	M
'Violet Pearl'	lilac	M
'Pink Pearl'	pink	M
'Oska'	purple	M
'Hollyhock'	pink	M
'Amethyst'	violet	L
'Distinction'	red purple	L
'Queen of Pinks'	pink	L
'Blue Giant'	blue	L
'City of Haarlem'	yellow	L
'Chestnut Flower'	pink	L
'Mme Haubensak'	pink	L

❦ *Hyacinthoides hispanica, Scilla hispanica,* or *Endymion hispanicus* are the Spanish bluebell of European woods. These delightfully fragrant bluebells are found in open woods, in great numbers in May. The flowers are very much like an open hyacinth but are taller 18" (45 cm) and the foliage is graceful. The bell-shaped flowers are blue, pink, and white, on sturdy stems, one stem per bulb. The flowers remain in bloom for three to four weeks. The fragrance is sweeter than that of hyacinths, the blue flowers being the most fragrant.

The native English bluebell *H. non-scriptus* (*Scilla nutans* or *Endymion non-scriptus*) is similar to the Spanish bluebell but the flowering stems arch gracefully as does the foliage. Both English and Spanish blue bells are magnificent plants for use in a shade garden. Unfortunately, the bulbs are not very hardy. Spanish bluebells are hardy from zones 5–9 and English bluebells are hardy from zones 6–9.

Hyacinthoides (Scilla)
BLUEBELLS
Liliaceae
Zones 5–9

Ecofunction
Bluebells produce both pollen and nectar. The latter is obtained from the side of the flower at the base. These plants are also a source of natural gum once used as a glue.

Organic Care
Bluebells prefer a well-drained, acidic soil which is moisture retentative. The addition of peat moss is ideal, as it ensures sufficient moisture during the growing time for the flower embryo to develop for the following year.

Design
Bluebells flower in May. Spanish bluebells flower with hyacinths, narcissus, and the single, double, triumph, and Darwin hybrid tulips. The English bluebells flower ten days later and flower with the double, greigii, Darwin, lily-flowered, and parrot tulips, as well as with the butterfly narcissus, the red *Dicentra eximia* 'Adrian Bloom'. The white 24" (60 cm) *Dicentra spectabilis* 'Alba' mixed with hostas are also exquisite with bluebells.

Hyacinthoides Species and Cultivars

NAME	COLOR	HEIGHT	MONTH	ZONE
H. hispanica 'Donau'	blue	18" (45 cm)	May	5-9
H. h. ' Excelsior'	violet	18" (45 cm)	May	5-9
H. h. 'Queen of the Pinks'	pink	18" (45 cm)	May	5-9
H. h. 'White City'	white	18" (45 cm)	May	5-9
H. non-scriptus	blue	18" (45 cm)	May	6-9

Ipheion
(syn. *Brodiaea uniflora*,
***Tritellia uniflora*)**
SPRING STARFLOWER
Amaryllidaceae
Zones 6–9

This bulb flowers in late spring. The bulb is hardy from zones 6–9. The solitary, large flowers are blue, violet, or white and have a mild, soapy fragrance. The strap-like foliage smells strongly of onion when crushed. The flower is 6–8" (15–20 cm) tall and goes completely dormant after flowering.

Ecofunction
The unusual alkaloids which are present in this family should be investigated chemically as the plant has a protective function in the garden against sucking insects.

Organic Care
Spring starflowers like a well-drained, good garden soil rich in potash, with full sun or light shade. The bulb needs dry conditions in late summer to cure, which also makes it an ideal bulb for rock gardens.

Design
These flowers make a nice succession flowering after scillas and chionodoxas. Ipheion is also useful for massing between shrubs and trees. *Ipheion uniflorum* 'Wisely Blue', with its silvery-blue coloring, is grown in many estate gardens in England. It can be used as an under planting in a sunny location for later flowering shrubs in warmer gardening zones.

Ipheion Species and Cultivars

NAME	COLOR	HEIGHT	MONTH	ZONE
I. uniflorum 'Froyle Mill'	violet	8" (20 cm)	March-April	6-9
I. uniflorum 'Wisley Blue'	pale blue	12" (30 cm)	March-April	6-9
I. uniflorum 'Alba'	white	12" (30 cm)	March-April	6-9

❧ Ixiolirion is also known as the Tartar lily. It is a late spring flowering bulb which produces 12–18" (30–45 cm), extremely long lasting, blue flowers which are hardy from zones 2–9.

Organic Care

Ixiolirion prefer a medium fertile, well-drained garden loam and full sun conditions. It requires a hot dry period in summer.

Design

This bulb is native of Asia Minor to Central Siberia. It is a useful bulb for massing in a city or suburban garden combined with shrubbery in a small area.

Ixiolirion
TARTAR LILY
Amaryllidaceae
Zones 2–9

Ixiolirion tartaricum is a dainty flower of spring.

Ixiolirion Specie

NAME	COLOR	HEIGHT	MONTH	ZONE
I. tartaricum (I. pallasii)	blue	12-18" (30-45 cm)	May-June	2-9

❧ Lilies are a huge group of flowering bulbs that lend great dignity and majesty to a border. Lilies can be grown in every gardening zone in Canada. There are magnificent native Canadian and North American lily species. Some have been crossed with lilies from other regions of the world to give a new challenge to Canadian gardeners. The early spring run off, hot mid-summer temperatures, and high solar exposures of the Canadian climate make the Canadian garden a far superior garden for growing lilies than her European and southern North American counterparts. These hybrids are hardier, more beautiful, and, in some instances, more disease resistant than the old lilies. They are divided into the following groups:

a) The Asiatic hybrid lilies which flower in June and July. The flowers face either upwards, outwards, or downwards. Tigerlilies *L. tigrinum* (syn. *L. lancifolium*) are in this group, zones 2–9;

b) The martagon lily hybrids (paisley hybrids), zones 2–9;

c) The madonna lily hybrids (the Cascade hybrids), zones 5–9;

d) The American lily hybrids (Bellingham hybrids and the Columbia-platte hybrids), zones 2–9. *Lilium canadense, L. humboldtii, L. pardalinum, L. parryi, L. philadelphicum* and *L. superbum, L. columbianum, L. michiganense,* and *L. washingtonianum* are some of the parents, zones 2–9;

e) The Easter lily (*L. longiflorum*), its hybrids, and *L. formosanum,* zones 7–9;

Lilium
LILY
Liliaceae
Zones 2–9

The oriental hybrid lily, *L.* 'Rose Elegance' follows the Trumpet with wonderful fragrance and vigor.

f) The Trumpet hybrids from the disease resistant *L. henryi,* including the Aurelian and Olympic hybrids. These lilies are fragrant and are the largest 5–7' (1.5–2.1 m) of the hybrid lilies, zones 2–9;

g) The Oriental hybrid lilies, the most useful in Canadian gardens as they are late flowering (August) and fragrant. The oriental parents are *Lilium auratum, L. japonicum, L. rubellum,* and *L. speciosum* crossed with *L. henryi,* zones 2–9;

h) The specie lily group. There are eighty or so lilies in this group of varying degrees of hardiness, most of which can be grown in the northern temperate garden.

Lilium regale 'Album' soaring above its blue-mauve flowering companion *Delphinium elatum* 'Guinevere'.

Ecofunction

Of the huge monocotyledon family group of plants, the lily family, which is part of it, is the most toxic. Many of the toxic compounds are known to be naturally occurring chemotherapeutic agents. These are chemicals used in the treatment and management of cancers, such as the now well-known story of the anti-tumor agent found in the rosey periwinkle (*Catharanthus roseus*). The alkaloid component reaches its maximum before and with flowering of these fragrant species.

The lily is a lepidopteroid flower. Night flying moths visit the flower for nectar.

Organic Care

The old fashioned *L. tigrinum* (syn. *L. lancifolium*) of the North American pioneer gardens and its hybrid forms should never be planted with other lily hybrids and specie lilies because this lily can carry a lily virus which could seriously damage other lily plantings, even though this lily would not show any viral infestation itself. It is a viral carrier plant and as such should be isolated 20–30' (8–10 m) from other species of lilies.

Alliums should be planted near lilies as they discourage aphids to which lilies are prone in some areas of North America. Aphids are responsible for the transfer of the lily mosaic virus. Alliums will also discourage bulb rot, rusts, and other fungal diseases to which lilies are prone in some gardening areas. Dusting the early spring ground around lilies with wood ashes as a fungicide for fungal spores is an excellent preventative garden practice.

All lilies like a rich, deeply drained garden soil. Drainage should be excellent in summer and winter as standing water will kill lilies. To aid drainage in questionable areas, sand can be used as infill before the bulbs are planted. The soil should be enriched with liberal quantities of bone meal, one year old, well-rotted manure, a small amount of dolomitic limestone (depending on the species), and wood ashes to a depth of 1.5' (45 cm). If acidic soil is needed, peat moss may be added, as in the case for *L. parryi* hybrids, oriental hybrids, and *L. duchartrei*. The Martagon lily and its hybrids *L. regale, L. pyrenaicum* and the Madonna lily and its hybrids require an alkaline soil. More promising results are obtained with these lilies if the soil is slowly made more alkaline a year in advance of planting. The Asiatic hybrids (a), the American hybrids (d), and the trumpet hybrids, except *L. regale*, prefer a neutral to very slightly alkaline soil. The majority of the specie lilies like a neutral soil, except for *L. henryii* which grows better in alkaline soil. *L. pardalinum giganteum,* unlike most lilies, will perform well in a clay soil. *L. auratum platyphyllum* prefers an acidic soil.

Planting depth for lilies varies for the groups: (a) the Asiatic hybrids 4–5" (10–12 cm) deep; (b) the Martagon hybrids 5–6" (12–15 cm) deep; (c) the Madonna lily and hybrids 2" (5 cm) deep in August; (d) the American lily hybrids 5–6" (12–15 cm) deep; (e) the Easter lilies 6" (15 cm) deep; (f) the trumpet hybrids 7–8" (17–20 cm) deep; (g) the oriental lilies 4–5" (10–12 cm) deep; and (h) the specie lilies should be planted twice the height of the bulb in depth, except for *L. concolor puchellum* at 3" (8 cm).

An old favorite, the Trumpet hybrid lily *Lilium* 'Golden Splendor' multiplies rapidly.

All lilies are particularly susceptible to late spring frosts. This problem is accentuated in zones 2–4 where early, warm day time temperatures tend to force commencement of bulb growth and subsequent hard frosts of 14°F (-10°C) and colder injure elongating shoots. Gardeners should be prepared to provide frost protection at short notice when cold weather threatens.

Lily bulbs do not have a heavy, protective exterior coat as do the alliums or narcissi. Therefore, it is essential that exposure of the bulbs be minimized. The lilies should be planted as soon after lifting or purchase as possible. New beds should be prepared well in advance of the fall planting. Prior to planting, the bulbs should be quickly and very gently shaken in a bag of wood ashes. This will kill off any migrating fungal spores and the mild sodium hydroxide solution produced by contact with the planting soil will act as a fungal shield for the growing bulb. A summer and winter mulch will considerably increase quality of flowering.

Design

L. longiflorum, 3–6' (1–2 m), can be grown in the June garden. These bulbs are usually forced for the Easter trade. *L. l. eximium* is the well known Easter lily. These bulbs are tender and can be grown in zones 7–9. They are intensely fragrant and beautifully formed with elongated flaring flowers 5–8" (12–20 cm) long with maroon striping on the outside of the trumpets. A particularly beautiful cultivar of this lily is 'Insulare'. The flower is at right angles to the flowering stalk. 'Praecox' is a more floriferous version of 'Insulare'. *L. formosanum* with its 8" (20 cm) long flower corollas from the Philippines is in this group. It is extremely easy to grow from seed. The August flowering strain should be grown from zones 6–7 and the October flowering strain can be used in zones 8–9. For gardeners in zone 9, *L. formosanum giganteum,* (syn. *Cardiocrinum giganteum*), 6–12' (1.8–3.6 m), which grows in rich acid soil, requires partial shade, flowers in June, with white elongated trumpets with delicate violet throat markings, is a stunningly marvelous beauty to behold. The cultivar 'Yunnanense' is slightly shorter, a little hardier, and could be grown in zone 8 with some winter protection.

In June, hybrid cultivars of the lilium species come into their own. The Asiatic hybrid lilies (a) can be grown in gardening zones 2–9. These lilies are extremely colorful and floriferous. Some species reach a height of 4–5' (1.2–1.5 m). The old favorite 'Enchantment', 36" (90 cm), with its large cup-shaped nasturtium-orange flowers, is a fine companion to *Campanula glowerata,* as is 'Connecticut King', a brilliant yellow cultivar, 3–4' (1–1.2 m). For softer color combinations, 'Unique' at 3' (90 cm) with pink and white blooms is very useful. In late June some of the American lily hybrids (d) begin flowering. These hybrids are especially disease resistant. 'Butterflies', 4' (1.2 m), is a mildly fragrant, dainty cultivar of *L. pumilum* and has beautiful small white wax-like flowers. 'Flander's Field' and 'Isaac Watts' are both red cultivars, remaining in bloom until the end of July. The Bellingham hybrids developed from Western natives, in pink, orange, and yellow nodding bells are particularly well adapted to shade, though they will grow in full sun. These lilies are particularly suitable for the prairies and eastern Canada. *L. parryi*, the lemon lily, 6' (1.8 m), is also adaptable to half-shade and is suitable for eastern gardens.

There are a large number of specie lilies flowering at the end of June and into July. *L. amabile* is a hardy, 2–3' (60–90 cm) lily with waxy orange nodding reflexed flowers, preferring full sun. *L. concolor pulchellum,* 3' (90 cm), is a fine starry orange-red lily from Manchuria, as is *L. cernuum,* 3' (90 cm), with purple-pink, nodding fragrant flowers. *L. monadelphum,* 5' (1.5 m), a Caucasian mountain lily, has

Lilium 'Thunderbolt' reflected against the blue-black flowers of *Delphinium elatum* 'King Arthur' with copper-colored diploid *Hemerocallis* in the foreground.

large fragrant, yellow, nodding bell-shaped flowers. *L. hansonii*, healthy and mouse proof, grows 4–5' (1.2–1.5 m) and has nodding waxy yellow-orange flowers. This Korean native can also grow in half shade. *L. tsing-tauense*, 3' (90 cm), with orange flowers and strangely whorled foliage, is acid-loving and can be used with rhododendrons, as can *L. parryi*, 5–6' (1.5–1.8 m), a North American native lemon lily (d) whose flowers are a beautiful luminescent yellow. Magnificent with *Campanula lactiflora* 'Alba' or *C. lactiflora* 'Loddon Anna' pink, *Lilium mackliniae*, 5' (1.5 m), zones 4–9, has white with pale pink flushing inside huge campanula-like nodding flowers. The natural hybrid *L. testaceum* (*L. candidum* crossed with *L. chalcedonicum*) or Nankeen lily is one of the oldest lily hybrids. It has airy, light buff-colored flowers on 5' (1.5 m) stems. This lily hybrid is extremely frost resistant and is useful for colder gardening areas. The sulphur yellow flowers of *L. pyrenaicum,* 2–4' (.6–1.2 m), flowers in June. This also has a naturally occurring cultivar *L. p.* 'Rubrum' with beautiful waxy orange-red flowers.

The *L. canadense* (syn *L. superbum*), 5' (1.5 m), with its orange to yellow fragrant, spotted trumpet flowers has a red cultivar 'Editorum' and a yellow cultivar 'Flavum'. Both cultivars flower in June. Similar and also June flowering is *L. michiganense*, 5' (1.5 m), but with darker spots. A smaller lily, *L. philadelphicum*, the wood lily, 2–3' (60–90 cm), also has orange-red flowers, but these are more campanulate in form, as is *L. grayi*, 3–4' (.9–1.2 m), a red spotted moisture loving lily with a nodding flower form.

A horizontal spread of buds from the Japanese *Lilium auratum platyphyllum* blending its woodbine fragrance into the white border.

Lilies are generally associated with the July garden, and with good reason, because of the wonderful fragrance of the trumpet lilies and the nodding daintiness of the Martagon lilies. In July, some Asiatic hybrid lilies are flowering. 'Corina', 4' (1.2 m), is a fine strong, red lily, and 'Yellow Blaze', 4–5' (1.2–1.5 m), has magnificent spotted, luminescent yellow flowers. The Martagon lily and its hybrid forms are tall and airy lilies, ideal for the July garden. *L. martagon*, 3–6' (.9–1.8 m), has mauve-pink flowers with tiny dark spots. There is an 'Alba' cultivar. The Backhouse hybrid, *L. m.* 'J.S. Dijt', is more cream colored, and *L. m.* 'Jupiter' has beige flowers with maroon spots.

The fragrance of the trumpet lilies is spell-binding in July. The various shades of pinks to deep rose of *L.* 'Pink Perfection', 5–6' (1.5–1.8 m), of the Olympic hybrid strain, the chaste, white purity of *L. regale* 'Album', 5' (1.5 m), L. 'Copper King', 5–6', (1.5–1.8 m), apricot, and *L.* 'Thunderbolt', 5–6' (1.5–1.8 m), melon, are the tallest of the trumpets and are also the most fragrant. A very useful border lily is *L.* 'Rosario', 4' (1.2 m), which blooms in mid-July, followed by *L.*

'San Souci', 4' (1.2 m), light pink, blooming a little later in the month. Both are fragrant oriental hybrids.

The American hybrids have less regal beauty than the trumpet lilies but are nonetheless handsome. *L.* 'Tiger Babies', 5' (1.6 m), bloom in mid-July and are richly colored pink with chocolate spots. They have the airyness of the martagon lilies. *L.* 'Windermere', 4' (1.3 m), is a magnificent rose-colored lily. *L.* 'Shuksan', 4–6' (1.3–2 m), with cadmium yellow flowers, is one of the finest of the Bellingham hybrids, an old strain of lilies obtained by crossing the native western American *L. pardalinum* and other native western species. These hybrids prefer dappled shade, which makes them ideal for a suburban garden. *L.* 'Harrisianum' is a huge 8' (2.4 m) hybrid obtained from *L. p. giganteum*, the Sunset lily, with red, gold, and burgundy flowers.

In July the specie lily *L. duchartrei* can grow to 7' (2.1 m). It has orange flowers spotted black with an interesting purple spotted flowering stalk.

In early August the *L. tigrinum* (*L. lancifolium*), 4' (1.2 m), bloom. There are many cultivars of the well-known Canadian tiger lily such as *L. t.* 'Orange Tiger', orange scarlet, *L. t.* 'Yellow Star', yellow, *L. t.* 'Pink', an attractive pink flowered cultivar, and L. t. 'White', a lovely white and bronze spotted flower. There is also a double 'Flore Pleno' cultivar.

Probably the most useful lilies for the Canadian gardener are the oriental hybrid lilies. They flower in mid-August when many plants are on the wane. They bring an incredible freshness, with their strong, spicy, honeysuckle smell, into the garden. The 'Imperial Gold, Silver and Crimson' strains have been improved considerably. *L.* 'American Eagle', 4–5' (1.3–1.6 m), is an improved 'Imperial Silver' lily. It has huge crisp white flowers with lavender spots. *L.* 'Casablanca' is the best white. It has enormous white fuzzy textured flowers. *L.* 'Journey's End' is a stunningly beautiful fuchsia flower with clear white running on the petals. *L.* 'Blushing Pink' and *L.* 'Rose Elegance' are outstanding soft pink colors.

Blooming at the end of August is the magnificent, fragrant *L. auratum platyphyllum*, 4' (1.2 m), a vigorous virus-free lily, with golden rays on each petal. There is also a natural cultivar with red-ray banding, *L. a.* 'Rubro-vittatum'. Still unsurpassed for virus resistance and vigor is *L.* 'Black Beauty', flowering in late August. In August the specie lily blooms, *L. speciosum*, 4' (1.2 m), into September, the fragrant flowers being white with carmine rays. This lily lives about four to five years in a Canadian garden. *L. henryi*, 5–9' (1.5–2.7 m), sometimes called the 'yellow speciosum', is an alkaline-loving, yellow lily thriving in partial shade. This is a very hardy disease resistant lily which is not bothered by burrowing creatures.

Lily Hybrids and Specie Lilies

	NAME	COLOR	HEIGHT	MONTH	ZONE
a)	**The Asiatic Hybrids**				
	L. 'Enchantment'	yellow	3' (.9 m)	June	2-9
	L. 'Connecticut King'	yellow	3-4' (.9-1.2 m)	June	2-9
	L. 'Unique'	pink	3' (.9 m)	June	2-9
	L. 'Corina'	red	3' (.9 m)	July	2-9
	L. tigrinum, (*L. lancifolium*)		4' (1.2 m)	August	2-9
	L. t. 'Orange Tiger'	orange	4' (1.2 m)	August	2-9
	L. t. 'Yellow Star'	yellow	4' (1.2 m)	August	2-9
	L. t. 'Pink'	pink	4' (1.2 m)	August	2-9
	L. t. 'White'	white	4' (1.2 m)	August	2-9
b)	**The Martagon Hybrids**				
	L. martagon	pink	4' (1.2 m)	July	2-9
	L. m. 'Alba'	white	4' (1.2 m)	July	2-9
	L. m. 'J.S. Dijt'	yellow	4' (1.2 m)	July	2-9
	L. m. 'Jupiter'	beige	4' (1.2 m)	July	2-9
c)	**The American Hybrids**				
	L. 'Butterflies'	white	4' (1.2 m)	June	2-9
	L. 'Flanders Field'	red	3-4' (.9-1.2 m)	June	2-9
c)	**The Madonna Hybrids**				
	L. canadium 'Cascade'	white	3-4' (.9-1.2 m)	June	5-9
	L. c. 'Cernum'	white	3-4' (.9-1.2 m)	June	5-9
	L. c. 'Salonikae'	white	3-4' (.9-1.2 m)	June	5-9
d)	**The American Hybrids**				
	L. 'Isaac Watts'	red	5' (1.5 m)	June	2-9
	L. 'Tiger Babies'	peach	5' (1.5 m)	July	2-9
	L. 'Windermere'	rose	4' (1.2 m)	July	2-9
	L. 'Shuksan'	yellow	4-6' (1.2-1.8 m)	July	2-9
	L. 'Harrisanum' (*L. pardalinum giganteum*)				
		red	4' (1.2 m)		2-9
e)	**The *L. longiflorum* and *L. formosanum* Hybrids**				
	L. longiflorum 'Eximium'	white	3-6' (.9-1.8 m)	May	7-9
	L. l. 'Insulare'	white	3-6' (.9-1.8 m)	May	7-9
	L. l. 'Praecox'	white	3-6' (.9-1.8 m)	May	7-9
	L. formosanum	white	5' (1.5 m)	Aug-Oct	6-9

NAME	COLOR	HEIGHT	MONTH	ZONE
L. f. giganteum	white	6-12' (1.8-3.6 m)	June	9
L. f. giganteum 'Yunnanense'	white	6-10' (1.8-3 m)	June	8-9

f)   **The Trumpet Hybrids**

L. 'Pink Perfection'	pink	5-6' (1.5-1.8 m)	July	2-9
L. regale 'Album'	white	4-5' (1.2-1.5 m)	July	2-9
L. 'Copper King'	apricot	4-6' (1.2-1.8 m)	July	2-9
L. 'Thunderbolt'	melon	4-6' (1.2-1.8 m)	July	2-9

g)   **Oriental Hybrids**

L. 'Rosario'	pink		July	2-9
L. 'San Souci'	pink	3-4' (.9-1.2 m)	July	2-9
L. 'Casablanca'	white	3-4' (.9-1.2 m)	August	2-9
L. 'Blushing Pink'	pink	5' (1.5 m)	August	2-9
L. 'Rose Elegance'	pink	4-5' (1.2-1.5 m)	August	2-9
L. 'Journey's End'	red	4-5' (1.2-1.5 m)	August	2-9
L. auratum platyphyllum	white	4' (1.2 m)	August	2-9
L. auratum 'Rubrovittatum'	white	4' (1.2 m)	August	2-9
L. 'Black Beauty'	red, white	4-5' (1.2-1.5 m)	August	2-9

h)   **Specie Lilies**

L. concolor pulchellum	red	3-4' (.9-1.2 m)	June	2-9
L. cernum	pink	3' (.9 m)	June	2-9
L. monadelphum	yellow	5' (1.5 m)	June	2-9
L. amabile	red	3' (.9 m)	June	2-9
L. hansonii	yellow	4-5' (1.2-1.5 m)	June	2-9
L. tsingtauense	orange	3' (.9 m)	June	2-9
L. parryi	lemon	5-6' (1.5-1.8 m)	June	2-9
L. mackliniae	white	5' (1.5 m)	June	4-9
L. testaceum	white	5' (1.5 m)	June	2-9
L. pyrenaicum	yellow	2-4' (.6-1.2 m)	June	2-9
L. pyrenaicum 'Rubrum'	red	2-4' (.6-1.2 m)	June	2-9
L. canadense (L. superbum)	orange	5' (1.5 m)	June	2-9
L. c. 'Editorum'	red	5' (1.5 m)	June	2-9
L. c. 'Flavum'	yellow	5' (1.5 m)	June	2-9
L. michiganense	orange	5' (1.5 m)	June	2-9
L. philadelphicum	orange/red	2-3' (.6-.9 m)	June	2-9
L. grayi	red	3-4' (.9-1.2 m)	June	4-9
L. duchartre	red	4-5' (1.2-1.5 m)	July	2-9
L. henryii	yellow	5-10' (1.5-3 m)	August	2-9
L. speciosum	red	4-5' (1.2-1.5 m)	August	2-9

❧ *Mertensia virginica* is known as the Virginia bluebell because of its nodding bell-like flowers in clusters. *M. virginica* is hardy from zones 4–9. *M. maritima*, found on shingle beaches of North America's eastern seaboard and the British Isles, has leaves with a refreshing flavor of oysters.

Mertensia
LUNGWORT
Boraginaceae
Zones 4–9

Mertensia virginica, just about to elongate and spread its powdery scent into the airways.

Organic Care

The fibrous roots should be planted 2.5" (6 cm) deep in the fall and mulched. It likes a neutral garden soil in partial shade with a high humus content to aid flowering in April to May.

Design

The flowers are 2' (60 cm), and the buds are pink when young, turning to blue when the flower corolla elongates. Flowering in April, *M. virginica* flowers appear with both the large cup narcissi and the small cup narcissi. The slightly taller and nodding aspect of *Mertensia* makes it an ideal companion for narcissi. *Trillium sessile* and *Fritillaria uva-vulpis* make unusually rich and colorful planting companions also.

For difficult areas near the coastline, there is the later blooming *M. maritima*, 2' (60 cm), with similarly nodding, pink-turning-to-blue, bell clusters. The plant is prostrate and mat forming.

It should not be forgotten, from a design point of view, that shade loving relatives of *Mertensia* are flowering at the same time. These are the beautiful, mottled foliage perennials, *Pulmonaria saccharata* also called Lungwort, with cultivars 'Bowles Red', 'Margery Fish', pink-to-blue, and 'Sissinghurst White', which may be used with *Mertensia* in great seas of long lasting color.

Mertensia Species and Cultivars

NAME	COLOR	HEIGHT	MONTH	ZONE
M. virginica	pink-blue	2' (60 cm)	April-May	4-9
M. virginica 'Rubra'	pink-rose	2' (60 cm)	April-May	4-9
M. virginica 'Alba'	white	2' (60 cm)	April-May	4-9
M. maritima	pink-blue	2' (60 cm)	July-Aug	5-9

Muscari
GRAPE HYACINTH
Liliaceae
Zones 3–9

Muscari comosum 'Plumosum', which flowers the second year after planting, is beautiful with late lilacs.

The *Muscari* bulb looks like a miniature hyacinth bulb, and the flowering spire resembles an elongated tiny hyacinth flower. These bulbs are hardy from zones 4–9 and a few species in zones 3–9. Gardeners in zone 2 should attempt to use them in a microclimatic area of their gardens. All the grape hyacinths stay in bloom for a long time. Some species are in flower at the end of March or beginning of April and *M. comosum* are in flower for most of May. Except for *M. botryoides* 'Album', all the flowers are bitonal in various shades of blue with white fringing.

Ecofunction

All of the muscari species are good sources of pollen and nectar for honeybees and other small beneficial insects.

The bulb of *M. comosum* yields chemotherapeutic drugs.

Organic Care

Although the bulbs prefer a well-drained, moderately rich garden soil in full sun, they will also do remarkably well in poor soils. The foliage should be allowed to die down in all species after flowering.

Design

The bulbs, if left alone, will form thick carpets which are useful for borders or rockeries or combination planting with mid-season short daffodils cyclamineus group narcissus, e.g., *N.* 'Jack Stripe', or early specie tulip such as the *T. tarda. M. azureum,* 4–6" (10–15 cm), has florets in two shades of blue and combines well with the Dutch crocii in late March and early April. The multi-stemmed *M. tubergenianum,* 12" (30 cm), and the various cultivars of *M. armeniacum,* which are larger, 6–8" (15–20 cm), bloom with early tulips. One cultivar, *M. armeniacum* 'Cantab', is delightfully fragrant and is a later bloomer than the other cultivars of *M. armeniacum.*

M. ambrosiacum (syn. *M. racemosum*), 6" (15 cm), the musk scented, lilac-colored grape hyacinth, can be used with the taller 12" (30 cm) *M. latifolium,* and combined with the cyclamineus *Narcissi* 'Dove Wings' or 'Jenny' cultivars.

M. botryoides, 8" (20 cm), the smaller *M. botryoides* 'Album', 6" (15 cm), combines well with the Kaufmanianna tulips, 6–8" (15–20 cm), or the candy striped *Tulipa clusiana,* 14" (35 cm), a delightful species tulip.

The violet-purple florets of *M. comosum* and its cultivar

'Plumosum', 12" (30 cm), combine well with many groupings in the May garden, such as the late *Leucojum aestivum* 'Gravetye Giant', *Fritillaria pontica, Camassias,* or lily-flowering tulips. Little known are the small May flowering 4" (10 cm) tall blue-black *M. commutatum,* zones 5–9, and the tall, 12" (50 cm), *M. neglectum,* zones 7–9, with its most unusual blue-black spire capped with light blue and a tiny rimming of white on the flowers.

Muscari Species and Cultivars

NAME	COLOR	HEIGHT	MONTH	ZONE
M. azureum	blue	4-6" (10-15 cm)	April	3-9
M. armeniacum 'Early Giant'	blue	6-8" (15-20 cm)	April	3-9
M. a. 'Blue Spike'	blue	6" (15 cm)	April	3-9
M. a. 'Cantab'	blue	6" (F) (15 cm)	April	3-9
M. a. 'Saphir'	blue	6" (15 cm)	April	3-9
M. tubergenianum	blue	12" (30 cm)	April-May	4-9
M. ambrosianum	blue	6" (15 cm)	April	4-9
M. latifolium	blue	12" (30 cm)	April	4-9
M. botryoides	blue	12" (30 cm)	April-May	3-9
M. botryoides 'Album'	white	8" (20 cm)	April-May	3-9
M. comosum	purple	8-12" (20-30 cm)	May-June	4-9
M. comosum 'Plumosum'	violet	12" (30 cm)	May-June	4-9
M. commutatum	blue-black	4" (10 cm)	April	5-9
M. neglectum	blue-black	12" (30 cm)	May-June	7-9

Narcissus
DAFFODIL AND
NARCISSUS
Amaryllidaceae
Zones 3–9

Narcissus is the Latin name given to the group of bulbs known commonly as the daffodils and narcissi. Narcissi are extremely hardy spring flowering bulbs. They have been grown, loved, and admired by gardeners for many centuries. The present day modern hybrids number in the hundreds. The flowers are yellow, white, orange, red, and green. Some are more fragrant than others. A new and exciting pink color has been bred into narcissi strains, giving modern hybrids a remarkable beauty which is a far cry from its dainty humble ancestor the *Narcissus bulbocodium*, the hoop petticoat daffodil.

The flowers of narcissi have a cup and saucer form. The new hybrid species have a large number of variations of cups and saucers. The description of these variations is called the flower's morphology. Based on this morphology, narcissi are classified into twelve divisions. Knowledge of these divisions, flower timing, and other growth characteristics is essential for the gardener's successful use of narcissi within a north temperate garden.

Narcissus 'King Alfred'.

The cup part of the narcissi flower is called the corona and the saucer part is called the perianth, which is a flare of sepals and petals surrounding the corona. Based on variations of the perianth and corona, the hybrid narcissi have been classified by the Royal Horticultural Society, London, England, 1989, into twelve main divisions, which are described as follows in the "Internatonal Daffodil Checklist," compiled by Sally Kingston:

Division I: Trumpet Daffodils
    One flower to one stem, the corona (trumpet) as long as or longer than the perianth (petals).

Division II: Large Cupped Daffodils
    One flower to one stem, the corona (cup) more than one third, but less than equal to the length of the perianth segments (petals).

Division III: Small Cupped Daffodils
    One flower to a stem, corona (cup) not more than one-third the length of the perianth segments (petals).

Division IV: Double Daffodils

One or more flowers to a stem, with doubling of the perianth segments or the corona or both.

Division V: Triandrus Daffodils

Characteristics of *N. triandrus* clearly evident, usually two or more pendent flowers to a stem, perianth segments reflexed.

Division VI: Cyclamineus Daffodils

Characteristics of *N. cyclamineus* clearly evident, usually one flower to a stem, perianth segments reflexed, flower at an acute angle to the stem, with a very short pedicel (neck).

Division VII: Jonquilla Daffodils

Characteristics of the *N. jonquilla* group clearly evident, usually one to three flowers to a rounded stem, leaves narrow and dark green, perianth segments spreading not reflexed, flowers fragrant.

Narcissus 'Articole' is a rare salmon pink double narcissus which is late flowering.

Division VIII: Tazetta Daffodils

Characteristics of the *N. tazetta* group clearly evident, usually three to twenty flowers to a stout stem, leaves broad, perianth segments spreading and not reflexed, flowers fragrant.

Division IX: Poeticus Daffodils

Characteristics of the *N. poeticus* group without admixture of any other, usually one flower to a stem, perianth segments pure white, corona usually disk-shaped with a green or yellow center and a red rim, flowers fragrant

Division X: Species, wild variants and wild hybrids

All species and wild or reputedly wild variants and hybrids, including those with double flowers.

Division XI: Split-Corona Daffodils

Corona split rather than lobed and usually for more than half its length.

Division XII: Miscellaneous Daffodils

All daffodils not falling into any one of the foregoing divisions.

Ecofunction

Narcissi supply early fresh pollen and nectar for honeybees, bumblebees, and many of the early Lepidoptera species. Honeybees bore a hole at the base of the corona to get to the nectar source which collects at the base of the flower tube. Hummingbirds, in turn, also make use of this entry mode.

Organic Care

Narcissi like a well-drained, rich loamy or sandy garden soil. The soil should be enriched with well-aged manure which should be at least one year old, if possible, bone meal, wood ashes, and a small amount

'King Arthur' flowers with *N.* 'Ice Follies' for a three-week period in the spring.

of dolomitic limestone. It is important that the soils in which narcissi are planted be loose and friable to aid curing of the bulb during its summer dormancy period, prior to fall growth. This curing process is very important for narcissi because, without it, the bulb will be unhealthy, prone to disease, and will be extremely short-lived. Gardening areas with a heavy clay soil should not consider growing this bulb until they have amended the soil with coarse sand. Usually, an equal volume of sand added to a given volume of enriched clay soil should open the soil and provide the desired friability.

Narcissi like full sun to half shade. If there is too much shade, the flowering will decline over a number of years to a non-flowering state.

Narcissi will grow to form large flowering clumps in four to five years. The clumps will require division approximately every eight years when flowering declines.

It is important to let the foliage of all the narcissi die back naturally. The food manufactured by the leaves is needed for the following year's bulb. When the leaves have faded and turned brown to half their length, they can be plaited and twisted out of sight.

If narcissi bulbs are naturalized in a grassy area, the lawn around them should not be cut until the foliage of the narcissi has turned brown.

Gardens in zones 2–4 will occasionally have late spring frosts. The flowers will be damaged by temperatures of -10°C to -15°C (14°–3°F). The stems will become frozen about 2" (5 cm) behind the flower-head and the flowers will flop over. However, the foliage will not show damage and will produce successful bulbs for the following year.

The large narcissi bulbs — the trumpet daffodils (Division I), the large cupped daffodils (Division II), the small cupped daffodils (Division III), the double daffodils (Division IV), and the split-corona daffodils (Division XI) — should be planted twice their height in depth. This will be about 5" (12 cm) above the bulb neck. Narcissi bulbs of the triandrus (Division V), the tazetta (Division VIII), and the poeticus (Division IX) daffodils should be planted 3.5"–4" (8–10 cm) above the neck of the bulb. For zones 2–5 this planting depth appears to be very important in the tazetta (Division VIII) group, as planting too deeply will eliminate flowering and not planting deep enough will cause cold injury to the flower embryo of the bulb. Narcissi bulbs of the cyclamineus group (Division VI) and the jonquilla group (Division VII) should be planted 3" (7 cm) above the neck of the bulb. The specie, wild variants and wild hybrid daffodils (Division X), should be planted 5" (12 cm) above the bulb neck for large bulbs and 3" (7 cm) above the bulb neck for smaller bulbs. The miscellaneous bulbs (Division XII) should be treated similarly to the specie group (Division X).

Narcissi bulbs should be planted in late August or early September to give the bulbs an opportunity to grow a good root system which is necessary for winter anchorage and early, rapid growth in the spring.

The split corona or butterfly narcissi are proving to be as hardy as they are healthy in colder gardening zones. *Narcissus* 'Colblanc' succeeds *Narcissus* 'Ice Follies' in a white border.

Design

Many gardeners like naturalized narcissi. Handfulls of bulbs are thrown onto a lawn area and where they land, they are planted. There are some mixtures of narcissi that are particularly good for naturalization in northern gardens, such as the trumpet narcissi (Division I), the large cupped narcissi (Division III), and the split-corona narcissi (Division XI). These narcissi are extremely large and will compete well with grass. Their foliage will die back rapidly in early summer, except for the split-corona narcissi group (Division XI), which is a later flowering group and is particularly useful in the prairie provinces or states. When planning to use bulbs for naturalizing, it should be taken into account that part of a lawn area will be uncut until the narcissi foliage has faded.

With careful planning, a flowering succession of six to eight weeks can be obtained using a mixture of early, mid-season, and late flowering narcissi in the garden. For ease of reference, the full flowering succession will be discussed. Decisions can then be made by the gardener as to which period of succession may be most useful to the gardening plan.

For zones 4, 5 and 6, April heralds some wild narcissi species, one of which is *Narcissus bulbocodium vernum,* 6–10" (15–25 cm), followed by the large trumpet narcissus group (Division I). These are the taller of the narcissi with the largest flowers and remain in flower for up to three weeks if the days are cool. Next comes the large-cupped narcissus group (Division II), followed closely by the smaller cyclamineus narcissi (Division VI), the small-cup narcissi (Division III), and the split-corona narcissi (Division XI). These narcissi have an extremely long period of bloom, from May into the beginning of June, and coincide with all May flowering plants. Flowering with them are the jonquilla narcissi (Division VII) with some of the wild hybrids group (Division X). In the middle of May, the double narcissi (Division IV) are in bloom, followed closely by the tazetta narcissi (Division VII), the poeticus narcissi (Division IX), and the triandrus narcissi (Division V). Flowering with these groups at the end of May into the beginning of June are some species of Division X, notably *N. juncifolius,* 4" (10 cm). The second week of June is generally the timing of the last of the narcissi spring flowers.

Narcissus 'Flower Drift' is a true double narcissus which is hardy, fragrant, and late flowering.

Spring in zones 7, 8 and 9 is heralded by the early blooming hardy miniature trumpet *Narcissus asturiensis minumus,* 5" (12 cm), in February or March. The following sequence of all the other narcissi groups is more spread out in the months of spring. Gardeners in zones 8–9 can enjoy a number of fall blooming narcissi of Division X, *N. viridiflorus* being the finest specie.

The first significant narcissi to use for garden design are the trumpet narcissi (Division I). These are the well-known trumpet daffodils with their large flowers, 20" (50 cm) tall, forming large clumps. *N.* 'King Alfred' and its white counterpart, *N.* 'Mount Hood', are still difficult to surpass for frost hardiness and freedom from disease. These narcissi flower with *Fritillaria imperialis* 'Lutea Maxima', and the three combine to make a backbone spring border to which *Tulipa fosteriana, kaufmanniana,* or *tarda* can be added in the forefront of the groupings.

A bulbous spring border should be superimposed on to and become part of an herbaceous perennial border for greater seasonal interest.

The large cupped narcissi (Division II) 'Ice Follies', 'Mrs. R. O. Backhouse', 'White Plume', or 'Peaches and Cream' can be used as a pink and white background for 'Jack Snipe' and 'Peeping Tom' and the extremely fragrant 'Baby Moon', a diminutive 6" (15 cm) daffodil mixed with *Muscari botryoides* 'Album', 6" (15 cm).

Next, the small cupped narcissi (Division III) is in bloom with the single hyacinths. Particularly attractive with them is the award-winning *Narcissus* 'Birma'. Blooming at approximately the same time is the split-corona group (Division XI). These are strikingly beautiful narcissi having a superb flower.

In the middle of May, the small and tiny miniatures (Division X) come into their own. *N.* 'Minnow', 12″ (90 cm), *N. canaliculatus,* 6″ (15 cm), *N. odoros rugulosus,* 8″ (20 cm), and its double form *N. odorus rugulosus plenus,* 8″ (20 cm), are particularly worth growing for their exquisite and abundant fragrance.

Also in mid-May, the double narcissi (Division IV) flower with the double late tulips or the paeony flowering tulips. Very dependable and hardy are the species *N.* 'Irene Copeland' and *N.* 'Tahiti', the award-winning double.

Flowering from mid-May until sometime into June are the tazettas (Division VIII), the poeticus (Division IX), and the triandrus (Division V) groups. These are all extremely fragrant narcissi and any of these three groups are a fine addition to the border. They should be planted near a walkway where their fragrance can be enjoyed. Generally the last narcissus to fade is the 'Yellow Cheerfulness' of the tazetta (Division VIII) group, although in some years *N. poeticus recurvus* 'Pheasant's Eye' vies for the last place. It should be noted by gardeners in zones 2–4 that these three groups of narcissi are not very cold hardy, and if killing frosts are part of a weather pattern, then these narcissi should be planted in a microclimatic area near the house or elsewhere in the garden that is protected.

Always unexpected when the narcissus rush is over, the *N. jonquilla,* 6–12″ (15–30 cm), and the smaller *N. juncifolius,* 4″ (10 cm), with its rush-like tubular foliage, comes into flower in early to mid June. Both lime loving, these miniatures are intensely fragrant and should have a tiny nook of their own in the garden.

In the autumn gardens of zones 8–9, there is a small seven-inch, green, fall narcissus, *N. viridiflorus,* which, despite its modest flower, is intensely fragrant and well worth growing. It can be tucked into a corner to add two to three weeks of fragrance into the September garden.

Narcissi Species, Specie Hybrids, and Miniatures

DIVISION I. TRUMPET NARCISSUS. ZONES 3-9

YELLOW PERIANTH YELLOW CORONA	HEIGHT	WHITE PERIANTH WHITE CORONA	HEIGHT	BICOLOR	HEIGHT
Dutchmaster	12" (30 cm)	Mount Hood	20" (50 cm)	Bravoure	18" (45 cm)
Golden Harvest	18" (45 cm)	Beersheba	20" (50 cm)	Honeybird	18" (45 cm)
King Alfred	18" (45 cm)	Magnet	17" (42 cm)		
Royal Victory	18" (45 cm)	Spellbinder	16" (40 cm)		
Unsurpassable	24" (60 cm)	Sweet Harmony	18" (45 cm)		

DIVISION II. LARGE-CUPPED NARCISSUS. ZONES 3-9

YELLOW PERIANTH COLORED CORONA	HEIGHT	WHITE PERIANTH COLORED CORONA	HEIGHT	WHITE PERIANTH WHITE CORONA	HEIGHT	PINK PERIANTH PINK CORONA	HEIGHT
Carlton	18" (45 cm)	Duke of Windsor	16" (40 cm)	Daydream	18" (45 cm)	Louise de Coligny	18" (45 cm)
Ultimus	18" (45 cm)	Flower Record	18" (45 cm)	Ice Follies	16" (40 cm)	Mrs. R. O. Backhouse	15" (38 cm)
Armada	18" (45 cm)	Manon Lescaut	18" (45 cm)	Mount Baker	18" (45 cm)	Pink Charm	16" (40 cm)
Fortune	18" (45 cm)	Peaches & Cream	18" (45 cm)	White Plume	20" (50 cm)	Romance	18" (45 cm)
St. Patrick's Day	18" (45 cm)					Roseworthy	10" (25 cm)
						Rosy Sunrise	14" (35 cm)
						Salmon Trout	15" (38 cm)
						Salome	15" (38 cm)
						Articole	20" (50 cm)
						Mon Cheri	18" (45 cm)
						Salmon Spray	17" (42 cm)

DIVISION III. SMALL-CUPPED NARCISSUS. ZONES 4-9

YELLOW PERIANTH COLORED CORONA	HEIGHT	WHITE PERIANTH COLORED CORONA	HEIGHT	WHITE PERIANTH WHITE CORONA	HEIGHT
Birma	18" (45 cm)	Verger	16" (40 cm)	Stainless	18" (45 cm)
Barrett Browning	17" (42 cm)	Angel	17" (42 cm)	Verona	16" (40 cm)
Edward Buxton	16" (40 cm)	Carnmoon	15" (38 cm)	Portrush	16" (40 cm)
		Limerick	18" (45 cm)		

DIVISION IV. DOUBLE NARCISSUS. ZONES 4-9

YELLOW	HEIGHT	BICOLOR	HEIGHT	WHITE	HEIGHT	PINK	HEIGHT
Rip Van Winkle	12" (30 cm)	Tahiti	16" (45 cm)	Ice King	20" (40 cm)	Pink Paradise	20" (40 cm)
Dick Wilden	18" (45 cm)	Unique	24" (60 cm)	White Lion	18" (45 cm)	Petit Four	20" (40 cm)
Yellow Cheerfulness	16" (40 cm)	Flower Drift	18" (45 cm)	White Marvel	14" (35 cm)		
		Texas	18" (45 cm)	Cheerfulness	16" (40 cm)		
		Mary Copeland	18" (45 cm)				

DIVISION V. TRIANDRUS NARCISSUS. ZONES 4-9

YELLOW	HEIGHT	WHITE	HEIGHT
Hawera	8" (20 cm)	Tresamble	14" (35 cm)
Liberty Bells	14" (35 cm)	Thalia	16" (40 cm)
		Petrel	14" (35 cm)
		Shot Silk	16" (40 cm)

DIVISION VI. CYCLAMINEUS NARCISSUS. ZONES 4-9

YELLOW	HEIGHT	BICOLOR	HEIGHT
February Gold	12" (30 cm)	Dove Wings	12" (30 cm)
Peeping Tom	14" (35 cm)	February Silver	12" (30 cm)
Tête-á-Tête	8" (20 cm)	Jack Snipe	10" (25 cm)
		Jetfire	12" (30 cm)
		Jenny	16" (40 cm)

DIVISION VII. JONQUIL HYBRIDS. ZONES 5-9

YELLOW	HEIGHT	BICOLOR	HEIGHT
Baby Moon	8" (20 cm)	Hillstar	15" (38 cm)
Quail	14" (25 cm)	Susy	18" (45 cm)
Jonquilla	8" (20 cm)		

DIVISION VIII. TAZETTA NARCISSUS. ZONES 4-9

YELLOW	HEIGHT	BICOLOR	HEIGHT	WHITE	HEIGHT
Early Perfection	18" (45 cm)	Germanium	16" (40 cm)	Cheerfulness	18" (45 cm)
		Minnow	6" (15 cm)	Sir Winston Churchill	14" (35 cm)
		Avalanche	22" (55 cm)		
				Sceleg	18" (45 cm)

DIVISION IX. POETICUS NARCISSUS. ZONES 3-9

BICOLOR	HEIGHT
N. actaea	20" (50 cm)
N. poeticus recurvus (Old Pheasant's Eye)	20" (50 cm)
N. p. 'Double White' (Flor Pleno)	14" (35 cm) (late)
N. p. 'Felindre'	20" (50 cm)
N. p. 'Hellenicus'	20" (50 cm)

DIVISION X. SPECIES, WILD VARIANTS AND WILD HYBRIDS. ZONES 4-9

Narcissus asturiensis (Minimus)	3" (7 cm)
N. bulbocodium 'Conspicuus'	6" (15 cm)
N. jonquilla	12" (30 cm)
N. jonquilla 'Rip Van Winkle' (old)	12" (30 cm)
N. juncifolius	4" (10 cm)
N. lobularis	8" (20 cm)
N. odorious rugulosus	8" (20 cm)
N. odorous rugulosus plenus	8" (20 cm)
N. viridiflorus	7" (18 cm)

DIVISION XI. SPLIT-CORONA NARCISSUS. ZONES 2-9

YELLOW PERIANTH COLORED CORONA	HEIGHT	WHITE PERIANTH COLORED CORONA	HEIGHT	WHITE PERIANTH WHITE CORONA	HEIGHT
Vivarino	18" (45 cm)	Cassata	17" (37 cm)	Papillon Blanc	16" (40 cm)
Tri Tomba	19" (47 cm)	Broadway Star	14" (35 cm)	Colblanc	16" (40 cm)
		Chanterelle	14" (35 cm)		
		Canasta	14" (35 cm)		
		Dolly Mollinger	18" (45 cm)		
		Marie José	12" (30 cm)		
		Parisienne	16" (40 cm)		
		Hoodsport	18" (45 cm)		
		Lemon Beauty	18" (45 cm)		
		Love Call	18" (45 cm)		
		Pick Up	16" (40 cm)		
		Tricolet	16" (40 cm)		

DIVISION XII. MISCELLANEOUS NARCISSUS

Naracissi in this group are not readily available from commercial plantsmen and therefore are not treated in this table.

❧ Nectaroscordums are closely related to the alliums and are some-times classified with them. The onion-like bulbs have a strong leek-like odor when injured. These bulbs produce sulphur proteins that have a fungicidal action. They are therefore protective bulbs, as are the alliums, and are highly desirable in a garden. Nectaroscordums, unfortunately, are only hardy from zones 6–9.

Nectaroscordum
NECTAROSCORDUM
Amaryllidaceae
Zones 6–9

Organic Care

Nectaroscordums like a sandy, damp, well-drained soil. The soil should be enriched with peat moss to acidify it slightly and to increase the water holding capacity. Phosphate and potassium in the form of bone meal and wood ashes should be used. Although they can grow in full sun, they prefer half shade. The bulbs should be planted twice their height in depth.

Design

Nectaroscordums are an ideal addition to a shade garden. The flowers of both species *N. siculum* and *N. bulgaricum* are white, pink, and green. *N. siculum* has a deeper rose color on the outside of the nod-ding bell-like flowers than *N. bulgaricum*. Both can grow in ideal condi-tions to 4' (1.2 m) They can be used as a background planting for the beautiful, fragrant *Arisaema candidissimum* whose spathe is remark-ably similar to the flowers of *N. bulgaricum*.

Nectaroscordum Species

NAME	COLOR	HEIGHT	MONTH	ZONE
N. bulgaricum	white-pink	3-4' (90-120 cm)	May-June	6-9
N. siculum	red-white	3-4' (90-120 cm)	May-June	6-9

❧ There are a number of species of ornithogalums which grow well in Canada and northern Europe. For the most part these bulbs are far hardier than is generally recognized by the gardening community. All of the species have bell-shaped green and white flowers, some species having attractively striped foliage which disappears by mid-summer.

Ornithogalum
ORNITHOGALUM
Liliaceae
Zones 3–9

Ecofunction

Ornithogalum species are important in the cut flower industry. The old favorite *O. umbellatum* has a cardiotonic drug which is thought by some experts to be safer than Digitalis.

Organic Care

The flowers like a moderately rich, well-drained soil, and full sun to half shade.

Design

O. balansae, zones 4–9, has an attractive, short, conical raceme of flowers, 4" (10 cm), and broad, plain leaves. This bulb, planted from 2–3" (5–8 cm) deep, flowers in April. Next to flower is *O. nutans*, zones 6–9, at the end of April and beginning of May. The flower is an open raceme with large, nodding bells, 12–14" (30–35 cm) tall. The leaves are very narrow with a silver mid-rib. *O. umbellatum*, 6–12" (15–30 cm), is also known as the Star of Bethlehem and was a favorite bulb of the early North American settlers. The flowers have green and white umbel-like clusters (corymbs) and fine silver and green foliage. This bulb is hardy from zones 3–9 and quite possibly in zone 2, flowering in mid-May. Both flower and foliage disappear remarkably rapidly after flowering. *O. nutans* and *O. umbellatum* make fine additions to a variegated foliage grouping.

Ornithogalum Species

NAME	COLOR	HEIGHT	MONTH	ZONE
O. balansae	white and green	4" (10 cm)	April	4-9
O. nutans	white and green	12-14" (30-35 cm)	April-May	6-9
O. umbellatum	white and green	6-12" (15-30 cm)	May	3-9

Pulsatilla
PASQUE-FLOWER,
PULSATILLA
Ranunculaceae
Zones 2–9

Pulsatillas are closely related to the anemones and are sometimes classified with them. Pulsatilla species occur throughout the northern hemisphere in the mountainous regions of Canada, Europe, Siberia, China, and Japan.

Ecofunction

Pulsatillas are a useful form of early pollen for honey bees and all the flying beneficial insects. The honeybee also mines the sap from the base of the flower.

All across the Northern biosphere wherever these plants occur, they have a strong and ancient medicinal history. Important pain-killers and nerve regenerative compounds are found in these plants.

P. occidentalis should be analysed chemically. All parts of pulsatilla species are poisonous when fresh and are even more so when dried.

Organic Care

Pulsatillas like a moderately rich, sandy, alkaline soil. The soil should be extremely well-drained, both in summer and winter. Pulsatillas like full sun.

Design

Pulsatilla patens (*Anemone patens*), zones 2–9, is also known as the Pasque flower, and is a handsome native of the dry prairies. It has a rhizomous root and varies in height from 8–10" (20–25 cm). When the flower emerges first in April, the whole plant is covered in fine silky hair, giving it a most unusual appearance. This fine hair is also a protection against late frosts. The flowers are a beautiful deep purple, blue, or white. They are most attractive massed in a rockery or near a sunny pathway or entrance.

The European pasque-flower, *P. vulgaris* (*A. pulsatilla*), zones 2–9, is a more refined plant with many cultivars of exquisite beauty. This plant also likes dry conditions after flowering.

A native pulsatilla from the Rocky Mountains of North America, *P. occidentalis* (*A. occidentalis*), zones 2–9, should be more widely grown in northern gardens. It grows up to 2' (60 cm) tall and has white or purple and white flowers. This specie has thick vertically growing tuberous roots and should be planted in a large rock-garden.

Pulsatilla Species and Cultivars

NAME	COLOR	HEIGHT	MONTH	ZONES
P. patens 'Wolfgangiana'	violet	10" (25 cm)	April	2-9
P. vulgaris 'Alba'	white	10" (25 cm)	April-May	2-9
P. v. 'Albicyanea'	pale blue	10" (25 cm)	April-May	2-9
P. v. 'Mallenderi'	purple	10" (25 cm)	April-May	2-9
P. v. 'Rubra'	red	10" (25 cm)	April-May	2-9
P. occidentalis 'Purple-White'	white or purplish	2' (60 cm)	May-June	2-9
P. o. 'Alba'	white	2' (60 cm)	May-June	2-9

Puschkinia
PUSCHKINIA
Liliaceae
Zones 3–9

Puschkinia scilliodes, happy in a little nook in front of the yellow rockery.

Puschkinias are early spring flowering bulbs that are extremely hardy, flowering from four to six weeks. The flowers open a few days later than the chionodoxas. The flower spike is from 4–6" (10–15 cm) and the flowers are white with a pale blue stripe on the outside of the petal. The flowers are very sturdy and frost resistant.

Ecofunction
Puschkinia species are a good source of early fresh pollen. Puschkinias are protective bulbs. They should be examined for antibacterial and antifungal compounds.

Organic Care
Puschkinias like a well-drained, slightly acid, garden soil. They prefer full sun.

Design
Puschkinias flower with the large Dutch *Crocus vernus* and early narcissus. However, the puschkinia should be mass planted alone. The *P. scilloides* 'Alba' looks splendid when used as a ground cover for the pink double flowering almond, *Prunus glandulosa* 'Rosea Plena' (zones 4–9).

Puschkinia Species

NAME	COLOR	HEIGHT	MONTH	ZONE
P. scilloides (*P. libanotica*)	pale blue	6" (15 cm)	April	3-9
P. scilloides 'Alba'	white	6" (15 cm)	April	3-9

Sanguinaria
BLOODROOT
Papaveraceae
Zones 2–9

Sanguinaria canadensis is also known as bloodroot and is native to eastern North America. It flowers at the end of April. Even though the white flowers are fleeting, flowering only ten to fourteen days, they are beautiful. Their blooms are set in their attractive and unusual, lobed foliage which disappears in mid-summer.

Ecofunction
The rhizome contains a red-yellow sap which is the source of its name. This sap is poisonous, the contents of which have several uses in traditional and modern medicine. It was used to treat rheumatism and also has a strong antiarrhythmic action on the heart, but most

interestingly, it appears to have been strongly effective in the treatment of cancers about a century ago in England based on knowledge gathered from indigenous North American peoples. With modern microtechniques, *Sanguinaria canadensis* extracts could well bear a closer scrutiny in medical research. The sap was also used as a body dye by indigenous populations and as a source of fabric dye. A fine yellow-orange dye is obtained from the sap using alum as a mordant. This plant has a place in pioneer gardens for that reason.

Organic Care

The plants like half-shade conditions and moist, neutral soil high in humus. The root is a thick, fibrous, rhizomous structure which grows horizontally a little below the soil surface in mats. The roots should be planted in the fall, about 3/4" (2 cm) deep with the flowering 'eyes', 1/2" (1–2 cm) below the surface. This plant benefits from a soil mulch high in humus.

Design

There is a sterile and extremely robust cultivar, *S. canadensis* 'Flore Pleno', which looks like a tiny paeony when in flower. Within a garden, to achieve flower form repetition, one can make use of *S. canadensis* 'Flore Pleno', white double late paeony flowering tulips 'Mount Tacoma', 18" (45 cm), and white early flowering paeonies.

 There exists also a rare and much coveted 'Rosea' cultivar of *S. canadensis*.

Sanguinaria canadensis, the maiden of the Canadian forests.

Sanguinaria Species and Cultivars

NAME	COLOR	HEIGHT	MONTH	ZONE
S. canadensis	white	4-8" (10-20 cm)	April	2-9
S. canadensis 'Flore Pleno'	white	4-8" (100-20 cm)	April–May	2-9
S. canadensis 'Rosea'	pink	4-8" (10-20 cm)	April	2-9

Scilla
BLUE SQUILL
Liliaceae
Zones 3–9

Scillas or blue squills are a group of very hardy, early flowering, spring bulbs. There are a number of varieties of these bulbs available. The bulb itself is like a miniature daffodil and is extremely poisonous. The flowers are white, blue, or rose-colored bells.

 The most hardy of all the scillas are *S. siberica*, 4" (10 cm), hardy to zone 3. With microclimatic protection they would be hardy in zone 2. The cultivar 'Spring Beauty' is larger, the flower being 6" (15 cm) tall. The flower has violet streaks mixed with blue and is very attractive. A

Scilla siberica is the hardiest of all scillas, being hardy to zone 3.

little less hardy, zones 4–9, is the *S. tubergeniana* (*S. miczenkoana*), whose bell-shaped pale blue flowers are borne on two to four flower spikes per bulb.

Another very early scilla is the *S. bifolia,* blue, and its pink cultivar 'Rosea'. These 4" (10 cm) flowers are like miniature hyacinths and naturalize very readily. These scillas are hardy from zones 4–9, but, because the chromosome number is so variable on these bulbs, they should be tested in zones 2 and 3 for hardiness, and hardy cultivars should emerge in some gardens.

Ecofunction

Because scillas naturalize so readily, they are an important source of pollen and nectar, sometimes in large quantities. Both pollen and nectar production appears to be abundant in these species.

Scillas are very poisonous. They are, in fact, used as rat poisons. The active chemical ingredients are cardiotonic drugs used in the treatment of heart failure.

Organic Care

Scillas like a good, sandy, well-drained garden loam in full sun to half-shade. All scillas like a soil which is enriched with lime, except for *S. monophyllos,* which likes an acidic, peat soil.

Design

Flowering with tulips and daffodils in May are *S. monophyllos,* with a dainty blue spire of flowers 5" (13 cm) tall, and *S. pratensis* (*S. amethystina*), with less delicate blue flowers. *S. monophyllos,* zones 5–9, likes a sandy, peat soil and could be used massed with azalea and rhododendrons. *S. pratensis,* zones 4–9, likes a soil enriched with lime.

Scilla Species and Cultivars

NAME	COLOR	HEIGHT	MONTH	ZONE
S. siberica	blue	4" (15 cm)	April-May	3-9
S. siberica 'Spring Beauty'	blue	6" (15 cm)	April-May	3-9
S. siberica 'Alba'	white	4" (10 cm)	April-May	3-9
S. tubergeniana (*S. miczenkoana*)	blue	5" (13 cm)	March-April	4-9
S. bifolia	blue	4" (10 cm)	April-May	4-9
S. bifolia 'Rosea'	rose	5" (13 cm)	April-May	4-9
S. monophyllos	blue	5" (13 cm)	May	5-9
S. pratensis	blue	5" (13 cm)	May	4-9

🌿 In Canada, the deciduous woods in May are carpeted with shining trilliums. The fondness for this flower is expressed by the *Trillium grandiflorum* being the flowering emblem of Ontario. The trillium is to the Canadian as the primrose is to the English. They are heralds of spring and warmer days to come. Many of these fine, trifoliate spring flowers are widely planted in European gardens and are highly treasured there.

Trillium
**WAKE-ROBIN,
BIRTHROOT**
Liliaceae
Zones 2–9

Ecofunction

It is no coincidence that the flower that heralds the spring in Canadian maple woods in such staggering numbers was used so ubiquitously for the treatment of birth and female complaints by the indigenous peoples of North America. *T. erectum* is also known as Squawroot, this flowering species being considered to be useful in the management of uterine haemorrhage in childbirth.

All trilliums are an important source of pollen and some nectar for honeybees' brood and all the flying beneficial insects emerging at the time of flowering.

Organic Care

Trilliums thrive in semi-shaded conditions and are ideal plants for a shade garden. They will grow in full sun, but the flowers last longer if they have at least afternoon shade. While some trilliums such as *T. grandiflorum* and *T. erectum* grow in alkaline soil, the other trillium species, except *T. nivale* which likes a neutral soil, prefer an acid medium. Trilliums like a good garden soil, high in humus, which is well drained. They require high moisture levels to achieve maximum growth and flowering in May. This is supplied naturally by snow run-off and spring rains. Trilliums, in a dry spring, will be considerably smaller in both flower and foliage.

Trilliums are hardy in all northern temperate zones. The trillium root is a rhizomous root that grows horizontally, putting down a large number of fibrous feeder roots with the flower and foliage growing from one end. They should be planted 2" (5 cm) deep and the root should be placed horizontally. The plant benefits greatly from a summer mulch. Root divisions or transplanting should ideally be done a week or two after flowering. The foliage will die back naturally and will do so rapidly, making the plant difficult to locate in its dormant state.

Trillium erectum blooms in the deciduous woods at Carrigliath.

Design

The dwarf trillium *T. nivale* or snow trillium, 6" (15 cm), is the first trillium to flower. Then comes the nodding trillium group, *T. cernum*, 1.5' (45 cm), white, *T. flexipes*, 15" (38 cm), white, and *T. rivale*, 10" (29 cm), which is white with pink markings. The white flowers turn a light pink with aging. The largest of all the trilliums are the *T. grandiflorum*, 18" (45 cm) with their large white flowers and *T. erectum*, the purple trillium or stinking Benjamin, which, curiously, has a strong, foul odor. There are many mutations of these two trilliums in the wild, some of which are quite beautiful and should be investigated by plant breeders. The western equivalent is *T. ovatum*, 20" (50 cm), which has a smaller white flower and is acid loving. All of these trilliums are in flower for the month of May.

The sessile trilliums are strikingly beautiful both for their pale mottling on the foliage and the ovoid flower form. *T. sessile* or toad-shade, 12" (30 cm), has two fine cultivars, T. sessile 'Rubrum' and 'Luteum'. These cultivars are magnificent when massed together and planted with primroses. The recurving prairie trillium *T. recurvatum*, 18" (45 cm), with its sepals reflexed or drooping and its fine purple flowers, are magnificent plants for garden design because of the strong horizontal planes created by the mottled foliate with flowers appearing at right angles to them. They can be massed with the reflexed flowering cyclamineus narcissi, *N.* 'February Gold' and 'February Silver', both 12" (30 cm), for an unusual floral display. The Japanese *T. tschonoskii,* 1.5' (45 cm), with smaller, nodding, white flowers can be used in denser shaded areas.

Last to bloom is *T. undulatum*, 1.5' (45 cm), the painted trillium, with its brilliant horseshoe of scarlet at the center of the somewhat nodding flower. Occasionally this flower will last into early June and can be planted with arisaemas and particularly with the Canadian native *A. triphyllum*.

Trillium Species and Cultivars in Order of Flowering

NAME	COLOR	HEIGHT	MONTH	ZONE
T. nivale	white	6" (15 cm)	May	2-9
T. cernuum	white	1.5' (45 cm)	May	2-9
T. rivale	white	10" (25 cm)	May	2-9
T. flexipes	white	15" (38 cm)	May	2-9
T. grandiflorum	white	1.5' (45 cm)	May	2-9
T. grandiflorum 'Flore Plena'	white	1.5' (45 cm)	May	2-9
T. erectum	purple, white, yellow, or green	2' (60 cm)	May	2-9

NAME	COLOR	HEIGHT	MONTH	ZONE
T. erectum	beige	2' (60 cm)	May	2-9
T. erectum 'Albiflorum'	white	2' (60 cm)	May	2-9
T. ovatum	white	20" (50 cm)	May	3-9
T. sessile	red-purple	1' (30 cm)	May	2-9
T. s. 'Rubrum'	red	1' (30 cm)	May	2-9
T. s. 'Luteum'	yellow	1' (30 cm)	May	2-9
T. recurvatum	purple	18" (45 cm)	May	2-9
T. tschonoskii	white	18" (45 cm)	May	3-9
T. undulatum	white-red bicolor	20" (50 cm)	May	2-9

The tulip has a long history spanning into the misty past. The introduction of ornamental gardening to the Northern European garden probably came as a spin-off of the great crusades at the end of the eleventh and thirteenth centuries when European noblemen returned home a great deal wiser having intermingled with a culture considerably more ancient and sophisticated than their own. These potential gardeners were aware of an exotic garden bulb which had been given greater value than the life of any man. This bulb was a tulip. There followed, after the first planting of a tulip 'Zomerschoon' in Leiden's University Hortus Medicus in the sixteenth century, an era where fortunes were lost or gained on the balance of one tulip bulb. Thus the tulip has changed from being the exclusive garden trophy of the rich into a massive industry based in Holland where plant breeders have genetically refined the tulip into the largest and most beautiful collection of tulip hybrids the world has ever seen. Now, these hybrid tulips and their cultivars are available to everyone.

Tulipa
TULIPS
Liliaceae
Zones 2–9

Tulip 'Prins Carnaval', a Rembrant tulip, is a glory in the spring.

Tulips represent a large group of bulbs with considerable variation in flowering times, color, height, growth habits, and physical structure. The flowering times begin in early spring and finish in early June. Tulips encompass the full color range from white through to black with the exception of a true blue. Modern genetic engineering and diligent plant breeding will undoubtedly produce this color, too. The plants may be multi-stemmed or single-stemmed. They range from 2–24" (5–60 cm) in height. The differences in the morphology of the tulip flower keeps growing from finely tapered petals to delicate fringing to viral striations of great beauty. The foliage of some tulips is plain, in others, beautifully mottled. The petals of the Kaufmanniana tulips are contractile, meaning that they open and close with solar intensity. Thus they open with mid-day sun and gradually close towards evening. Movement in plants is rare but greatly increases interest and design potential within a garden.

Tulips are classified into fifteen distinct groups from "The Classified List and International Register of Tulip Names" (K.A.V.B. Hillegom, 1981), and are as follows:

The parrot tulip, *Tulipa* 'Firebird', and *Viburnum farreri* combine to make an identically tonal, fragrant composition in May.

NAME	FLOWERING TIMES
1. Single Early Tulips	Early
2. Double Early Tulips	Early
3. Triumph Tulips Chiefly the result of hybridization between single and late flowering tulips.	Mid-season
4. Darwin Hybrid Tulips Chiefly the result of hybridization between Darwin tulips and *Tulipa fosteriana* and the result of hybridization between other tulips and botanical tulips which have the same habit and in which the wild plant is not evident.	Mid-season
5. Single Late Tulips This class includes Darwin Tulips and cottage tulips. Owing to hybridization, the borderline between the former classes is no longer visible.	Late
6. Lily-flowered Tulips Flowers with pointed, reflexed petals.	Late
7. Fringed Tulips Tulips whose petals are edged with crystal shaped fringes.	Late
8. Viridiflora Tulips Tulips with partly greenish perianths.	Late
9. Rembrandt Tulips Broken tulips, striped or marked brown, bronze, black, red, pink or purple on red, white or yellow ground.	Late
10. Parrot Tulips Tulips with laciniate flowers.	Generally late
11. Double Late Tulips Paeony flowered tulips.	Late
12. Kaufmanniana (species)	Very early

Varieties and hybrids, sometimes with
mottled foliage.

13. Fosteriana (species)   Early
Varieties and hybrids, large, some cultivars
with mottled or striped foliage.

14. Greigii (species)   Early
Varieties and hybrids, always with mottled
or striped foliage.

15. Other species and their   Variable
varieties and hybrids.

Ecofunction

Pollen of the early flowering species is used by honeybees. The bulbs
are severely purgative to cattle and horses.

Organic Care

Tulips thrive in a light, fertile, sandy, well-drained soil. Manures used
for tulip enrichment should be at least one year old and well-com-
posted. Bone meal and a small amount of wood ashes should be
added and mixed well with the planting soil. This gives an ideal growing medium for tulips. Clay soils should be amended with .25 volume
of sand to lighten the soil prior to fertilizing, as tulips are not long
lived in heavy clay soils.

Tulips like a minimum of five hours of direct sunlight to full sun
conditions. If given less sun than this, they will become ethiolated,
growing at an angle toward their main light source, giving them an
ungainly appearance.

Tulips are hardy in all north temperate gardens, zones 2–9. Some
careful selection of tulip groups and planting sites should be done in
zones 2 and 3 to ensure success. Heavy clay soils in these cold gardening areas have to be amended with sand and high potassium and
high phosphate fertilizers, as the combination of a cold soil and climate will seriously hamper the bulbs longevity.

In zones 2–4, because of the rapid onset of warm temperatures
of spring and early summer, together with a high solar exposure and
a longer day, especially in the northern latitudes, the mid-season and
late season blooming times of tulips are telescoped together. This phenomenon is not found in zones 5–9, where early, mid-season, and late
season hybrids can be enjoyed from March to the beginning of June.

Tulip bulbs should be planted as late in the fall as possible. For
zones 2–4, this is September; for zones 5–6, the end of September
into mid-October; and for zones 7–9, mid-October into mid-
November. In all garden zones this allows for three to four weeks
of cool root growth before the ground freezes or, in zones 7–9,
temperatures stay consistently low. The single late tulips, including

The viridiflora tulip, *Tulipa* 'Spring Green', combines with late flowering narcissi and bitonal *Iris pumila* hybrids in a fine composition of color and foliage.

the Darwin, Cottage, and Mendel tulips, the viridiflora and the Rembrandt tulips should be planted 8" (20 cm) deep, measured from the neck of the bulb. The Darwin hybrid tulips, the lily flowered tulips, and the fringed tulips should be planted 6–7" (15–18 cm) deep. The single early, double early, Triumph, Parrot, Double late, and Greigii tulips should be planted 5–6" (10–12 cm) deep. The Kaufmanniana, the Fosteriana, and some of the specie tulips such as *Tulipa tarda* should be planted from 4–5" (10–12 cm) deep. The specie tulips of Group 15 vary considerably in bulb size. The larger bulbs should be planted 4" (10 cm) deep and the smaller bulbs 2.5–3" (6–8 cm) deep. In clay soils, tulip bulbs should be planted 1–1.5" (2–4 cm) less deeply than in sandy soils.

The larger flowering bulbs should be placed 6" (15 cm) apart, while the Kaufmanniana and Fosteriana tulips should be planted 4–5" (10–12 cm) apart. Other specie tulips, e.g., *T. tarda,* should be planted 8" (20 cm) apart because these tulips, within two to three years, will form large flowering clumps which can be divided every five to six years or as needed.

Gardeners should pay particular attention to new cultivars of the Botanical or specie tulips. These are Kaufmanniana varieties and hybrids, Fosteriana varieties and hybrids, Greigii varieties and hybrids, and some botanical tulips, notably *T. tarda, T. chrysantha* 'Tubergen's Gem', *T. clusiana,* and *T. humilis.* Most of these tulips are very early flowering except Greigii varieties and hybrids. All of these tulips are exceptionally frost hardy, disease free, and long-lived. These tulips, together with the single late tulips, the Darwin hybrid tulips, the Rembrandt and the Viridiflora tulips, should be considered as perennial plantings. All the other tuliips, the single and double early tulips, triumph, lily-flowered, fringed, parrot, and double late tulips should be considered to be annual bulbs. This is because some of these bulbs will flower for an extra year or two, but the bulbs have an annoying habit of dividing, at which point flowering discontinues. The tulips should be dug up. The large bulbs should be replanted. Small bulbs should be well spaced in propagation beds for two to three years to allow the bulb to reach sufficient size for flowering. Because of the time and energy involved in doing this, many gardeners leave this to professional bulb growers and simply order a new supply regularly.

Bulb Protection

One planting of *Fritillaria imperialis* per 20 feet of bed will deter foraging mice, voles, and moles. Unfortunately, chipmunks and ground squirrels are inordinately fond of the small botanical tulips and, the smaller the bulb, the more highly they prize them. These bulbs, especially *T. bataliniiI* and *T.clusiana,* are high on the risk scale. When these bulbs have been planted, two small 1 x 2" (2 x 5 cm) stones placed directly over the bulb appear to deter these creatures, most probably by limiting their ability to smell the fresh bulb. The stones can later be removed.

Design

From a design, color, and work perspective it is better to add tulips to an existing garden plan or area than it is to work spring material around the tulip itself. Tulip beds of any of the tulip groups, except the botanical or specie tulips, are magnificent in themselves. These beds can later be planted with colorful annuals or biennials. For example, one may intermingle the fragrant Siberian wallflowers or *Cheiranthus allionii* 'Orange', 12" (30cm), with any of the mid or late flowering tulips. The reflexed petals of the lily flowering tulips are particularly elegant in this combination.

Tulipa tarda opening its buttery yellow center to greet the spring sun.

    A magnificently colorful flower succession can be obtained from April into the beginning of June for zones 4–7. Spring is much longer for zones 8 and 9 and, consequently, the first flowering will be in the beginning of March or the end of February, depending on spring temperatures. The first tulips to come into flower are the almost sessile *T. kaufmanniana* and hybrids, 6-8" (15–20 cm), the *T. chrysantha* 6-8" (15–20 cm), *T. fosteriana* and its hybrids 8-18" (20–45 cm), *T. tarda* 6" (15 cm), *T. pulchella humilis* 'Persian Pearl' 6" (15 cm), *T. praestans* 'Van Tubergen' 8" (20 cm) or *T. praestans* 'Fusilier', 10" (25 cm). Any of these tulips can be massed with erythoroniums, especially the *E. denscanis*, which is rose-colored and combines with the pink Kaufmanniana hybrids 'Ancilla', a bicolor tulip. This tulip, like many of the Kaufmanniana tulips, is closed when the sun is low, showing the exterior of the flower which is one color, in this case, a pale pink. When the sun is high in the sky, the flower opens fully to its water-lily form exposing an exquisite orange center, rimmed with crimson and tapering white petals. An alternative would be to combine *T. pulchella humilis* 'Persian Pearl' with *Erythronium revolutum* 'White Beauty'. Both are 6" (15 cm) tall and the golden-yellow eye of the erythromium compliments the buttery central cup of this small tulip. The chocolate-marbled foliage of the erythroniums compliments a similar,

Tulipa greigii 'Red Riding Hood' formalizes an espaliered standard pear tree of Russian ancestry.

darker marking in the foliage of some of the Kaufmanniana and Fosteriana tulips.

For vertical contrast, the white *Muscari botryoides* 'Album', 6–8" (15–20 cm), may be massed with the extremely long lasting *T. fosteriana* 'White Emperor' 20" (50 cm) tulip. For spectacular color, groupings of the *T. fosteriana* 'Flaming Emperor', 16" (40 cm), a red and orange bicolor, may be mixed with 'Red Emperor' 18" (45 cm), with scarlet flowers. Looking at the general overview these tulips can be set in a sea of *Arabis* 'Alba' or the rich rose colors of aubrietas. The larger, taller tulip flower succession comes in May with the single and double early tulips, the triumph tulips, and the Darwin hybrid tulips. There is an enormous array of hybrids in these groups. For the most part, gardeners in zones 2–5 have to plant these tulips in a protected spot in the garden to minimize occasional frost damage to the flowers, as these tulips, except for the Darwin hybrids, seem to be the least cold tolerant of all the tulips. These tulips flower at the same time as hyacinths. However, both groups do not stand well together. They need to be interspersed with large horizontal areas. Any of the mat forming, dwarf phlox species will supply this. Later on in May come the most ornamental of the large tulips, the single and double late tulip vying for a place with the smaller, spectacularly mottled-foliaged Greigii tulips which are smaller, the Darwin hybrid tulips, 8–10" (20–30 cm), the lily-flowered tulips, the streaked Rembrandt tulips, the fringed and the parrot tulips. Of most interest to the gardener is the Greigii tulip hybrid group. If this tulip is planted on the shallow side, it becomes an extremely early hardy tulip and can flower at the end of March and into April. It can be massed with chionodoxas. If the tulip is planted deeper, then the fine mottled foliage may be enjoyed into May. 'Oratorio' 8" (20 cm), 'Red Riding Hood', 8" (20 cm), and 'Easter Surprise', 14" (35 cm), are the most useful hybrids for the front of the border or for nooks in the spring garden that need color.

For garden interest there are the multiflowered tulips 18–20" (45–50 cm), which appear to be tulip bouquets coming out of a single bulb. The parrot tulips add a touch of fantasy to the garden. As an accent and for longevity of bloom, the Viridiflora tulips, a cultivar of the late Darwin tulips, may be employed. If carefully used, these can extend the tulip season into June. 'Spring Green' is particularly fine because it can be used to good advantage with June flowering eremurus lilies.

The Tulips

NAME	COLOR	HEIGHT	MONTH	ZONE
DIVISION 1: SINGLE EARLY				
Beauty of Volendam	burgundy pink	14" (36cm)	May	4-9
Flair	red yellow bicolor	14" (36cm)	May	4-9
Diana	white	14" (36cm)	May	4-9
DIVISION 2: DOUBLE EARLY				
Schoonoord	white	15" (40cm)	May	4-9
Peach Blossom	rose	15" (40cm)	May	4-9
Hytuna	yellow	15" (40cm)	May	4-9
DIVISION 3: TRIUMPH				
Design	yellow pink	15" (40cm)	May	5-9
Peer Gynt	pink	15" (40cm)	May	5-9
Babylon	cream	15" (40cm)	May	5-9
DIVISION 4: DARWIN HYBRIDS				
Apeldoorn	scarlet	18" (46cm)	May–June	3-9
Elizabeth Arden	pink	18" (46cm)	May–June	3-9
Shirley	white-mauve	18" (46cm)	May–June	3-9
DIVISION 5: SINGLE LATE TULIP				
Halcro	wine	18" (46cm)	May	3-9
Ester	pink	18" (46cm)	May	3-9
Sorbet	cream red	18" (46cm)	May	3-9
DIVISION 6: LILY FLOWERED				
Aladin	scarlet	18" (46cm)	May	3-9
White Triumphator	white	18" (46cm)	May	3-9
Ballade	mauve	18" (46cm)	May	3-9
DIVISION 7: FRINGED TULIPS				
Burgundy Lace	red	18" (46cm)	May	4-9
Fancy Frills	rose	18" (46cm)	May	4-9
Laverock	yellow	18" (46cm)	May	4-9
DIVISION 8: *T. VIRIDIFLORA* CULTIVARS				
Spring Green	cream/green	16" (40cm)	May–June	3-9
Artist Green	salmon	16" (40cm)	May–June	3-9
Greenland	pink-green	16" (40cm)	May–June	3-9

DIVISION 9: REMBRANDT

May Blossom	purple and cream	17" (43 cm)	May	4-9
Zomerschoon	purple and cream	17" (43 cm)	May	4-9

DIVISION 10: PARROT

Black Parrot	purple-black	18" (46 cm)	May-June	3-9
White Parrot	white	18" (46 cm)	May-June	3-9
Pink Fantasy	pink	18" (46 cm)	May-June	3-9

DIVISION 11: DOUBLE LATE OR PEONY FLOWERED

Lilac Perfection	pink	18" (46 cm)	May	3-9
Angelique	rose	18" (46 cm)	May	3-9
Mount Tacoma	white	18" (46 cm)	May	3-9

DIVISION 12: *T. KAUFMANNIANA* CULTIVARS

Ancilla	red white	6" (15 cm)	April	2-9
Heart's Delight	red white	6" (15 cm)	April	2-9
Shakespeare	apricot red	6" (15 cm)	April	2-9

DIVISION 13: *T. FOSTERIANA* CULTIVARS

White Emperor	white	8" (20 cm)	April	2-9
Orange Emperor	orange	8" (20 cm)	April	2-9
Pink Emperor	pink	8" (20 cm)	April	2-9

DIVISION 14: *T. GREIGII* CULTIVARS

Oratorio	pink	9" (23 cm)	April-May	2-9
Easter Surprise	orange	9" (23 cm)	April-May	2-9
Red Ridinghood	scarlet	9" (23 cm)	April-May	2-9

DIVISION 15: SPECIE TULIPS AND HYBRIDS

T. tarda	yellow	6" (15 cm)	April-May	2-9
T. turkestanica	yellow	6" (15 cm)	April-May	2-9
T. batalinii 'Bronze Charm'	yellow	3" (8 cm)	June-July	2-9
T. chrysantha 'Tubergen's Gem'	red orange	6" (15 cm)	May-June	2-9
T. pulchella humilis 'Persian Pearl'	pink	6" (15 cm)	May-June	2-9
T. praestans 'Fusilier '	orange-red	8" (20 cm)	June	2-9

Zantedeschia
CALLA LILY
Araceae
Zones 7–9

Zantedeschia rehmannii in the herb garden.

The calla lily has a tender, cormous rhizome which is perennial in the milder zones 7–9. In zones 2–6 it is necessary to winter store the dormant rhizome. The flowers are quite exotic and have an outside corolla-like structure called a spathe which can be white, yellow-rose, flame, or light pink. Some of the foliage has extremely attractive white speckles. The plants can grow up to 2' (60 cm).

The species lily _Z. albomaculata_ was very much a favorite of Victorian gardens, and this lily was very often used as a subject for art nouveau design work both in Europe and North America in the early twentieth century.

Ecofunction

Calla lilies collect water and dew around the leaf bases. They are miniature drinking pools for tiny beneficial insects in the garden. Their leaves provide shade for frogs, toads, and salamanders.

Organic Care

Callas like a good, slightly acid, garden soil which is very high in humus. Peat moss should be added to the soil to increase its water-holding capacity. However, the soil should not be water-logged. A summer mulch will supply the coolness they need for root growth. Gardeners in zones 2–6 should plant the lilies in May, 2" (5 cm) deep. The rhizome should have one or more cream-colored, curved growing shoots as soon as the soil temperature warms up at the end of May. They will begin growth in June, growing extremely rapidly to flower in July and August. The roots should be spaced 8–10" (20–25 cm) from one another.

In October, after killing frosts, the roots should be dug up, cleaned off, air-dried for several hours, and placed in dry, milled peat moss in a cool dry place with temperatures above 32°F (0°C). Very little storage space is needed for these roots.

Any ripened seed capsules should be added to the stored roots. The large, dark seeds may be planted in May. The first year they will produce tiny miniature plants which should be stored in the same fashion as mature plants.

Design

Calla lilies are a fine addition to a shade garden, blooming in July and August. Their ideal location is under the dappled shade of high arching trees mixed with other shade plants such as hostas. They mass well in small suburban gardens. These lilies may be used to advantage in a tiny garden with some small water feature, the splashing and dampness giving freshness to both flowers and foliage.

Zantedeschia Species and Hybrids

NAME	COLOR	HEIGHT	MONTH	ZONE
Z. albomaculata	white	18" (45 cm)	July-Aug	7-9*
Z. elliottiana	yellow	30" (75 cm)	July-Aug	7-9*
Z. rehmannii	pink	18-24" (45-60 cm)	July-Aug	7-9*
Z. r. 'Rose Lavender Gem'	lavender	18-24" (45-60 cm)	July-Aug	7-9*
Z. r. 'Flame'	orange-red	18-24" (45-60 cm)	July-Aug	7-9*

*Frost free storage required in zones 2-6

Zephyranthes
**ZEPHYR LILY, RAIN
LILY, FAIRY LILY**
Amaryllidaceae
**Zones 7–9
Tender bulb
in zones 2–6**

Zephyranthes are native to the western hemisphere. They like rain and have dainty, fairy-like, white, pink, or yellow flowers with grass like foliage.

Organic Care

Zephyranthes like a very rich, slightly acid, garden soil. Peat moss should be added to the planting mixture to encourage the damp conditions of which these bulbs are fond. Winter drainage should leave the bulbs damp but not completely waterlogged. Zephyranthes should be planted 2½–3" (5–8 cm) deep and will form attractive clumps in two to three years.

Design

Z. atamasco, 3–12" (8–30 cm), zones 7–9, is the hardiest. *Z. candida*, *Z. citrina,* and *Z. grandiflora* are hardy in zones 8–9. *Z. rosea* is the least hardy, needing protection in zone 9. *Z. atamasco* and *Z. grandiflora* flower in the spring while the others flower in the fall.

These lilies are useful for the milder gardening areas of Canada. In zones 2–6, they must be lifted after the first killing frost. *Z. candida* is native to river marshes of South America as in *Z. rosea* in Cuba. This and their summer to fall flowering habit make them a useful bog or water garden specie in zones 8 and 9. Clumps of zephyranthes are also very dainty in the fall rock-garden or in garden containers.

Zephyranthes Species

NAME	COLOR	HEIGHT	MONTH	ZONE
Z. atamasco	white	3-12" (8-30 cm)	April-May	7-9
Z. candida	white	12" (30 cm)	July-September	8-9
Z. citrina	yellow	8-12" (20-30 cm)	July-September	8-9
Z. grandiflora	pink	12" (30 cm)	May-June	8-9
Z. rosea	rose	12" (30 cm)	September	9

Finnegan's Wake, the dog who insists
on garden control.

FLOWERING SEQUENCE OF BULBS, CORMS, AND TUBERS

March

Eranthis (Winter Aconite)	
E. cilicicus	Yellow
E. hyemalis	Yellow
Crocus	
C. ancyrensis	Yellow
C. tomasinianus	Violet
Bulbous Iris	
I. dandfordiae	Yellow
I. histrioides 'George'	Violet
Galanthus (Snowdrops)	
G. elwesii	White
Scilla (Squill)	
S. bifolia	Blue
S. b. 'Rosea'	Rose
Chionodoxa (Glory of the Snow)	
C. luciliae	Blue
C. l. 'Pink Giant'	Pink
C. sardensis	Blue
Narcissus	
N. asturiensis	Yellow
Scilla (Squill)	
S. siberica 'Alba'	White
S. s. 'Spring Beauty'	Blue
S. tubergeniana	Blue
Galanthus (Snowdrops)	
G. nivalis	White
G. 'Allenii'	White
G. n. 'Viridapicis'	White
G. ikariae ssp.	
'Latifolius'	White
G. nivalis 'Flor Pleno'	White
G. n. 'Scharlockii'	White
Iris	
I. 'Cantab'	Blue
I. 'Reticulata'	Orange
Crocus chrysanthus	
Crocus vernus	
Muscari azureum	Blue
Puschkinia	
P. libanotica	Blue
P. l. 'Alba'	White
Ipheion uniflorum	
I. u. 'Froyle Mill'	Violet
I. u. 'Wisley Blue'	Blue
I. u. 'Alba'	White

April

Erythronium (Dog's Tooth Violet)	
E. japonicum	Lilac
Fritillaria	
F. persica 'Adiyaman'	Plum
Colchium	
C. luteum	Yellow
Bulbocodium vernum	Magenta
Anemone blanda	
A. b. 'Charmer'	Pink
A. b. 'Blue Star'	Blue
A. b. 'White Splendour'	White
Narcissus	
N. bulbocodium	Yellow
Erythronium	
E. dens-canis	Rose
E. revolutum	
'White Beauty'	White
E. grandiflorum	Cream
E. 'jeanette brickell'	Pink
E. tuolumnense 'Pagoda'	Pink
Chionodoxa (Glory of the Snow)	
C. luciliae 'Gigantea'	Violet
Tulipa	
T. fosteriana	
T. chrysantha	
T. kaufmanniana	
T. puchella humulis	Pink
T. Praestans	
'Van Tubergen'	Scarlet
Fritillaria	
F. lutea 'Maxima'	Yellow
Narcissus	
Trumpet narcissus	
N. 'King Alfred'	
N. 'Mount Hood'	
Camassia (Wild Hyacinth)	
C. leichtlinii	
Muscari	
M. ambrosiacum	Blue
M. botryoides 'Album'	White
M. armeniacum	Blue
Bulbous iris (Juno)	
I. aucheri	Blue
I. bucharica	Yellow
I. hollandica hyb.	
Trillium	
T. erectum	Red
T. grandiflorum	White
T. sessile	Red
T. s. 'Luteum'	Yellow
T. undulatum	White
Mertensia	
M. virginica 'Rubra'	Red
M. v. 'Alba'	White
Large cup narcissus	
N. 'Ice Follies'	White
N. 'Mrs. R. O. Backhouse'	Pink
N. 'Articole'	Apricot
Cyclamineus narcissus	
N. 'Jack Snipe'	Yellow
Fritillaria	
F. uva-vulpis	Purple
Sanguinaria canadensise	
S. c. 'Flor Pleno'	White
S. c. 'Rosea'	Rose

May

Jonquil Narcissus	
N. 'Baby Moon'	Yellow
N. 'Suzy'	Yellow
Muscari	
M. 'Comosum'	Lilac
M. c. 'Plumosum'	Lilac
Small Cup Narcissus	
N. 'Birma'	Yellow
N. 'Peridot'	White
Split-corona narcissus	
N. 'Papillion'	White
N. 'Cassata'	Yellow
Hyacinth	
H. 'L'innocence' E	White
H. 'Violet Pearl' M,	Lilac
H. 'Queen of Pinks' L	Pink
Ornithogallum	
O. umbellatum	White
Scilla	
S. monophyllos	Blue
S. amethystina	Blue
Tulipa	
T. Single early	
T. Double early	
T. Triumph	
T. Darwin hybrid	
Hyacinths-double	
H. 'Madame Sophie' E.	White
H. 'Hollyhock' M.	Pink
H. 'Chestnut Flower' L.	Pink
Tulipa	
T. batalini 'Bright Gem'	Yellow
Miniature narcissus	
N. minnon	Yellow
N. canaliculatus	Yellow
N. odorus	Yellow
N. o. 'Plennus'	Yellow
Double narcissus	
N. 'Tahiti'	Yellow
Tulipa	
T. greigii	
T. Single late	
T. Lily flowering	
T. Fringed	
T. Rembrandt	
T. Parrot	
T. Double late	
Narcissus	
N. Tazetta	
N. Poeticus	
N. Triandrus	
Fritillaria	
F. imperialis 'Rubra'	Red
Viridiflora tulip	
Alliums	
A. neapolitanum	
(A. cowanii)	White
A. karataviense	Lilac
A. elatum (A. Macleanii)	Lilac
Leucojum	
L. aestivum 'Gravetye Giant'	White
Camassia	
C. Quamash 'Orion'	Blue
C. cusickii	Blue
Delphinium	
D. semibarbatum (D. Zalil)	Yellow

June

Fritillaria
F. meleagris	Bronze, Grey
F. m. 'Alba'	White
F. michailovskyi	Plum

Narcissus juncifolius	Yellow

Eremurus (Fox-tail Lily)
E. robustus	Pink
E. himalaicus	White

Arisaema
A. amurense	Green
A. atrorubens	Green
A. triphyllum	Green

Allium
A. aflatunense	
'Purple Sensation'	Violet
A. azureum (A. caeruleum)	Blue
A. christophii	Mauve
A. moly	Yellow
A. oreophilum	
'Zwanenburg'	Red
A. rosenbachianum	Violet
A. roseum	Pink
A. triquetrum	Green
A. ursinum	White
A. nigrum	Green
A. unifolium	Pink

Ixiolirion (Siberian Lily)
I. tartaricum 'Pallasii'	Plum

Nectaroscordum
N. bulgaricum	Green
N. siculum	Violet

Asiatic hybrid lily
L. 'Enchantment'	Orange
L. 'Connecticut King'	Yellow
L. 'Unique'	Pink

Gladiolus
G. byzantinus	Violet
G. byzantinus 'Alba'	White

Specie lilium
L. concolor 'Puchellum'	Red
L. cernuum	Pink
L. amabile	Red
L. hansonii	Yellow
L. tsingtauense	Orange
L. parryi	Yellow
L. mackliniae	White
L. testaceum	White
L. pyrenaicum	Yellow

American lily hybrids
L. 'Butterflies'	White
L. 'Flanders Field'	Red
L. 'Isaac Watts'	Red

N. american native lilies
L. superbum L. canadense)	Orange
L. grayi	Red/Orange
L. michiganense	Red/Orange
L. philadelphicum	Red/Orange
L. longiflorum	White
L. formosanum giganteum	White

Delphinium
D. menziesii	Blue

July

Eremurus
E. 'Stenophyllus'	Yellow

Asiatic hybrid lily
L. 'Corina'	Red
L. 'Yellow Blaze'	Yellow

Martagon lily hybrid
L. martagon	Pink
L. m. 'Alba'	White
L. m. 'J. s. Dijt'	Yellow
L. m. 'Jupiter'	Beige

Eremurus
E. 'Shelford Hybrids'	Pastels

Alliums
A. narcissiflorum	
'Insubricum'	Plum
A. flavum	Yellow
A. giganteum	Red
A. sphaerocephalon	Violet
A. odorum	Red

Arisaema
A. 'Candidissimum'	Pink
A. 'Consanguineum'	Purple

Trumpet hybrid (Aurelian) lily
L. 'Pink Perfection'	Pink
L. 'Regale Album'	White
L. Copperking	Apricot
L. Thunderbolt	Melon

Lilium species and specie hybrids
L. duchartrei	Red

Oriental hybrid lily
L. 'Rosario'	Pink
L. 'San Souci'	Pink

American hybrid lilies
L. 'Tiger Babies'	Peach
L. 'Windermere'	Rose
L. 'Shuksan'	Yellow
L. harrisanum (L. padalinum	
giganteum)	Red

Tuberous begonia	Mixed
Caladium	Mixed
Crinum	Pink
Gladiolus	Mixed

Zantedeschia
(Calla Lilies)	Mixed

Zephyranthes	Pink
Dahlias (Dwarf)	Mixed

August

Alliums
A. cirrhosum	Violet
A. c. 'Album'	White
A. tuberosum	White
A. t. 'Mauve'	Mauve

Dahlia (Tall)	Mixed
Galtonia candicans	White

Asiatic hybrid lilies
L. tigrinum 'Orange Tiger'	Orange
L. t. 'Yellow Star'	Yellow
L. t. 'Pink'	Pink
L. t. 'Alba'	White

Oriental hybrid lilies
L. 'Casablanca'	White
L. 'Blushing Pink'	Pink
L. 'Rose Elegance'	Pink
L. 'Journey's End'	Red
L. auratum	
platyphyllum	White/Yellow
L. a. 'Rubrovittatum'	White/Red
L. 'Black Beauty'	Pink

Colchicum
C. agrippinum	Pink
C. byzantinum	Violet
C. autumnale 'Album'	White
C. a. 'Pleniflorum'	Pink
C. speciosum	Violet
C. s. 'Waterlily'	Lilac

Leucojum
L. autumnale	White

Narcissus
N. viridiflorus	Green

Crocus
C. longiflorus	Violet
C. laevigatus	Lilac
C. sativus	Lilac
C. speciosus	Lavender
C. zonatus (C. kotschyanus)	Rose

Sternbergia
S. lutea	Yellow
S. clusiana	Yellow

Lilium Specie
L. henryi	Yellow
L. speciosum	Red

Lilium formosanum	White

Garden Controls

Description

Garden Care

Toxicity

Human Precautions

Ecodamage

A northern American green tree frog, *Hyla cinerea evittata*, rests on a trumpet hybrid lily *Lilium regale* 'Album'.

Garden Controls

 Chemicals which are used for controlling, or, indeed, sometimes killing, biological activity which has acquired a pestilent character are called pesticides. They are generally classified by their target group. For the purpose of classification, the following, among others, are the more common pesticides and their targets encountered by the gardener:

Pesticide	Target
Acaricide	Mites
Miticide	Mites
Algicide	Algae
Avicide	Birds
Bactericide	Bacteria
Fungicide	Fungi
Herbicide	Plants
Insecticide	Insects
Molluscicide	Snails and Slugs
Nematicide	Nematodes
Piscicide	Fish
Predacide	Vertebrate Animals
Rodenticide	Rodents
Silvicide	Trees and Woody Growth
Slimicide	Slime Moulds

Within the arena of flower gardening, the gardener sometimes has to resort to using bactericides, fungicides, herbicides, insecticides, and, in some damper garden areas, a molluscicide for slugs. For normal garden purposes bluebirds and wrens act as very efficient insecticides. Unwanted vertebrates and rodents can be managed by trapping or chemical deterrents.

Chemicals used for controlling a system will subdue it, alter its behavior, or kill it. Most of the controlling chemicals are toxic to their target group or organism. However, it is the lack of relative toxicity they have for other organisms, man included, and their minimal chemical amplification in nature which makes a controlling chemical or pesticide useful to gardeners interested in minimizing injury to our ecosystem.

All chemicals, including pesticides, when used within a closed system, can act as poisons. Even sugar or common table salt come into this category. A closed system is a system, chemically speaking, where there is no exit. Each unit of life is a closed system from virus to man. The world is a chemically closed system. Therefore, it is important for a poison or pesticide to do its job and then to dissipate or break down into harmless components and not to amplify into sub-fragments, for example, radionucleides, that are even more toxic to a larger group than the parent compound.

Tree swallow chicks taking their first steps in garden patrol.

When chemists, biochemists, or biologists are assessing the toxicity of a pesticide, they subject a given number of experimental animals to an increasingly higher amount of the pesticide until 50 percent of them die. At this stage the lethal dosage of pesticide used, which is measured in milligrams per kilogram of animal body weight, is called the LD_{50}. The rat is the accepted test specie. This measure is now used for the laboratory assessment of all pesticides. A high LD_{50} rate means that the animal can tolerate ingesting a large amount of the chemical before it becomes ill. A high LD_{50} rate, therefore, is an indicator of relative non-toxicity, and a low LD_{50} rate indicates that a chemical is extremely toxic to the test animal, and, by extrapolation, also to man and his environment.

Because the world is a closed system, with its enormous chemical buffering capacity, biological evolution has produced many extremely interesting and complex natural pesticides. These pesticides, to date, seem to be the least toxic for general garden use. The natural or botanical pesticides are presently being refined by industry all over the world for present and future sale. In some instances, compounds are being added to the pesticide to increase its killing action. These compounds are called synergists. Further refinement is being carried out in the formulation of these pesticides, or the way they are chemically hung together with their dispensing agent, for ease of use and application. Pesticides come in granules, pellets, powders, dusts, solvents, wettable powders, and in emulsions.

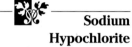

Sodium Hypochlorite

Description

Sodium hypochlorite is a potent bactericide which can safely be used in the garden. Sodium hypochlorite is also sold as common household bleach and used as an algicide in swimming pools. It is sold as a colorless 5 percent solution in plastic containers. It has a strong alkaline, or caustic, reaction. Sodium hypochlorite is a commonly used medical laboratory chemical. It is used to disinfect the communal water supply for towns and cities. The household sodium hypochlorite solution may be further diluted with water in the ratio of one part 5 percent sodium hypochlorite solution to ten parts water to provide an effective bactericide and fungicide.

Garden Use

In the garden, sodium hypochlorite is used as a bactericide and a fungicide. Sodium hypochlorite is invaluable as a bacterial sterilant in all garden pruning. The aforementioned 1:10 solution of household bleach to water is useful as a sterilant for secateurs, saws, and all pruning tools. The tools should be surface sterilized to prevent the spread of bacterial or fungal diseases within the garden. When pruning, the secateurs should be dipped into the solution after every cut and should have a thorough dipping when changing from specie to specie. As the solution is also caustic, it will remove some of the machine oils from the moving mechanisms which should be replaced prior to storage. This 0.5 percent solution is extremely useful as a surface sterilant for cuts on plants when pruning. The open cut of the plant should be wiped with sodium hypochlorite. Bleeding ends of trimmed vines may be wiped to prevent entry of fungi and bacteria. Pruning all maple species and nut species in the fall should also involve surface sterilizing the newly cut area with 0.5 percent sodium hypochlorite. This is extremely important to do in areas of high acid rain as the trees are weakened by stress. Sterilizing the cut area gives the trees additional 'clean' time for their immune system to form callus tissue. Callus tissue is the natural healing of a tree which excludes fungal and bacterial penetration and infections due to its high phenol content. It is similar to scab tissue in humans and other mammals.

A 0.5 percent solution of sodium hypochlorite can be used as a fall fungicide on all rose species against black spot disease (*Diplocarpon rosae*) when the roses have shed their leaves and have become dormant. Many species of rust fungus (*Phragmidium*) are severely inhibited by a similar treatment. Because this solution is caustic and raises the pH of the surrounding soil, a counter buffer of either tea or tea-leaves, the ordinary household orange pekoe variety, should be put on the soil 12–18" (30–45 cm) around the rose bush in the spring when growth commences. Tea is high in tannic acid.

A 0.5 percent solution of sodium hypochlorite can be used as soil drench in pots or in flats of plants if the fungus disease damp-off (*Pythium de Baryanium*) is encountered. A counter-buffer of tea (tannic acid) should not be used in this instance, as damp-off will not grow well in a caustic medium.

Toxicity
The LD_{50} of 0.5 percent sodium hypochlorite solution for rats is 150 mg/kg when used as an oral poison. Although this LD_{50} is low for rats, when the solution is diluted it is relatively safe for human use.

Human Precautions
Sodium hypochlorite is caustic to the eyes and defats the skin. Protective glasses and rubber gloves should be worn when using this solution. Sodium hypochlorite can be washed harmlessly from a domestic area using water. Sodium hypochlorite, as all pesticides, should be kept out of the reach of children. It should not be ingested.

Ecodamage
Sodium hypochlorite breaks down rapidly in soil to its molecular constituents and does not create a significant hazard in small, diluted amounts.

Sulphur

Description
Sulphur has been used as a fungicide for hundreds of years domestically. Fortunately, with modern chemical manipulation, sulphur, in all its various forms, may be used as an extremely potent fungicide with little or no consequential environmental damage. Sulphur is an element and is, like carbon, oxygen and nitrogen, one of the building

blocks of all life forms. As a fungicide, sulphur may be used alone. It also has a fungicidal action when it is part of a bridging structure within molecules, as it is in horticultural oils, neem oils, and garlic. Sulphur, in its unique bridging function, is also found in many protein structures of all life forms, the human included.

New technology has presented sulphur products for public use in three formulations. Sulphur dust, or elemental sulphur, which has large particles, is mixed with a small percentage of inert clay or talcum powder to increase its spreadability on and adherence to foliage. This is sold as garden sulphur. The second sulphur form is ground extremely finely until it becomes so fine a dust that it will mix with water as a spray. This is sold as a sulphur fungicidal spray. The third sulphur form is ground into a minute form until it becomes a colloid and mixes well with water. This, too, is sold in a spray form.

Garden Use

Sulphur, when used as a dust or in a spray form, is an extremely effective fungicide. From a flower gardener's point of view, the spray form is handier, easier to use, and covers an affected surface rapidly. The spray form also helps the fungicide to reach some out-of-the-way or higher areas that would be difficult to treat with dust alone. For maximum usefulness and minimum foliage damage, sulphur sprays should be used early in the morning or in the evening when the plants are fully turgid. Because sulphur solutions are colloidal, it greatly helps to shake the sprayer when in use to give a greater dispersion of sulphur in the fungicidal mist.

Sulphur is an efficient fungicidal spray against such common garden fungi as powdery mildew, rusts, black spot, apple scab, black knot, and brown rot of stone fruit. In the greenhouse it is also an extremely useful miticide.

Sulphur and horticultural oils have a synergistic effect on one another. An horticultural oil should not be sprayed on foliage until three to four weeks after a sulphur spray, as it will increase the burning effect of sulphur on foliage. However, in areas of acid rain or heavy rainfalls, a sulphur spray can precede a horticultural oil spray by two to three weeks. Sulphur sprays should not be used during periods of intense drought or when the temperatures are above 90° F (32° C). If it is absolutely necessary to spray in hot, dry weather, the plant material should be well-watered one to two hours, at least, before spraying, and spraying should be done only in early morning or late evening.

Sulphur is also used to acidify soil for acid loving plants: 25 lb. (11 kg) of sulphur added to 100 square feet (9 square meters) of garden surface soil will change the pH from 7.0 to 5.0.

Toxicity

Sulphur is less toxic than other fungicides.

Human Precautions

Sulphur is a strong irritant to the mucous membranes, lungs, eyes, and nasal passages. Sulphur will form a percentage of sulphurous and sulphuric acids on contact with body moisture. When spraying with this fungicide, protective clothing, rubber or neoprene gloves, and a respirator should be used. Pets and children should be removed from the spray area for approximately one half hour after the spraying procedure is completed to ensure that the droplets will have settled.

Ecodamage

Sulphur in large amounts acidifies the soil. Sulphur garden sprays do not significantly damage garden ecologies, as soil organisms are well equipped to handle this naturally occurring element.

Horticultural Oils

Description

The observation that oils act as an efficient pesticide has been both known and recorded since early Roman times. Since 1970, a world demand for environmentally safe pesticides has led to a review of oils being used as fungicides, insecticides, miticides, and selective, broad leaf herbicides. Incredible though it may seem, a very simple answer lay as a solution to this research. This was oil viscosity. Oils, because of their inherent design, have the ability to flow slowly. A slow moving oil, like treacle, is said to be very viscous and a fast moving oil, like water, is said to have low viscosity. It appears that the faster an horticultural oil will flow, the greater its potential as a summer oil spray. Many of these new summer oils are from plant sources, such as corn oil, and are highly refined. The cruder or less refined oils make excellent winter and spring dormant oil sprays.

Both forms of oil spray, the low and high viscosity sprays, are potent fungicides. In the formulations of the spray mixtures, oil is diluted with water. As oil and water do not mix, a third component, soap, is added. The long molecular chains of the soap help to mechanically dissolve the oil in the water by increasing surface tension. The resultant mixture is called an emulsion. The emulsion form of the spray has a synergistic effect because the soap enables the oil to be spread in one thin sheet all over either the dormant tree or, in the summer time, all over the infected foliage, thereby increasing its intended action.

It would greatly benefit the horticulturist if some enterprising scientist or corporation were to add target botanical sprays such as Azadirachtin as a foliar feed deterrent to these emulsions.

Garden Use

Horticultural oils are potent insecticides. Winter applications as a dormant oil spray are effective against scale insects, aphids, and mites. They have the action of sterilizing the entire surface of a tree, shrub, rose, or plant to ground level for a short period of time. This gives a chance for subsequent beneficial predation to make a greater kill. The summer applications of horticultural oils have a similar effect. Horticultural oils can also be used safely and efficiently in the home for most household potted plants. Both low and high viscosity sprays will kill fungal growth in all its phases by direct contact. These include the mycelia, zoospores, bacidiospores, and ascospores of the higher fungi. Powdery mildew, rusts, black spot, black knot, and brown rot of stone fruit may all be controlled with oil sprays. The oil acts as a barrier respiration inhibitor. When horticultural oils are being used as a summer foliage spray, care should be taken that only the low viscosity horticultural oils are used, as the high viscosity oils will block the stomata and lenticels of the plants. Stomata and lenticels are found in all plants and are the organs for gaseous exchange also called respiration or breathing. If those organs are blocked, the plant cannot breathe and will either be badly damaged or will die. Stomata are analagous to the human mouth. In times of drought and when the plants are under water stress, oil sprays should be avoided. The stomata will semi-close, and thus a low viscosity oil will act as a high viscosity oil and will be able to clog the stomata, resulting in the burning of leaves or some foliage damage. In these circumstances, care should be taken to water the plants extremely well one to two hours before spraying to ensure that the stomata and lenticels are fully open.

Toxicity

Horticultural oils consist of complex molecules composed entirely of carbon and hydrogen called hydrocarbons, linked by sulphur bridges. When used in such small amounts within a garden, horticultural oils are considerably less toxic than most other sprays.

Human Precautions

As with all sprays, eye and skin protection should be worn as well as a suitable respirator. Although horticultural oils are not seriously toxic to humans, sensitivity reactions to the oils may occur along with eye irritation caused by the emulsifiers.

Ecodamage

Horticultural oil sprays used in the garden are broken down rapidly on contact with the soil by beneficial soil organisms.

Horticultural oils will dissolve the upper cuticular layer of all blue-green evergreens, thus reducing their blue effect. For aesthetic purposes only, these oils should not be sprayed on such evergreens. If an accident does occur, the evergreen will resume its blue-green hue in two to three years.

Wood Ashes

Description

Wood ashes, to date, are not commercially available but are an excellent fungicide for the home garden. Wood ash has a long history of horticultural use. Small wood ash storage houses can be seen dotted all over North America in older settlements. Wood ash, for general garden purposes, should come from burning untreated wood only. The ash should be stored dry. Ash from a woodstove or fireplace is excellent for garden uses. Wood ash from hardwood trees contains up to 10 percent potash when it has been kept in a dry state. Wood ash which has been exposed to rain will only contain about 2 percent potash, hence the reason for storing the ash dry. Wood ash also contains about 40 percent lime, which is the basis of its alkaline caustic action. Wood ash, as well as being a fungicide, is an excellent source of potassium for the home garden.

Garden Use

Wood ash is used as a dusting powder. In the spring, a dusting can be applied around delphiniums, gypsophilums, phlox, paeonies, hollyhocks, clematis, alliums, dictamnus, dwarf, intermediate, tall and remontant iris.

Wood ashes can also be used as a molluscicide. The wood ash is applied in the garden in such a way that both slugs and snails have physical contact with the woodash. Injured plants are surrounded by a 1' (30 cm) band of wood ash, 1/4" thick. Ants will also refrain from crossing this barrier.

Wood ash is useful as a fungicide because it has a strong caustic or alkaline reaction in contact with moisture. This caustic reaction inhibits the growth of all fungal spores and fungal mycelium. It is thus an excellent preventative fungicide if used in the spring because the fungal spores cannot germinate in such an adverse medium.

Wood ash being used as a fungicide.

Toxicity
Wood ashes are toxic due to their caustic or alkaline reaction with water.

Human Precautions
Wood ashes defat the skin, so gloves should be worn when handling the dust. A dust mask will prevent the inhalation of the fine ash particles. Children should not play with wood ash because of its caustic action.

Ecodamage
Wood ashes in large amounts are so caustic that they will inhibit plant growth. Woodashes, when used in small amounts, have a beneficial effect on the soil as added nutrients.

Garlic

Garlic, or *Allium sativum*, is a flowering allium and is a member of the *Amaryllidaceae* family. Garlic has been used domestically as a food enhancer for thousands of years both in eastern and western civilizations. Garlic has also been used traditionally as a medicinal plant. It was used by Hippocrates, a brilliant and ingenious Greek physician who lived four hundred years before Christ, as an anti-carcinogenic compound. Cancer, as a scourge, has been with the human race for at least a million years as traces of cancer have been found in the bones of pre-historic man. Both in China and ancient India, garlic has been used as an anti-tumor agent. In modern times epidemiological studies have shown both the French and Bulgarians, who eat the highest amounts of fresh garlic, to have the lowest incidence of cancer. It is important for domestic or household use to know that fresh garlic contains a powerful anti-bacterial and anti-fungal agent called Allicin (2-Propene-1-Sulfinothioic acid S-2-propenyl ester). Allicin is responsible for the true odor of garlic. This chemical is destroyed by distillation.

There is now a spray made from garlic oil on the market, which is a potent fungicide and is also a bactericide. Garlic oil is obtained from freshly crushed garlic cloves by steam distillation. The oil and resulting spray, too, has an onion or garlic-like smell which comes from the sulphur component of the molecule. Garlic oil is a volatile oil of allicin (S-allyl-L-cysteine sulphoxide) and other compounds such as citral, geraniol, and linalool. Allicin will also be found in garlic oil but only in trace amounts because of degradation due to steam distillation.

Garden Use

Recent research has indicated garlic spray to be far more potent a pesticide than was earlier thought. It is useful as a nematicide, fungicide, a broad spectrum insecticide, being toxic, for example, to the cabbage butterfly, *Pieris brassicae*, the larvae of the Colorado beetle, *Leptinotarsa decemlineata*, and mosquito larvae. Because garlic spray is a broad spectrum insecticide, it will kill both pest and beneficial insects. In the instance of its garden use as an insecticide against garden aphids, garlic spray will kill both aphid and the syrphid fly, *Syrphus carnea*, this fly being the natural predator of aphids. It is suggested, therefore, that insecticidal soap be used in the first two rounds against aphids, and if this does not work, then garlic spray may be used as the natural incidence of this beneficial fly must be low in the garden being treated. Generally, protection of beneficial garden insects must be borne in mind when using this spray.

Toxicity

Garlic spray is essentially non-toxic to humans. The LD_{50} of Allicin in mice is 60 mg/kg intravenously and 120 mg/kg subcutaneously.

Human Precautions

Because garlic contains geraniol, long sleeves should be worn when spraying. Pets and small children should be removed from the area when spraying is taking place because as geraniol can cause some contact dermatitis is some susceptible individuals, dogs and cats included.

Ecodamage

Garlic and its derivatives pose a minimal threat to the environment, except, as previously mentioned, its toxicity to certain beneficial insect populations. Care should be taken to note beneficial populations and, subsequently, to weigh the beneficial effect of the spray against its potential injury to these populations.

Neem Oil

Description

Neem oil is also called Margosa oil which is extracted primarily from the seeds of the neem tree or *Azadirachta indica*. This tree is a sub-tropical tree which grows in Africa, India, and in many parts of Asia. It can also be grown in the southern United States. There are also a number of rare trees of the Canadian Carolinian forest which can be compared to *Azadirachta indica*. All parts of this tree, the leaves, the bark, the roots, and, most especially, the seeds, have been known for centuries to be most remarkable in many ways. All parts of the tree have been used as pesticides for such insects as migratory locusts, *Locusta migratoria*, and have also been used in traditional medicines. Because of the alarming damage done to beneficial ecosystems, man, and our world's water supply by organically synthesized agricultural and domestic pesticides, there is a world-wide search underway for alternatives. Neem oil is one of the many potential answers that have emerged from this scientific hunt.

The neem tree has obviously developed, through its tough evolutionary course, a formidable arsenal of target protective compounds for its own protection and safety against its myriads of pestilent enemies. The oil extracted from the seed kernels has the highest pesticide activity. On chemical analysis, this oil is a fascinating mixture of complex three-dimensional chemicals which are mostly glycerides and limonoids, including a very interesting terpinoid called Azadirachtin, which is a highly active insect feeding deterrent and growth regulator. Neem oil has a strong garlic odor coming from its sulfur containing molecular constituents. Neem oil is sold as Margosan-O®, as an oil emulsion spray.

Garden Use

Neem oil emulsion spray works both as a systemic and contact pesticide and can be used as a regular garden fungicide for mildews, rusts, and bacterial rots. It has great potency as an insecticide against cockroaches, mosquitos, Japanese beetles, cucumber beetles, corn earworm, Colorado beetles, leafminers, nematodes, plant hoppers, flea beetles, locusts, army worms, two-spotted spider mites, clothes moths, and cabbage loopers. Because neem oil spray is an emulsion, the container should be agitated while spraying for an even cover. All plant material should be well watered and fully turgid before spraying. Spraying for maximum impact should be done in early morning or evening.

Toxicity

Neem oil shows very low toxicity to all mammals. The LD_{50} for rats is 13,000 mg/kg. It also appears that neem oil is not mutagenic or cancer causing.

Human Precautions

Young children and animals should be removed from the spray area for four to five hours. As neem oil is still undergoing scientific investigation, the usual precautions for mists and sprays should be taken. The skin should be covered and gloves, eye protection, and a respirator should be worn. Ingestion of the oil should be avoided as the intestinal mucosa also contains beneficial bacteria which could possibly be harmed.

Ecodamage
Neem oil products naturally degrade in sunlight and will also rapidly degrade in the soil. At the present state of the research, it appears that many beneficial systems are not harmed by this oil.

Pyrethrum

Description
Pyrethrum and its derivatives are extracted from *Chrysanthemum cinerariifolium,* which is also known as pyrethrum or the dalmation insect flower, and *Chrysanthemum coccineum* (syn. *C. roseum; Pyrethrum atrosanguineum*), which is also called pyrethrum, the painted daisy, or the Persian insect flower. The dried flower head is the source of the insecticidal compounds, which are Pyrethrin I, II, and Pyrethrosin. These chemicals are fairly easy to synthesize and are called pyrethroids. Both natural and synthetic pyrethrins are often used in combination with a synergist which increases the killing action. Piperonyl butoxide (PBO) obtained from sesame seeds is the synergist usually used with pyrethrins. Since this synergist has some negative effects on the nervous system, pyrethrins without this synergist are a safer pesticide to use.

Chrysanthemum coccineum 'Brenda' is a source of the chemical, pyrethrum.

Garden Use
Pyrethrins in combination with insecticidal soap are the most useful formulations for garden use. They control aphids, white-flies, spider mites, beetles, fleas, flies, leaf hoppers, and caterpillars, among other pests. This formulation is far safer than the aerosol formulations because the mist droplet size is less fine and more pyrethrin can be aimed at the target area without getting additional unwanted spray elsewhere in the garden. Formulations with naturally occurring pyrethrins are more desirable for garden use than the synthetic pyrethroids. Pyrethrum sprays should be stored in a cool, dark place, away from children.

Toxicity
Pyrethrin I and II have an oral LD_{50} of 1,200 mg/kg rat weight. No genetic mutations have been found to date with these compounds.

Human Precautions

Pyrethrins can be toxic to cats. Pyrethrins can also cause allergic reactions in some people. Children, and especially cats, should be removed from the spray area. Skin should be covered and eye protection and respirators should be worn. Small potted plants can be sprayed in and sealed within plastic bags for maximum effect.

Ecodamage

Pyrethrins are oxidized readily by both air and sunshine and break down readily in the soil. Because of its low persistence and rapid action, it is most useful as a specific spot treatment pesticide.

 Rotenone

Description

The powerful and well-known pesticide rotenone is extracted from the root tissue of *Derris elliptica, D. malaccensis,* and *D. urucu,* which occur in South America, and *Lonchocarpus* species, which are tropical members of the *Leguminosae* family. Derris root is also called cubé root.

Rotenone and its related derivatives are powerful inhibitors of the mitochondrial electron transport chain. Their mode of action is not entirely understood but death of the organism is due to oxygen deprivation. The spray or dust acts as a contact or stomach poison.

Garden Use

Rotenone is sold in a formulation with a carrier as a wettable powder or as a dust. Rotenone is non-toxic to plant tissue of all kinds in all stages of growth. It should be applied early in the morning to gain maximum effect from dew. Dew will act as a surface active agent on the leaf. In other words, it will assist in spreading the insecticidal film over the leaf surface, thus increasing the chance of contact with the target insect. Early morning spraying also reduces the possibility of contact with honeybees. Rotenone in minute amounts is extremely effective against Colorado beetle larvae, flea beetles, grape hoppers and other leaf hoppers, aphids, cattle grubs, overwintering scale insects, and also most species of the *Lepidoptera* family, in all its stages.

Toxicity

Rotenone is moderately toxic to animals. Its oral LD_{50} is 132 mg/kg rat body weight. Rotenone is a potent pesticide. It has been used as such by South American native people for centuries. Rotenone is highly toxic to fish and to some amphibians.

Human Precautions

Because the site of action of rotenone is believed to be in the electron transport system of the Kreb's tricarboxylic acid cycle, care should be taken handling this material. This cycle is found in all living tissue, both man and plant alike. The cuticular and lignin cell lining in plants obviously affords cytoplasmic protection which is not present in man. Skin should be covered. Eye protection and a respirator should be worn. Clothing should be separately washed and sun dried for 24 hours. All children and animals should be kept away from the spray area for 24 to 48 hours.

Ecodamage

Rotenone decomposes rapidly upon exposure to light and air. Damage to the soil from minimal amounts is not significant. Rotenone should never be used near a water source, such as a well head, stream, pond, or river, as it is an extremely potent and damaging piscicide. Accidental poisoning of ornamental water gardens should be carefully avoided. Even minute quantities of rotenone are toxic to all fish. Because Rotenone is toxic to the *Lepidoptera* family, spraying of feeding plants for these species should be avoided.

Pesticidal Soaps

Description

Soaps have been used as a pesticidal agent for almost three hundred years. In the western world, they were probably the most widely used of all pesticidal materials. Unfortunately for the environment, their use was eclipsed by the left-over chlorinated hydrocarbons from the Second World War's arsenal. In a short forty to fifty years, the world has felt the load of the deadly menace of millions of tons of the halogen family within its closed chemical system. This has prompted further research into less toxic products such as soaps. Soaps as pesticides have been refined into a most sophisticated group of products and the research goes on.

Soaps are either sodium or potassium salts combined with fats from any source. The potassium soaps are the common domestic soaps, such as hand soap and shampoos. These soaps have a gentle washing action. The pesticidal soaps are a salt of sodium with unsaturated fatty acids. These fatty acids are chains of carbon of ten to eighteen atoms. They can be thought of as beads in a necklace. This number of carbon atoms seems to have maximum toxic effect on soft bodied insects. The soap penetrates the body of the insect or grub and kills it. It stands to reason that the slow moving insects are killed and the fast moving insects escape. By chance, more than design, the fast moving insects are the adult beneficial insects that have also a higher cuticular layer and are left relatively untouched.

Pesticidal soaps are toxic to the lower orders of plants, the algae, the mosses, liverworts, lichens to some extent, and ferns. The gymnosperms and the angiosperms, including the monocotyledons and the dicotyledons, are untouched. This means that most garden foliage is not affected. Some foliage that is hairy, such as verbascums and geraniums, should have a little test area sprayed to check if the leaf will burn. If it does, a second spray of lukewarm water following the pesticidal soap spray by two to five minutes will remedy the problem without neutralizing the insecticidal effect of the soap.

All soaps in their general use have a bactericidal and fungicidal action because they significantly change surface tension. This is enhanced by the addition of sulphur into pesticidal soaps to give a very efficient fungicidal action.

When the soap's fatty acid molecular structural chains are lengthened, soap can be used as a non-selective herbicide. Because young growth of all plants is highest in moisture and has not as yet developed a wax infiltrated cuticle, it is most susceptible to this spray.

Garden Use

Pesticidal soaps are a valuable garden tool. These soaps kill aphids, caterpillars, crickets, earwigs, fungal gnats, grasshoppers, some leaf hoppers, mealybugs and mites, pear psylla, sawflies, slugs, scales, spittle bugs, thrips, and white flies. In areas of North America and Europe where acid rain is a problem, mosses, some unicellular algae, and liverworts will infest lawns. This spray will reduce the population of these groups in the lawn. The pesticidal spray should be applied in April to May, followed by a lawn application of ground dolomitic limestone to neutralize the effect of the acid rain. One application will last for up to five years.

The pesticidal soap broad spectrum herbicide should be applied in the spring when growth is commencing. It can be used against poison ivy *Rhus toxicodendron* in North America and bracken fern *Pteridium* species in Europe.

Toxicity

Pesticidal soaps are almost non-toxic unless they are ingested in huge amounts. Even then they merely cause gastric upset. The LD_{50} for rats is 16,500 mg/kg.

Human Precautions

Soap solution is a mild irritant to the eyes. Pesticidal soaps can be washed safely from skin surfaces. Dogs and cats should be removed from spray area to avoid their ingesting the soaps through grooming. The manufacturer's label should be carefully read, as always, and precautions should be heeded. It should be remembered that many formulations of pesticidal soaps may also contain other additives such as pyrethrins.

Ecodamage

Pesticidal soaps are biodegraded rapidly in the soil by the bacteria of the naturally occurring nitrogen cycle.

d-Limonene

Description

d-Limonene is a potent pesticide and is extracted from the oil of citrus fruits. All citrus fruits have circular glands just below the epidermis of the fruit's skin. These glands are packed with oil which is under tension. This citrus oil consists mostly of a terpene called *d*-limonene and a terpene alcohol called linalool. These terpenes occur also in neem oil, in the *Monarda* species, in dill, *Anethum graveolens,* and caraway, *Carum carvi.* The red field ants in North America seem to use a related compound as a chemical nest protector. Terpenes occur in all essential oils, which makes them universal in the plant kingdom.

Garden Use

Presently, *d*-limonene is formulated in aerosol and liquid sprays for use against fleas, aphids, and mites. Research is being conducted on this terpene for much broader domestic and industrial application.

Toxicity

The oral LD_{50} for limonene is 5,000 mg/kg in rats. Limonene seems to have some effect on motor nerves in animals. A cursory observation of the chicken-yard will show that hens, who are not in the least selective food-wise, will not touch citrus peelings of any kind. Dogs, cats, and other preening animals are all loathe to get this oil on their fur. Possibly this oil reacts with the deoxy form of vitamin D, resident on the fur of these animals.

Human Precautions

Although generally non-toxic to humans, limonene or citrus oil will induce an allergenic reaction in sensitive individuals.

Ecodamage

The citrus oils, limonene and linalool, are rapidly broken down by soil organisms.

Boron

Description

Boron is one of the naturally occurring elements or atoms that make up the building blocks of life like carbon. It occurs in nature as a mineral known as sassolite. Boron is commonly used domestically as Borax. Borax is sodium tetraborate. Boron salts and acid are used universally in commerce from glassmaking to a 1.5 percent solution as contact lens fluid. Boron is an extremely useful, mild antiseptic and fungicide and is commonly used pharmaceutically as such. A lack of boron in the soil in some areas of North America and Europe is found by the appearance of dark hollow areas in turnips and cabbage. A 2 percent soil drench of borax will rapidly remedy this lack.

Garden Use

Boron products, especially the acid, are most useful to the gardener and to his domicile as an effective ant poison. Boron products for ant control are usually supplied in a liquid bait. Properly baited ants from the tiny sugar ants to the large carpenter ants will be killed over a period of three weeks through ingestion of boric acid. The main route of the ant is discovered either in the garden or in the house. The boric acid containing bait is put directly on this route. Ants track and find their way chemically. The bait, placed in such a way, becomes a source of desirable food which the ants will carry back to the nest, poisoning the entire colony. A continuing supply of bait must be available over the three week period.

Boron products are being used in Europe as alternatives to toxic wood preservatives, such as chromated copper arsenate compounds. The wood is pressure treated and is sold under the registration Tim-Bor®.

Toxicity

The LD_{50} for rats ranges from 3,200 mg/kg to 6,000 mg/kg body weight. Boron products have low toxicity to man and other animals when used in dilute solutions. However, the accidental ingestion of concentrated boron products is extremely hazardous.

Human Precautions

When using boron products, hands should be well washed. Care should be taken that Borax is not stored with household staples. It should be out of the reach of children and treated as a poison. For normal garden purposes, dilute solutions of boron products can be treated as non-toxic by its user.

Ecodamage
Boron, when used in the garden environment in its diluted form, has a beneficial effect in the soil.

Calcium Oxide

Description
Calcium oxide is also known as quick lime, lime, burnt lime, and calyx. In commerce, it is available as lime. It is crystaline, composed of whitish or gray lumps which rapidly combine with carbon dioxide and moisture from the air to form slaked lime. When water is added, it becomes calcium hydroxide, a caustic solution. This chemical reaction generates a great quantity of heat. This mixture, with or without stabilizers and binding agents such as casein, is applied with a large brush. The water evaporates leaving a white coating of calcium carbonate, which is known as white-wash. White-wash has been used over the centuries as a fungicide and an insecticide. It was much used in Victorian gardens. Calcium oxide should not be confused with granular or powdered agricultural limestone, stonedust, or dolomitic limestone.

Garden Use
One use of white-wash in a north temperate garden is against southwest injury. This injury is the result of splitting of the bark on the southern facing trunks of trees due to frost damage. The injury is in the form of a long slash vertically opening the bark of the tree and exposing the internal tissue of the tree. This tissue will be further injured by fungal and insect damage subsequently. Damage most often occurs in trees with dark trunks, such as cherries and maples. The southern face of the tree is warmed by low altitude winter sunshine, while the rear of the tree is still in a frozen state. The differential in expansion explodes the tree trunk in one big rip. White-wash stops this action by light and heat reflection in the winter months. White-wash is also applied to flowering apple, cherry, and all fruit-trees as a winter control mechanism to reduce coddling moth, over-wintering insects, fungal spores, and bacteria. It also serves as a useful surface coating for greenhouses, potting sheds, and shelves where planting containers are stored as it inhibits the growth and subsequent transfer of bacterial and fungal disease organisms.

Toxicity

The hydrated form of calcium oxide orally in rats has an LD_{50} of 7.34 mg/kg. This is because of the extreme caustic action of this chemical internally.

Human Precautions

Care should be taken to protect the eyes when water is being added to calcium oxide as the solution may bubble violently and may splash. Calcium oxide defats the skin so gloves should be worn. Exposed skin should be well rinsed with running cold water. A respirator should be worn as protection against calcium oxide dust while handling and mixing the powder. Children and pets should be kept away from the area of preparation of a white-washing mixture.

Ecodamage

White-wash forms calcium carbonate. The addition of calcium, a divalent cation, is beneficial to the soil structure and organisms in small quantities.

Diatomaceous Earth

Description

Diatomaceous earth is a naturally occurring earth left behind from the death of diatoms and desmids, which are tiny unicellular silica encrusted sea organisms. There is some debate as to whether they are indeed algae, from a biochemical and evolutionary point of view. These organisms are active in all warm shallow seas to the present day. If the climate remains stable over a considerable period of time, huge layers of diatomaceous fossil earth results, which later can be mined for use. Diatomaceous earth has considerable use within a laboratory as a filtration tool. It is used as such in swimming pools also. In this instance the commercial partially melted grade which contains the crystalline silica is used. Diatoms and desmids are a fascinating study under light microscopy or electron microscopy as the organisms are covered with sharp sword-like structures of the most unimaginable shapes, all useful as minute killing barbs.

Garden Use

The mechanical, minute killing effect of the barbs or spines of diatoms and desmids punctures the exoskeletal structure and thus the insect dies. As such it is also a potent molluscicide. It is sometimes formulated with pyrethrins to enhance its killing power. In garden centers it is normally sold in its naturally occurring powder. This is used as a powder within the garden and has a slightly heavier consistency than talcum

powder. When it is being used as a molluscicide within the garden, bar-
riers of diatomaceous earth are circled around the offended plants or
group of plants so that the slugs are forced to cross them. Diatomaceous
earth mixed with wet cat food used as bait is a useful earwig control. The
bait should be placed into narrow tubing of some kind, discarded garden hose or split bamboo stakes, and placed at the back of the border
or in the coolest and darkest spot in the garden. Earwigs have recently
become a tremendous problem in some suburban areas in North
America. Gardeners should remember that earwigs are beneficial scavenger insects, but, in this case, are out of control. Every effort should
be made to induce at least one mating pair of house wrens *Trogolodytes
aëdon* into the garden as a natural control to reduce the offending numbers of earwigs. Diatomaceous dust controls aphids, caterpillars, mealy
bugs, and white flies as well. Diatomaceous dust can also be used with
seeds in storage as a non-toxic insecticide.

Toxicity
Diatomaceous earth is non-toxic, the oral LD_{50} for rats being from
3,160 to 8,000 mg/kg of weight. Food that has been dusted should be
washed. Diatomaceous earth may act as an irritant in intestinal diver-
ticular disease. Diatomaceous earth is considered to be a relatively
safe pesticide.

Human Precautions
Diatomaceous earth is relatively safe for human handling. A respirator should be worn to avoid inhaling the dust. It should be stored out
of the reach of children as silica dust can cause minor eye irritations.

Ecodamage
Diatomaceous earth is non-toxic to the environment. In garden
amounts it is beneficial to the earth. Care should be taken in the garden to avoid accidental application on beneficial garden reptiles as
diatomaceous earth may cause them minor irritation.

Silica Gel

Description
Silica gels are inert amorphous materials which have considerable
industrial application as dehydrating agents. Silica gels are used universally in a positive or negative electrostatic form of molecular filtration tools within laboratory systems for protein purification and
determination. Silica gels, used as electrostatically charged dehydrating agents, are very efficient insecticides and are also called silica
aerogels. Aerogels are formed by the precipitation of silicic acid,
which is further formulated for the adsorption of various vapors,

including linseed oil, which is chemically similar to the waxy cuticular layer of insects. Silicic acid, approximately H_2SiO_3, from which silica areogels are obtained, is found naturally as the semi-precious stone opal. Silica aerogel formulated with a grinding agent is sold as Dri-Die®. A mixture of 40 percent silica aerogel together with 1 percent pyrethrins as an active ingredient with the synergist piperonyl butoxide, held in a petroleum carrier, is sold as Drione®. This mixture of compounds carries a positive electrostatic charge which acts as an insect sticking agent.

Garden Use

For garden use Drione®, a non-specific insecticide and arachnicide, kills ants, cockroaches, crickets, fleas, weevils, spiders, ticks, and especially bees and wasps. It is a formidable pesticide. Aerogels are more useful for direct target killing within a closed area rather than in open spaces such as a garden. Because many beneficial organisms, such as spiders, bees, and wasps are also affected, this pesticide should be applied with caution.

Toxicity

Dri-Die® has an LD_{50} of 3160 mg/kg of rat body weight and Drione® has an LD_{50} of 8,000 mg/kg. Silica is an extremely inert material, but some inert materials have been known to lay dormant in the endoplasmic reticulum for years before becoming a severe cell irritant.

Human Precautions

When using silica aerogels, care should be taken that natural fabrics are worn as polymerized synthetics can also carry an electrostatic charge and increase the breathing hazard of this material. Silica gel should be kept out of the reach of children because of its fascinating ability to stick. A respirator is advisable.

Ecodamage

Silica aerogels are efficient piscicides and should not be used near waterways or where fish are likely to become contaminated.

Sodium Bicarbonate

Description

Sodium bicarbonate can also be called sodium acid carbonate. Sodium bicarbonate is baking soda. Baking soda, in its other guise, has considerable industrial and medicinal use. Baking soda has been found to have considerable fungicidal activity when used as a spray. This is an extremely useful spray for an allergenic household. In its baking function, sodium bicarbonate is changed to sodium carbonate and releases carbon dioxide as the baking temperature increases. The carbon dioxide is the rising or leavening agent. When it is used as a foliar spray, both the daytime increase in temperature on the leaf's surface and the standing misted solution releases carbon dioxide and the alkalinity increases. This alkaline film acts as a potent anti-fungal agent.

Garden Use

If a solution of roughly 0.1 molar is used as a foliar spray, it will attain an alkalinity of pH 8.3 on the foliage surface. An approximate 0.1 molar solution is prepared as follows: 1/3 oz. (8.4 grams or 1 teaspoon) dissolved in one quart (one liter) of water.

Sodium bicarbonate spray is effective against powdery mildews, rusts, and rose black spot. When used as a soil drench, it is effective against crown rot and many other fungal diseases.

Toxicity

Sodium bicarbonate is used as an antacid medicinally. It is not generally considered toxic to humans.

Human Precautions

None.

Ecodamage

None. Sodium bicarbonate is one of the universal buffer systems of life.

Seaweed Powder

Description

Seaweed powder should have the following brown algae as a portion of the algae mixture, *Fucus vesiculosus, Chorda philum* and any *Laminaria* species, and some red algae called *Chondrus crispus*. These species have naturally occurring broad-spectrum antibiotics.

Garden Use

Soluble seaweed powder used as a foliar spray has both bactericidal and fungicidal action. Seaweed powder is used as a nutritional foliar spray, which is increasing in popularity because of the healthy plant material such spraying produces. The use of seaweed as a fertilizer is as old as recorded history. Present agricultural technology has shown us that some soils are deficient in many micro-elements. Using a seaweed spray adjusts for these deficiencies and is an extremely good garden practice. Soluble seaweed powder used as a foliar spray is useful against bacterial rots, crown-rots, rusts, powdery mildews, black spot disease of rose, and many other fungal diseases. Seaweed powder gives a continuing degree of protection against these diseases in the garden.

Toxicity
Non-toxic.

Human Precautions
None.

Ecodamage
Generally beneficial. The removal of aged, spent seaweed from coastal areas should take place in September and October after the sexual conceptacles have released their oogonia and antheridia. Sea mining of any seaweed involving the cutting of holdfasts is to be avoided absolutely.

Spunbonded Polyester Fabric

Description
This fabric is ultraviolet light stable and extremely light. The fabric is porous to water, is self-ventilating, and allows 80 percent transmission of sunlight.

Garden Use
It is mainly used in a north temperate garden as a frost protector, providing a temperature increase of approximately 10 degrees. This fabric also acts as a barrier material over the cabbage family and prevents the cabbage looper butterfly from laying its eggs on members of this family. It can be floated over an area and pinned in place with old fashioned wooden clothes pegs.

Toxicity
LD_{50} not applicable.

Human Precautions
None.

Ecodamage
This cloth is entirely broken down by hydrogen peroxide producing organisms in the soil to naturally occurring constituents.

Bacterial Insecticides

Description
Bacterial insecticides are part of a large, general group of new pesticides which are called microbial pesticides. This new group of pesticides has been developed because of the hazards to the environment of the chemical pesticides now in use. Microbial pesticides

consist of algal, bacterial, fungal, mycoplasmic, parasitic, nematodal, protozoal, Rickettsial, viroidal, and viral organisms that kill their host organism. Thus microbials are living organisms or the toxic products of these organisms. Sometimes they are combined with other chemicals to enhance their killing action or their life-span on the host organism. Microbial research is in its infancy. There are about 2,000 naturally occurring microorganisms which wait to be investigated as potential pesticidal products. To date there are three bacterial insecticides of interest to the flower gardener. There is *Bacillus thuringiensis* var. Kurstaki (BTK), a naturally occurring bacillus whose toxins are lethal to the larva of moths and butterflies. This product is most commonly marketed as Thuricide®. Another bacterial insecticide consists of naturally occurring *Bacillus lentimorbus* and *B. popilliae*, the two bacteria that cause the milky spore disease of the accidentally introduced Japanese beetle, *Popillia japonica*, which decimates areas of lawn, especially in disturbed ground in new suburban areas.

Bacterial insecticides are formulated similarly to chemical products, in liquid concentrates, wettable powders, dusts, and granules. Like all bacterial insecticides, to be effective they must be eaten. The bacillus is formulated in the dormant spore stage. The spore, as part of its normal biochemistry, carries a strong toxin in crystaline form, which, when eaten by an insect, dissolves in its gut, puncturing the gut's wall and releasing the endotoxin into the insects blood stream, paralyzing it and finally killing it. The bacterial spores invade the body, but new spores and toxins are rarely produced, though in the case of *Bacillus popilliae* and *B. lentimorbus*, new spores are produced and can remain active in the soil for up to 25 years. This product is sold as Doom® or Milky Spore Disease™.

Garden Use

Doom® is formulated as a dust with an inert carrier which is dusted in a grid system on an infected area of the lawn. Rain will carry the product into the soil, where it will act as a bacterial insecticide against the invading populations of Japanese beetle. Thuricide® is used as a spray against all caterpillars. This spray is not to be used if a butterfly garden is desired. Since about thirty-five new varieties of *Bacillus thuringiensis* have been discovered, new host specific sprays for moths and butterflies can be expected to be available in the near future.

Toxicity

The oral LD_{50} for BT spray in its presently formulated form is 8,100 mg/kg of rat body weight.

Human Precautions

Long sleeve clothing, gloves, goggles, and a mask or respirator should be used when handling bacterial insecticides. Bacterial spores act as proteinaceous foreign bodies, similar to pollen, and in some susceptible allergenic people can pose a serious health hazard. The respirators worn by these people should have a carbon filter cartridge. Dogs, cats, and children should be removed from the spray area.

Ecodamage

The ecodamage caused by using the naturally occurring organisms in microbial sprays is minimal. However, the patented organisms produced by the genetically engineered chromosomal change of existing species being held by industry pose a problem for the environment of insect resurgence similar to what was seen in the 1940s, '50s and '60s after the insect populations developed resistance to our current arsenal of chemical insecticides. Uncontrolled mutation by unnatural selection may also pose a problem both for man and his environment.

Common Garden Controls

CHEMICAL	BACTERICIDE	FUNGICIDE	INSECTICIDE	HERBICIDE
Bacterial Insecticide			X	
Boron	X	X	X	
Calcium Oxide	X	X	X	
Diatomaceous Earth			X	
Garlic	X	X	X	
Horticultural Oils	X	X	X	X
d-Limonene			X	
Mulch 6" (15cm)				X
Neem Oil	X	X	X	
Seaweed Powder	X	X		
Silica Gel			X	
Sodium Bicarbonate		X		
Sodium Hypochlorite	X	X		
Spunbonded Polyester Fabric			X	
Sulphur	X	X		
Pesticidal Soaps	X	X	X	X
Pyrethrum			X	
Rotenone			X	
Wood ash	X	X	X	X

Glossary

Acid: any chemical which will produce free hydrogen ions. To a gardener, it means that the soil is acidic if it will turn moist litmus paper red. The stronger the red color, the more acidic the soil. Litmus paper is a paper impregnated by an indicator dye which will turn red or blue, depending if it is steeped in an acid or an alkaline (base) solution.

Acaricide: a pesticide which will kill mites.

Allopolyploid: has three or more basic sets (diploid number) of chromosomes in the normal or non-sexual plant cell.

Annual: a plant which will live, flower, and set seeds in one season.

Anther: the male pollen bearing part of a plant.

Androecium: the male organs of a flower.

Algicide: a pesticide which kills algae.

Alkali: can also be called a base, which is quite often a hydroxide, which can neutralize acids. An alkali can turn moist litmus paper blue: the more blue the color, the stronger the alkali. To a gardener, it is an alkaline soil. It is a soil containing calcium carbonate ($CaCO_3$), which is the fifth most abundant of the elements on the planet.

Ascospore: a spore produced from the ascus which is inside an ascocarp. This is the sexual reproductive organ of the ascomycete fungus. The haploid ascospore will germinate like a primitive seed. Yeasts are ascomycetes.

Bacidiospores: a spore produced in the life cycle of a basidiomycetous fungus.

Bactericide: a pesticide which will kill bacteria. Antibiotics are bactericides.

Biomass: the summation of living material on the planet Earth.

Bioplan: a planning system, in gardening, whereby habitat is incorporated into the general garden design.

Biosphere: living beings together with their environment.

Bonemeal: an inorganic fertilizer. It contains tricalcium orthophosphate, tricalcium phosphate, and tertiary calcium phosphate.

Bract: a modified leaf, sometimes reduced, found below a flower.

Bulb: an underground modified leaf bud with a reduced stem and crowded fleshy scales, which are food stores.

Bulbil: a small bulb sometimes produced on a plant, in a leaf axil.

Calyx: the outer whorl of separate or united sepals.

Callus: thick new tissue covering plant injury for protection and healing.

Carpel: the part of the ovary which produces the seed.

Cathodoluminescence: light produced by excited pye electrons.

Cell: the structural unit of higher life forms, in plants, consisting of cytoplasmic and nuclear structures enclosed by a firm wall for rigidity.

Chromosome: rod-shaped structures found in cells that are constant in number for a given species. They carry the genes responsible for the inheritance of all traits.

Corolla: the inner parts or whorl of the flower comprised of petals which are usually united into a tube.

Corona: a crown or circle of appendages in a flower.

Corymb: a short or somewhat broad flower grouping or inflorescence which is flattened at the top.

Cotyledon: the first primary seed leaf coming usually in pairs, from the germinating seed embryo.

Cultivar: a cultivated variety of any plant given its name which is denoted by single quotation marks. For example, the white cultivar of columbine would be called *Aquilegia vulgaris* 'Alba'.

Diploid: a cell which has two basic sets of chromosomes (two genomes). The regular or somatic cells of plants or animals have this number.

Dolomitic Lime: a mineral stone consisting largely of calcium magnesium carbonate ($CaMg(CO_3)_2$). Several technical and agricultural grades are available. In gardening it releases calcium cations slowly over a five-year period into the garden environment, and is thus said to be a slow release fertilizer. It is used to neutralize an acid soil.

Ecodamage: damage done to an ecosystem.

Ecofunction: a purpose, an action, or a reaction of an organism within its ecosystem.

Ecosystem: an interacting system of living organisms and their non-living environment.

Fall: the drooping, sometimes wider, lower part of the perianth of the Iris and related species.

Filament: the stalk which holds the anthers in the stamen or male organ of a flower.

Flower: an appendage bearing one or more pistils (female) or one or more stamens (male) or both. The former flower is referred to as a *pistillate* flower, the latter a *staminate* flower. When both are present, the flower is said to be *perfect*. When such a flower is then surrounded by a perianth and a calyx, the flower is said to be a *complete flower*. Flower classification and identification pivots around flower form.

Fluorescence: electron excitation causing visible and/or invisible light.

Fungicide: a pesticide which kills fungi.

Genus: a grouping of similar species such as *Aquilegia* or *Iris*.

Gland: a secreting body on a plant, seen as a prominence or appendage such as the secretory hairs.

Habitat: a plant's or an animal's natural environment.

Herbaceous: dying back to the ground each year, not woody.

Herbicide: a pesticide that kills herbaceous species.

Hybrid: the offspring of two different species that are genetically different.

Hydrocarbon: a molecule containing hydrogen and carbon within its framework.

Humus: the organic or decaying component of the soil, comprised of plant and animal parts.

Hyphae: the thread-like growing portion making up the mycelial body of a fungus.

Inflorescence: the pattern of arrangement of a flower or flowers on a plant.

Insecticide: a pesticide which kills insects.

LD$_{50}$: a scientific estimation of the killing rate of a pesticide to which all pesticides are subjected. An increasingly higher amount of a pesticide is fed, usually to rats, until 50 percent of them die. The lethal dosage is measured in milligrams per kilogram of rat body weight. The resulting figure is said to be the LD$_{50}$ in mg/kg of body weight.

Lenticels: lens-shaped breathing apparatus of woody plants.

Meristem: embryonic apical tissue that is genetically capable of growing into different plant organs.

Mesophyll: the spongy layer of tissue, underneath the leaf epidermis, responsible for photosynthesis.

Miticide: a pesticide that kills mites.

Monocarpic: a single flowering and fruiting followed by plant death.

Monoecious: the pistillate and staminate flowers on the same plant.

Molluscicide: a pesticide that kills snails and slugs.

Mycelium: the thallus or vegetatively growing body of a fungus made of hyphae.

Mycorrhiza: a mutually beneficial fungal growth on higher plants.

Nectary: the nectar secreting gland found in a flower.

Nematicide: a pesticide that kills nematodes.

Node: the place on a stem where one or more leaves are attached.

Orris: ground root of many *Iris* species used in perfumery.

Ovary: the lower part of a pistil which contains the ovule.

Parasite: an organism living at the expense of others.

Pedicel: the stalk of a flower.

Peduncle: the stalk of an inflorescence.

Perianth: the floral envelope, either the calyx, the corolla, or both.

Petal: a unit of the inner floral envelope usually colored.

pH scale: a logarithmic scale of the potential of hydrogen ion concentration measured in an acid or base. Pure water is said to be neutral reading pH 7.0. pH values from zero to seven indicate acidity, and pH values from seven to fourteen indicate alkalinity. Since the scale is a logarithmic scale, each pH unit of one has a value of ten, so pH 6.0 is ten times more acidic than pH 7.0 and pH 5.0 is a hundred times more acidic than pH 7.0, etc.

Piscicide: a pesticide which kills fish.

Predacide: a pesticide which kills vertebrate animals.

Raceme: an unbranched elongated inflorescence with the oldest flowers at the base.

Ray: a ray flower, or a circle of ray flowers.

Rhizome: a modified stem on or under the ground, often swollen and fleshy.

Rhodopsin: red plant pigments.

Rickettsia: a gram-negative microorganism causing certain diseases, e.g., typhus.

Rosette: a ring of radiating leaves.

Rodenticide: a pesticide that kills rodents.

Scale: a small dry leaf or bract.

Scape: a leafless peduncle which may have scales bearing one or many flowers.

Seed: a fertilized ovule, encasing the embryonic plant.

Sepal: one of the separate units of a calyx, usually green.

Sessile: without a stalk.

Silvicide: a pesticide that kills woody growth.

Slimicide: a pesticide that kills slime moulds.

Spadix: a thick or fleshy flower spike usually surrounded by a spathe, e.g., *Araceae*.

Spathe: a bract around the flower spike or spadix which may or may not be colored.

Species: the basic unit of plant classification, a group of individual plants having characterization in common which are distinct from other groups of plants. A logical division of a genus.

Spore: a simple reproductive body, usually from the lower groups of plants, the algae, ferns, fungi, and mosses. The spore contains encased nuclear and protoplasmic material needed for germination.

Stamen: consists of the anther (male) and usually the filament. The anther produces pollen.

Staminode: a sterile stamen, e.g., *Canna*.

Standard: the upper, usually broad part of the perianth of the *Iris*.

Sterile: non-functional sexual flower organs, no flowers or fruits produced.

Stoma: (pl. **Stomata**) microscopic mobile pores in the epidermis areas of a plant, through which gas exchange takes place for photosynthesis and respiration. Turgidity in the whole plant affects the guard cells of the stoma, which thus are responsible for the opening of the pore.

Tepals: the perianth undifferentiated into typical corolla and calyx, e.g., *Begonia* and *Tulipa*.

Tetraploid: a cell with four times the basic set of chromosomes.

Triploid: a cell with three times the basic set of chromosomes. Triploid plants are ususally sterile.

Tuber: a modified stem which is short, thick, and fleshy sometimes underground, usually with buds or 'eyes', e.g., *Begonia*.

Umbel: an inflorescence in which the branches come from a common point forming a flower head which is approximately flat.

Variety: a group of plants within a species which has a variant of one or two characteristics differing from the common unit. In general terms, a variety occurs naturally and a cultivar is bred artificially or naturally.

Vascular: describes plants which have xylem and phloem conduction systems for transport. These are ferns, mosses, gymnosperms, and angiosperms. Non-vascular plants are algae and fungi.

Viviparious: forming plantlets while still on the parent plant.

Wilt-point: the point of water loss beyond which a plant will not recover.

Wood ash: a fertilizer which is a valuable source of potash. Wood ash from hardwoods contains 10 percent available potash. Wood ash from softwood trees contains 2 percent potash stored dry. It also contains approximately 40 percent lime ($CaCO_3$).

Xerophyte: a plant with a modified morphology to reduce water loss.

Zoospore: mobile spores.

Zygomorphic: bilaterally symmetrical.

References

Allison, James. *Water in the Garden.* Toronto: Little, Brown and Company, 1991.

Buckley, A.R. *Canadian Garden Perennials.* Toronto: Hancock House Publishers Canada, 1977.

Budavari, S. *The Merck Index, Eleventh Ed. An Encyclopedia of Chemicals, Drugs and Biologicals.* Rahway, N.J.: Merck & Co., Inc., 1989.

Borror, Donald J., White, Richard E. *A Field Guide to the Insects of America North of Mexico.* Boston: Houghton Mifflin Co., 1970.

Bush-Brown, James and Louise. *America's Garden Book.* New York and London: Charles Scribner's Sons, 1958.

Clausen, Ruth Rogers, and Ekstrom, Nicholas H. *Perennials for American Gardens.* New York: Random House, Inc., 1989.

Cody, W. J. *Ferns of the Ottawa District.* Ottawa: Canada Department of Agriculture, 1956.

Flint, Harrison L. *Landscape Plants for Eastern North America* New York: John Wiley & Sons, 1983.

Grant, John A. and Caroll. *Garden Design Illustrated.* Seattle: University of Washington Press, 1954.

Glasener, E. *The Winter Garden 47,* (4), 1991. Brooklyn: Brooklyn Botanic Garden, 1991.

Glattstein, J. *Gardener's World of Bulbs 47,* (2), 1991. Brooklyn: Brooklyn Botanic Garden, 1991.

Hernick, James W. *Iroquois Medical Botany.* Syracuse, Syracuse University Press, 1995.

Hosie, R. C. *Native Trees of Canada.* Ottawa: Department of Fisheries and Forestry, 1969.

Howes, F. N. *Plants and Beekeeping.* London: Faber and Faber, London, 1979.

Kingsbury, John M. *Poisonous Plants of the United States and Canada.* Englewood Cliffs, NJ: Prentice-Hall, Inc., 1964.

Krochmal, Arnold and Connie. *The Complete Illustrated Book of Dyes From Natural Sources.* New York: Doubleday & Co., 1974.

Klots, Alexander B. *A Field Guide to the Butterflies of North America, East of the Great Plains.* Boston: Houghton Mifflin Co., 1951.

Lewis, Walter H., Lewis-Elvin Memory P. F. *Medical Botany Plants Affecting Man's Health.* Toronto: John Wiley & Sons, 1977.

Liberty Hyde Bailey Hortorium. *Hortus Third: A Concise Dictionary of Plants Cultivated in the United States and Canada.* New York: MacMillan Publishing Company, 1976.

McEwen, F. L., and Stephenson, G. R. *The Use and Significance of Pesticides in the Environment.* Toronto: John Wiley & Sons, 1979.

Olkowski, William; Daar, Sheila; Olkowski, Helga. *Common-sense Pest Control.* NP: Taunton Press Inc, 1991.

Pirone, P. P. *Tree Maintenance* New York: Oxford University Press, Inc., 1988.

Peterson, Roger Tory, and McKenny, Margret. *A Field Guide to Wildflowers of Northeastern and North-Central North America.* Boston: Houghton Mifflin Co., 1968.

Paul, Anthony, and Rees, Yvonne. *The Water Garden.* Toronto: Penguin Books, 1986.

Phillips, Roger, and Rix, Martyn. *Perennials* Vol. (I), (II). New York: Random House, 1991.

Raven, Peter H., and Curtis, Helena. *Biology of Plants.* New York:. North Publishers Inc., 1970.

Rix, Martyn, and Phillips, Roger. *The Bulb Book.* New York: Pan Books Ltd., 1981.

Scutz, Walter E. *How to Attract, House and Feed Birds.* New York: Collier Books, 1970.

Stuart, Malcolm. *The Encyclopedia of Herbs and Herbalism.* London: Orbis Publishing Ltd., 1979.

Taylor, Norman, and DeWolf, Gordon P. Jr. *Taylor's Guide to Perennials.* Boston: Houghton Mifflin Co., 1961.

Taylor, Kathryn S., and Hamblin, Stephen F. *Handbook of Wildflower Cultivation.* Toronto: MacMillan Publishing Co., Inc., 1963.

Warburton, Bee, and Hamblle, Melba. *The World of Irises:* The American Iris Society Wichita, Kansas. Salt Lake City: Publisher's Press, 1978.

Wright, Michael, ed. *The Complete Handbook of Garden Plants.* NP: The Rainbird Publishing Group Ltd., 1984.

Plant and Seed Sources

Seeds of Diversity
PO Box 36, Station Q
Toronto, ON
M4T 2L7 Canada

Early's Farm & Garden
Centre Inc.
2615 Lorne Ave.
Saskatoon, SK
S7J 0S5 Canada
Tel: (306) 931-1982
Fax: (306) 931-7110

Florabunda Seeds
641 Rainbow Rd.
Salt Sprng Island, BC
V8K 2M7 Canada

Gardens North
5984 Third Line Rd. N.
North Gower, ON
K0A 1T0 Canada
Tel: (613) 489-0065
Fax: (613) 489-1208
<garnorth@istar.ca>

The Herb Farm
323 Parleeville Rd.
RR 4, ON
Norton, NB
E0G 2N0 Canada
Tel: (506) 839-2140

Jardin Marisol
111 Blvd. Bromont
Bromont, PC
J0E 1L0 Canada
Tel/Fax: (514) 534-4515

Rawlinson Garden Seed
269 College Rd.
Truro, NS
B2N 2P6 Canada
Tel: (902) 893-3051
Fax: (902) 897-7303

Vesey's Seeds Ltd
York, PEI
C0A IP0 Canada
Tel: (902) 368-7333

Corn Hill Nursery Ltd.
RR 5
Petitcodial, NB
E0A 2H0 Canada
Tel: (506) 756-3635
Fax: (506) 756-1087

Salt Spring Seeds
PO Box 444 Ganges
Salt Spring Island, BC
V8K 2W1 Canada
Tel: (614) 537-5269

Stokes Seeds Ltd.
30 James St., PO Box 10
St. Catharines, ON
L2R 6R6 Canada
Tel: (800) 396-9238

Moore Water Gardens
PO Box 70
Port Stanley, ON
N5L 1J4 Canada

Wrightman Alpines
1503 Napperton Dr., RR 3
Kerwood, ON
N0M 2B0 Canada

Cooper's Garden
2345 Decatur Ave., N.
Golden Valley, MN
55427 U.S.A.
Tel/Fax: (612) 542-9447

Hollingsnorth Nursery
RR3, PO Box 27
Maryville, MO
64468 U.S.A.
Tel: (816) 562-3010

Hardy Roses for the North
PO Box 2048
Grand Forks, BC
V0H 1H0 Canada
or PO Box 273
Danville, WA
99121-0273 U.S.A.

Sempervivum tectorum, an extremely hardy plant, spilling out of an old leather shoe.

Hortico Inc
723 Robson Road, RR 7
Waterdown, ON
L0R 2H1 Canada
Tel: (905) 689-6984
    (905) 689-3002
Fax: (905) 689-6566

Cruickshank's
The Garden Guild
1015 Mount Pleasant Road
Toronto, ON
M4P 2M1 Canada
Tel: (416) 750-9249
    (800) 665-5605

Garden Import Inc.
P.O. Box 760
Thornhill, ON
L3T 4A5 Canada
Tel: (905) 731-1950
Fax: (905) 881-3499
www.gardenimport.com
e-mail: flower@gardenimport.com

North Green Seeds
16 Witton Lane
Little Plumstead
Norwich, Norfolk
NR135DL England

Sweet Grass Gardens
Native North American
Plant Reference Guide
RR 6
Hagersville, ON
N04 1H0 Canada
Tel: (519) 445-4828
Fax: (519) 445-4826

Richters
The Herb Specialists
Goodwood, ON
L0C 1A0 Canada
Tel: (905)640-6677
Fax: (905) 640-6641
www.richters.com
e-Mail: orderdesk@richters.com

Acknowledgements

For his continuing encouragement and enthusiasm I would like to thank Mr. Bill Roberts.

For their technical assistance, I wish to acknowledge Mr. Don Hollingsworth of the American Paeony Society; Mr. Joseph K. Mertzweiller of The Society for Louisiana Irises; Mr. A. C. Whitely of the Botany Department of the Royal Horticultural Society of England; Mr. James A. Bauml, senior plant taxonomist of the Department of Arboreta and Botanic Gardens of the County of Los Angeles, California; Mr. Colin Rigby of the American Iris Society; Mr. John Cable of Ensata Gardens, Galesburg, Michigan; Mr. R. Vick of the Devonian Botanic Garden, University of Alberta, Edmonton, Alberta; Mr. Howard R. Crum of Lilypons Water Gardens, Buckeystown, Maryland; Dr. Fritz Bender, Spangenberg, Germany; Prof. Yu-tang, Normal University, Changchun, China; Dr. Henri Ouellet, Canadian Museum of Nature.

For information with regard to availability of specific cultivars, I wish to acknowledge the staff of Moore Water Gardens, Port Stanley, Ontario, Canada; Mrs. Sally Gregson, Mill Cottage Plants, North Wells, Somerset, England; Mr. & Mrs. H. Wrightman of Wrightman Alpines, Kerwood, Ontario, Canada; the late Mr. Richter of Richter's, Goodwood, Ontario, Canada; Mr. Dugald Cameron, Garden Import, Thornhill, Ontario; Mrs. Gloria McMillen, McMillen's Iris Garden, Norwich, Ontario; Yana Maltais, Prism Perennials, Castlegar, British Columbia, Canada; Will McLewin, Phedar Nursery, Romiley, England; Belle Durio, Louisiana Nursery, Opelousas, Louisiana, U.S.A.; Mr. G. Dempster, Waterperry, Wheatley, Oxon, England; Mrs. Nora O'Flynn, Irish Garden Plant Society, Dublin, Ireland; Diana Nicholls, Nicholls Gardens, Gainsville, Virginia, U.S.A.; Hortico Inc., Waterdown, Ontario, Canada; Melody Wilhoit, Redbud Lane Iris Garden, Kansas, Illinois, U.S.A.; W. E. Th. Ingwerson, Ltd., East Grinstead, West Sussex, England; Kristl Walek of Gardens North, North Gower, Ontario; Stokes Seeds, Ltd., St. Catharines, Ontario; Cruikshanks', Toronto, Ontario; and Park Seed, Greenwood, South Carolina.

For their provision of word processing services, I wish to acknowledge Mrs. Barbara Franks, Mr. W. Douglas Ross, and Mr. Wayne B. Poapst of Popskraft, Merrickville, Ontario.

For her assistance in maintaining the garden during the production of this volume, I wish to acknowledge Jane A. Hilborn, Ottawa, Ontario.

For their assistance in obtaining reference material with a smile, I wish to thank Mrs. J. Larsen and Ms. Mary Kate Laphen of the Merrickville Public Library, Merrickville, Ontario. Finally, I wish to acknowledge the support, inspiration, and encouragement given to me by all the anonymous individuals with whom I've had contact over the last several years.

—Diana Beresford-Kroeger

The water-garden at
rest, so happily is
the gardener.